Worlds of Common Prayer

Worlds of Common Prayer

Liturgical Time and Poetic Re-enchantment, 1827–1935

Chene Heady

FAIRLEIGH DICKINSON UNIVERSITY PRESS
Vancouver • Madison • Teaneck • Wroxton

Published by Fairleigh Dickinson University Press
Copublished by The Rowman & Littlefield Publishing Group, Inc.
4501 Forbes Boulevard, Suite 200, Lanham, Maryland 20706
www.rowman.com

6 Tinworth Street, London SE11 5AL, United Kingdom

Portions of chapter two were published in an earlier form as "'Tun'd to Hymns of Perfect Love: The Anglican Liturgy as Romantic Object in John Keble's *Christian Year*" in the article anthology *Romantic Objects*, ed. Larry Peer (2009), and are reproduced with permission of Palgrave Macmillan.

Portions of chapter three were published in an earlier form as "'Earth has clear call of daily bells: Nature's Apocalyptic Liturgy in Christina Rossetti's Verses" in *Religion and the Arts* 15.2 (2011), and are reproduced with permission of Koninklijke Brill NV.

Excerpts from *Murder in the Cathedral* and *The Cocktail Party* from *The Complete Poems and Plays, 1909–1950* by T.S. Eliot. Copyright © 1950 by T.S. Eliot, renewed 1978 by Esme Valerie Eliot. Reprinted by permission of Houghton Mifflin Harcourt Publishing Company. All rights reserved.

Excerpts from the poem "From an Evening Service" by Dorothy L. Sayers are reprinted by permission of the trustees of the estate of Anthony Fleming.

Fairleigh Dickinson University Press gratefully acknowledges the support received for scholarly publishing from the Friends of FDU Press.

British Library Cataloguing in Publication Information Available

Library of Congress Cataloging-in-Publication Data
Names: Heady, Chene, author.
Title: Worlds of common prayer : liturgical time and poetic re-enchantment, 1827–1935 / Chene Heady.
Description: Lanham, Maryland : Fairleigh Dickinson University Press, [2019] | Includes bibliographical references and index.
Identifiers: LCCN 2019016424 (print) | LCCN 2019022100 (ebook) | ISBN 9781683931737 (cloth : alk. paper)
Subjects: LCSH: Religious poetry, English—19th century—History and criticism. | Christian poetry, English—20th century—History and criticism. | Liturgy and literature. | Christianity and literature. | Literature and society—England—History—19th century. | Literature and society—England—History—20th century.
Classification: LCC PR595.R4 H43 2019 (print) | LCC PR595.R4 (ebook) | DDC 821/.8093823—dc23
LC record available at https://lccn.loc.gov/2019016424
LC ebook record available at https://lccn.loc.gov/2019022100

™ The paper used in this publication meets the minimum requirements of American National Standard for Information Sciences—Permanence of Paper for Printed Library Materials, ANSI/NISO Z39.48-1992.

For Emily

Contents

Acknowledgments

I would like to thank Longwood University and the supportive administration and colleagues I have encountered there. Special thanks are due to Wade Edwards and Roger Byrne, who as department chair and dean advocated for the sabbatical that made completion of this book possible. I owe a debt of gratitude to Sean Barry and Michael Lund, my Romanticist and Victorianist colleagues, who thoughtfully critiqued earlier versions of individual chapters. I fondly remember and thank the students in my seminars on the detective fiction of Dorothy L. Sayers and the verse dramas of T. S. Eliot; I am sure our discussions have influenced the shape of this book. Finally, I appreciate Longwood's interlibrary loan office, whose indefatigable labors made it possible for a professor at a small, rural university to conduct thorough research.

I would like to thank Chad Griffiths for the use of his personal collection of Anglo-Catholic liturgical manuals, many of which were identical to those employed in T. S. Eliot's parishes.

I would like to thank James Gifford, the director of Farleigh Dickinson University Press, for his insightful feedback and support. I would also like to thank the anonymous peer reviewer, whose detailed comments helped to improve the book's argument and prose style.

I owe thanks to Emily Walker Heady twice. First, as spouse, for enduring my tendency to bring the Book of Common Prayer into any conversation, regardless of the putative subject. Second, as literary critic, for invaluable feedback on multiple drafts of the complete manuscript.

An earlier version of portions of the second chapter was published in *Romantic Objects* (2009), edited by Larry Peer. An earlier version of portions of the third chapter was published in *Religion and the Arts* 15.2 (2011), edited by James Najarian. Both are reproduced with the permission of the publishers and with thanks to the editors.

Introduction

The Cultural Project of the Anglo-Catholic Liturgical Long Poem

Although he has fallen out of favor with twentieth-century readers, Guy Morville was one of the best-loved Romantic heroes of the Victorian era. The titular *Heir of Redclyffe* of Charlotte Yonge's 1853 novel is a Byronic, almost Gothic figure: raised in seclusion after the death of his parents by a grandfather who believes the family cursed, he grows into a rich and titled young man both devoutly religious and psychologically tormented, equally impetuous in generosity and anger, giving the impression of hidden depths. He risks his life saving the survivors of a shipwreck, woos a beautiful girl whose branch of the family had historically feuded with his own, rescues his new bride when she is falling off a cliff, and finally dies young while attempting to end the familial feud. Little wonder, then, that he was adored by the more Romantic and idealistic sectors of Victorian youth. *The Heir of Redclyffe* went through five editions in its first year before being "reprinted almost annually" for half a century.[1] Charlotte Yonge was an ardent Anglican whose parish pastor was the prominent High Churchman John Keble—the author of the bestselling collection of liturgical poetry *The Christian Year* (1827)—and her characters often quote Keble's poetry and endorse his theological views.[2] But her hero's appeal extended far beyond the borders of the High Church subculture. Guy Morville was idolized by the young pre-Raphaelites William Morris and Edward Burne-Jones, for instance, as "a pattern for actual life."[3]

Guy may have seemed a plausible "pattern for actual life" because in the end no clear line separates him as a person from the Book of Common Prayer as a text, and the Prayer Book comprises the Church of England's normative model of life. While Guy attends Anglican services earlier in the novel, it is only after he fully becomes an adult by entering into marriage—in a ceremony conducted according to the forms of the Prayer Book (382)—that he seems to become synonymous with the sacred text. Guy marks his marriage by giving his wife Amabel a Prayer Book inscribed with her new name (386). One might expect newlyweds to spend a honeymoon reading romantic poetry, if any literary text at all. But since Anglican churches are rarely found in continental Europe, Guy spends his honeymoon reading his new bride the daily and Sunday Anglican services, as well as the daily Psalter—and it thrills her. Although she has always thought that he reads the liturgy with "peculiarly beautiful expression," he has now come to read the service with "so remarkable a melancholy and a beauty in his voice that she could hardly refrain from tears" (431).

In fact, the Prayer Book may itself be the most Romantic object in this realist mid-Victorian novel. It possesses an oracular function, predicting events that have yet to transpire. When Guy reads Amabel the first lesson for Evensong on the Seventeenth Sunday after Trinity, "Weep ye not for the dead, neither bemoan him" (Jer. 22:10), neither he nor his wife suspect that he will not survive their honeymoon, but she is strangely moved nonetheless. The Prayer Book also possesses the capacity to control and even break the order of nature. Later the same day, Guy and Amabel sit alone under a tree, watching the sun set over the Italian Alps. Amabel looks at Guy and remarks that "[t]here is only one thing wanting" to make the moment perfect. "A kiss?" the modern reader assumes. "Suppose we chant the afternoon's psalms," she instead suggests (432). The Anglican monthly cycle of the Psalms does not alter for Sundays or feast days, and the newlyweds cap off this beautiful honeymoon day by chanting the Psalms for the evening of the fifth day of the month together. As they chant from Psalm 29, "the voice of the Lord shaketh the wilderness," a "peal of thunder" replies; when they chant, "The Lord shall give his people the blessing of peace" a distant echo both "solemn and mysterious" answers back "The blessing of peace" (432). Like Rochester's call across the miles to Jane Eyre in Charlotte Brontë's novel,[4] the Anglican Psalter provokes the only supernatural occurrence in an otherwise realist text.

Not many days later, Guy dies from a deadly fever contracted while selflessly nursing back to health Philip Edmundstone, his rival heir to the Redclyffe title, who had also been traveling in Italy. True to the Common Prayer to the last, Guy requests with his final words that his wife recite for him the "Commendatory Prayer" from the Anglican service for the Visitation of the Sick (468). And, thanks to the Prayer Book, Guy lives on after his death, as his copy of the Book of Common Prayer completes the tasks he was personally unable to finish in his short life. When his widow in grief and bewilderment is unsure what to do or how to act, she picks up Guy's Prayer Book and finds her course clear (469). At his request, his Prayer Book is bequeathed to Philip Edmundstone, his former antagonist and the new heir of Redclyffe; the ancient family feud ends the moment Guy's widow inscribes

Philip's name in the book (470–71, 486–87). This Prayer Book allows the now guilt-stricken Philip to have the courage to assume his new aristocratic responsibilities, and to begin to reform England, both at his estate and in parliament; "but for the prayer-book . . . how could he have borne it?" (520). At his death, Guy has left behind a pregnant Amabel; their child physically embodies their newly unified extended family, a fitting end to the book's marriage plot. Guy cannot see his child's birth or attend her baptismal service—but his Prayer Book does so in his stead (543).

At this point, the modern critic may feel somewhat bewildered. The great Romantic hero of this work of Victorian literature is . . . the Book of Common Prayer? In the standard narrative of English cultural history, the nineteenth century—as a period of massive scientific advances, changing technologies, increasing political pluralism and individualism, and new awareness of global cultures—is an age of rising secularization. In J. Hillis Miller's classic work of the same title, this epoch witnesses *The Disappearance of God.* Even in Charles Taylor's influential and controversial revisionist account of secularization, *A Secular Age*, the nineteenth century still marks the moment when a social world that functions without reference to transcendence first becomes fully inhabitable;[5] at least for the educated elite, vertical structures of order and meaning have become dismantled in favor of the horizontal. So how could the Book of Common Prayer—the collective ritual voice of the established church—become the romantic lead of one of the most popular of all of Victorian novels?

Admittedly, Guy Morville did not begin life as a Prayer Book. He was originally a much more conventional Romantic or Victorian hero. His upbringing, as I have mentioned, was positively Byronic. And as a teen, he is an unstable, unpredictable soul whose future cannot be foreseen, full of Romantic potential and full of Romantic omens of doom; he quotes Byron's poetry from memory (87). The turning point seems to occur as he starts college. In many a Romantic and Victorian text—such as, memorably, William Wordsworth's *Prelude*, Book III—the college years are the period in which one breaks with childhood and sets a new direction in life, for better or worse. The impetuous young student who becomes by the end of college a terribly indebted reprobate eventually becomes something of a stock literary type. Philip Edmundstone has read his Byron (399), and over and over predicts precisely such a future for Guy. But just as Guy is leaving for college, he promises to quit reading Byron and instead accepts the kindly Mrs. Edmundstone's gift of "a Christian Year," the Reverend John Keble's book-length poetic meditation on the Anglican liturgy and liturgical calendar (87, 90). And like many a Victorian, Guy seems to have learned through Keble and his admirers to modulate his restless interior emotional life to the tune of the Anglican liturgy. When on their honeymoon Amabel recites Keble's liturgical poetry to him, both she and Charlotte Yonge know that no attribution is necessary (432).[6] *The Christian Year* provides epigraphs for some of the novel's most pivotal chapters (XXXIII, XXXVI), and the Book of Common Prayer prevents Guy Morville from becoming a self-destructive Byronic hero. Liturgical poetry helps him to reconnect as an individual subject with a divine collective order, and thus (after his death) enables a reformed and remade England. To paraphrase Thomas Carlyle's famous injunction from *Sartor Resartus*: Put down thy Byron, pick up thy Keble.

The Heir of Redclyffe vividly captures an Anglo-Catholic cultural milieu in which it seemed possible that through the mediation of liturgical poetry, the Book of Common Prayer might refashion both self and world. The novel's mass popularity for half a century also shows that this hope was not confined to a peripheral religious subculture; rather, Anglo-Catholic liturgical poetry occupied an important place in the Victorian literary and cultural imagination. In the pages that follow, I will trace the critically neglected story of the Anglo-Catholic liturgical long poem from its birth at the end of the Romantic period to its precipitous decline following World War II.

The story begins—and in most scholarly accounts also ends—with Charlotte Yonge's parish priest, John Keble. With fellow Oxonians John Henry Newman and Hurrell Froude, Keble founded the articulate, energetic, and organized High Church party that came to be known as the Oxford Movement. The Oxford Movement—also called the "Tractarian Movement," after its polemical series the *Tracts for the Times*—reshaped world Anglicanism by recovering the ritualistic, ancient, and medieval elements of that church. Prior to the nineteenth-century, as G. B. Tennyson has shown, Anglicans produced relatively little liturgical poetry.[7] Keble's *Christian Year* (1827), as its title suggests, is an attempt to restore the older Christian conception of time in place of its now-dominant secular counterpart; the work attempts to re-enchant an increasingly industrialized and disenchanted England. And it was the great literary success of its era. During the Victorian age, *The Christian Year* was commonly considered a literary classic, and it "sold an average of 10,000 volumes a year" for "fifty years"; Keble was indisputably "the most popular English poet of his age."[8]

Most literary scholars who have not ignored Keble altogether have treated the success of *The Christian Year* as an anachronism or an anomaly. The received story is that the Victorian age ultimately has no place for Keble's liturgical vision; the Tractarians' extreme sense of "religious communality" and belief in a unified order of creation were "at odds with" and in the end could not contend with the rise of individualism and "the increasing fragmentation of their world."[9] The most influential scholar of nineteenth-century religion and literature, Stephen Prickett, speaks for the critical tradition as a whole when he asserts, "Keble's *The Christian Year*, and, indeed, the entire poetic output of the Oxford Movement, must be seen as . . . a dead end, theologically and aesthetically alike."[10]

The present volume contests this consensus. Anglo-Catholic communality, which leads to a mystical regard for the collective liturgy, did not comprise an early Victorian literary dead end, but for over a century inspired innovative and ambitious volumes of poetry. From the birth of the Oxford Movement in the late 1820s and early 1830s until the liturgical reforms of the 1960s, prominent Anglo-Catholic writers wrote book-length poetic works inspired by the structure of the Anglican liturgy and liturgical calendar. Bestselling mass-market writers as diverse as John Keble and the Golden Age detective writer (and poet) Dorothy L. Sayers and canonical writers as disparate as Christina Rossetti and T. S. Eliot participated in this literary project.

Far from the minor literature of a conservative subculture, the Anglo-Catholic liturgical long poem was broadly popular and possessed lofty, and sometimes radical, political and philosophical aims. Since human subjects orient themselves in reference to their cultural construction of time and perceive the rhythms of nature in temporal terms, poetry that attempts to restructure time according to the liturgical calendar also inevitably reshapes the self and reconfigures the human relationship with nature.[11] Further, since liturgy is by definition a communal endeavor, liturgical poetry inherently grapples with, and often reimagines, the idea of community. During the period I study, England was in the process of redefining itself as a nation, moving from the explicitly confessional and oligarchical Georgian state, through the Victorian and Edwardian extensions of religious freedom and popular franchise, and on to the highly secularized postwar Welfare State. By reimagining the English community in liturgical terms, liturgical poetry intervenes in these cultural transformations, sometimes offering unexpected visions of a post-capitalist, post-industrial English future. For the literary critic or cultural historian, the Anglo-Catholic liturgical long poem provides a fresh lens through which these alterations in the English imagined community can be productively analyzed. From Romanticism to Late Modernism, the Anglo-Catholic liturgical long poem constitutes an important site of literary innovation and cultural and philosophical debate.

I

Liturgy

If the literary project of the Anglo-Catholic liturgical long poem has not previously been studied, this omission probably stems from a general critical tendency to ignore English liturgical poetry or minimize its significance.

The literary influence of particular liturgies on particular English authors demonstrably remains a subject largely unexplored. No liturgy has been more central in post-Reformation English experience and religious identity than that contained in the Book of Common Prayer. As Timothy Rosendale has persuasively argued, "By regulating the conduct of public worship, the aural delivery of the Word, and by implication the format of the individual encounter with the divine, it [the Book of Common Prayer] was the central textual mediator of social and religious experience" in the Reformation era and afterwards; it became "the cornerstone of a complex and powerful new collective identity."[12] But Rosendale also observes (and complains about) the Book of Common Prayer's "history of near-spectacular neglect among literary scholars."[13] Daniel R. Gibbon also laments that "few literary scholars . . . have focused on the literary and cultural impact of the peculiar rhetorics of the Book of Common Prayer"; the work of "trac[ing] the complicated lines of influence that these ubiquitous liturgical texts had upon the English language and imagination" is "just starting."[14]

I suspect that critics have neglected liturgical poetry—and, more broadly, the influence of liturgy on English literature—for reasons derived from both the standard anthropological account of liturgy and the basic premises of literary theory. The noted anthropologist Roy Rappaport offers both a clear definition of liturgy and a perceptive account of the cultural work that liturgy performs. Rapport defines liturgy as "religious ritual" and in turn defines ritual as "the performance of more or less invariant sequences of formal acts and utterances not entirely encoded by the performers."[15] He notes the performance of such sequences logically entails "the sealing of the social contract . . . the construction of time and eternity; the representation of a paradigm of creation; . . . . and the construction of orders of meaning transcending the semantic."[16] To perform a liturgical sequence is to enact an ideal model of both society and world, is to structure time by tropological rather than chronological order, is to arrange signs by vertical rather than horizontal points of reference.

The operating assumptions of literary criticism as a field may lead it to minimize or miss the creative potential of liturgy thus defined. In its fixed structure, liturgy could be assumed to thwart individual innovation. Given its inherently collective nature, liturgy could be taken to function merely as a means of social control. Despite their many differences, each of the late nineteenth-century thinkers whose work most influenced the development of literary theory—Karl Marx, Friedrich Nietzsche, and Sigmund Freud—considered religion as a whole to be primarily a mechanism for social control, and critiqued religious faith on those grounds. Many critics, especially in the Marxist tradition of Louis Althusser, have followed in this tradition by analyzing the ways in which literary texts unconsciously reveal religion's function as a mechanism of identity formation that is ultimately subservient to state power (in Althusser's terminology, an Ideological State Apparatus). In the final section of his famous essay "Ideology and Ideological State Apparatuses," Althusser explicitly extends this line of inquiry to the forms of the Catholic liturgy—"the well-known rituals of baptism, confirmation, communion, confession and extreme unction, etc."—and concludes that they are vehicles by which individuals are interpellated by the Religious State Apparatus into an identity subservient to the capitalist state.[17]

By contrast, critics have considered *authorial* religion to be interesting primarily when it seems to function as a means of resisting or subverting such social control—which is to say, when it seems to be an individual rather than a collective property and can thus be to some degree exempted from the general critique. To cite only Victorian examples, one might reference the many affirmative and nuanced studies of Christina Rossetti's faith performed by feminist scholars[18] or the boom in queer readings of Gerard Manley Hopkins.[19] Within the dominant critical frame, then, scholars are not likely to consider seriously the possibility that the collective aspects of religion, such as liturgy, might make constructive contributions to literature, politics, or human subjectivity.

However, scholarship has over the last two decades begun to reevaluate the political potential of collective liturgical performance. In her influential work *Ritual Theory, Ritual Practice* Catherine Bell asserts—against sociologists who view ritual simply as a means by which social power relations are internalized—that liturgy can inspire acts of subversion or protest. She grants that since it enacts a social ideal and typically involves hierarchy, liturgical ritual necessarily constructs a power relationship. But she adds that, since the force of liturgy depends on its fixed and inherited form, liturgical ritual represents a social authority to some degree prior to and different from power in its present state. Hence, ritual is a site not just of "consent" but also of "resistance," a space that provides "a sense of community *without* overriding the autonomy of individuals or subgroups" (Bell's italics).[20] Talal Asad takes the point further: in secular modernity, a liturgically derived individual subjectivity *must* be subversive, as the liturgical body has internalized a sense of time that "cannot be translated into the homogenous time of national politics" and possesses "memories, feelings, and desires" that "necessarily escape the rational/instrumental orientation of such politics."[21] The theologian Catherine Pickstock, whom I will discuss at more length in my chapter on John Keble, has asserted the creative and politically liberative power of liturgical performance still more strongly.[22] I am indebted both to her major work *After Writing: On the Liturgical Consummation of Philosophy* (1997) and more generally to the Radical Orthodox school of thought to which she belongs, which places theology in dialogue with literary theory.[23] Although in this volume I will sometimes employ the Althusserian concept of interpellation as a useful model of the relationship between individual identity and external social forms such as liturgy, I follow Bell, Asad, and Pickstock in resisting the assumption of passivity on the part of the religious believer that the term seems to imply.

The work of applying this theoretical reevaluation of liturgy to nineteenth and twentieth-century English religious poetry has only recently begun. Kirstie Blair (who will be discussed below) and Karen Dieleman, the author of the only monograph specifically on this subject, have been pioneering in this regard. In her valuable work, *Religious Imaginaries: The Liturgical and Poetic Practices of Elizabeth Barrett Browning, Christina Rossetti, and Adelaide Proctor*, Karen Dieleman defends the "thesis—that distinctive religious-poetic voices can arise from religious imaginaries formed by and in response to liturgical practice."[24] She asserts that just as theology can be an intricate intellectual exercise, to which one does not merely submit but in which one creatively participates, so too liturgy can be understood as a set of cultural practices that do not merely shape the passive believer, but by which the believer actively reshapes the community and world. She finds this insight also to be applicable to poetics, which means that the recognition that an author's poetry is liturgically inflected should no longer necessitate a dismissal of his or her work to imitative or pejoratively devotional status.

The communal nature of liturgy suggests that an author's liturgical poetics will usually be derived not from abstract liturgical theories of the sort I have discussed above, but from the particular liturgical practices of a given community. Unlike Dieleman's study, which discusses the influence of several different Christian liturgical traditions on English poetry, the present volume embraces liturgical particularity as an intellectually fruitful methodological limitation. For, while there were occasional efforts (in conscious imitation of John Keble) to structure book-length poetic works around the Roman Catholic or Jewish liturgical calendars, the nineteenth- and twentieth-century attempt poetically to remake the world and reorder time via the liturgical calendar was largely an Anglican—and, more specifically, Anglo-Catholic—enterprise. Each author I analyze writes as a member of the Church of England, which possesses a liturgical tradition in many ways unique in Western Christianity.

As many historians of religion have noted, Anglicanism has historically been a religion held together more by a common worship than a common creed. Roman Catholics may liturgically belong to the more common Western (or Roman) Rite or a wide variety of Eastern Rites derived from the religious traditions of Eastern Europe, North Africa, and the Middle East. In their liturgical diversity, they are bound together by a common body of doctrine (the pronouncements of the Catholic General Councils from Nicaea in 325 to Vatican II in 1962–1965) and allegiance to a common spiritual authority (the Pope). Anglicanism is doctrinally defined by the Thirty-Nine Articles, which were crafted to accommodate the diverse factions within the Anglican Church, while excluding Roman Catholicism and dissenting Protestantism, and which are consequently clearer in their negations than in their affirmations. The Articles have also never received a definitive interpretation. John Henry Newman famously reconciled them with the decrees of the Council of Trent and, and on the other side of the spectrum, some liberal Anglicans assent to them while denying Jesus's physical Resurrection. Anglicanism is formally defined by allegiance to the Archbishop of Canterbury, whose headship of the communion is deliberately symbolic and without judicial force.

Perhaps uniquely in Christian experience, Anglicanism has historically been a religion defined primarily and most positively in liturgical terms. As Rowan Williams, himself Archbishop of Canterbury, observes, the "Book of Common Prayer is unique among the worship books of Christendom in having become the touchstone for the ethos and even, for hundreds of years, the unity of a whole church."[25] The Book of Common Prayer was, historically, the primary force holding together a theologically diverse community that possessed no single vision of episcopal authority; it was the distinctive object of devotion that marked members of the community and the primary element of the Anglican religious experience that was remembered with nostalgia by those who had left it. To a large extent, the Anglican Communion *is* its liturgy, a claim that has important ramifications for liturgical poetry that also attempts to reconstruct the English church and nation.

An explanation of the contents and history of the Book of Common Prayer is then in order. J. Neil Alexander succinctly defines the "unique and unmistakable shape" of the Prayer Book:

> At its core is a fivefold set of liturgical texts: the daily offices, the Litany, the Holy Communion, the pastoral offices, and the ordinal. Each liturgical text is for use in public worship and to be followed by both clergy and congregation on Sundays and holy days. Auxiliary components, such as the Psalter, the calendar of the church year, and tables setting forth the scriptures to be read on various occasions, complete the book. ("The Shape," 64)

The Book of Common Prayer was designed during the English Reformation to create, as its title suggests, uniform national worship. Uniformity of worship was unknown in the medieval English church, whose liturgy possessed many local variants.[26] The creation of a common religious imagination through a uniformly shared liturgical practice was one of Archbishop Thomas Cranmer's principal innovations, and it was enforced by law. The 1559 Act of Uniformity required that all worship was to be conducted according to the

Prayer Book. From 1662 until 1828–1832, religious observance according to the Prayer Book was required for political position and for legally recognized marriages and funerals;[27] until the mid-nineteenth century, it was required for education at Oxford or Cambridge.

The compulsory nature of the English *Book of Common Prayer* did not preclude the possibility of revision, and it exists in four basic versions. Though emphases vary, each version of the Prayer Book assumes the continuity of the established church with the medieval church that came before it, and presents Anglican worship as an improved and purified or "rationalized" version of the earlier tradition.[28] The Book of Common Prayer was first compiled by Archbishop Thomas Cranmer as a loose translation of the medieval English Sarum Rite (with a few Lutheran and Eastern Orthodox additions) in 1549, revised in a more Calvinist direction in 1552, revised again so as to synthesize (especially in its communion rite) medieval Catholic with Reformation Calvinist convictions in 1559, and revised again so as to emphasize its nationalist character in 1662 (adding the "State Services," which I will discuss later). Some Anglo-Catholics have preferred the 1549 Prayer Book, as better illustrating continuity with the medieval church, while some evangelical Anglicans have argued for the 1552 Prayer Book, as better representing the Protestant character of the Church of England. However, for over three hundred years, from 1662 to 1966, the 1662 Prayer Book remained in force as the sole licit public liturgy of the Church of England.[29] Like the language of the King James Bible, the language of the Prayer Book came to be commonly regarded as both ancient and sacred.

Since the 1662 Prayer Book combines multiple liturgical and theological traditions, it has been defined as either a fundamentally Protestant document or a fundamentally Catholic document; the judgment largely depends on whether one wishes to emphasize its continuity or disjunction with the medieval liturgies it revises.[30] Many scholars and individual believers have noted that the Anglican communion rite, for instance, can be read so as to either affirm or deny the Roman Catholic doctrine of the Real Presence of Christ in the elements.[31] The Anglo-Catholic writers I analyze, and whose beliefs I will shortly define, place a particular stress on continuity. Dorothy L. Sayers speaks for all the authors in this study when she writes, "There was never any break with tradition so violent as to destroy altogether the liturgical framework which preserved the continuity of form between the pre-Reformation and post-Reformation worship of the Church."[32] The present volume is a study of Anglo-Catholic poetics, and hence will share this emphasis on the Prayer Book's elements of continuity with earlier liturgies. I take this emphasis pragmatically, because it will best elucidate the philosophy and concerns of the authors whom I am studying. I should not be understood as taking a side in the still ongoing polemical debates within the Anglican Communion as to whether Cranmer's Prayer Book—and Anglicanism itself—is fundamentally Catholic or Protestant in nature, or some via media between the two.

II

Liturgical Time

Although previous scholarship on the literary impact of the Book of Common Prayer has focused primarily on the baptismal, marriage, communion, and funerary rites—and how they create both an imagined community and shared picture of human life[33]—the present volume will focus primarily on poetic uses of the liturgical calendar. The Anglo-Catholic liturgical long poem—a book-length poetic work structured around the Anglican liturgical calendar—is obviously and explicitly concerned with the nature of time. And liturgical time differs significantly in its nature and dynamics from the homogenous clock time that is normative in secularized Western modernity. In *A Secular Age*, Charles Taylor usefully delineates the cultural and philosophical foundations of the experience of liturgical time. He asserts that traditional societies—including the *ancien régime* Europe of the 1700s—construe the world as "enchanted" and inherently meaningful and ordered. They imagine time not as an endless succession of uniform moments, but as consisting of two separate orders: the ordinary and sequential, "horizontal flow of secular time" and "higher times" that transcend these limitations.[34] Taylor suggests that for medieval Western Europeans, higher times took three basic forms: "Plato eternity," which consists of abolishing time; "God's eternity," which consists of gathering and ordering time into graced moments; and a national and/or religious "time of origins."[35] For Christians, the life of Jesus—who in the graced moment of the incarnation brings together the finite and the infinite, time and eternity, and who founds the church—is the ultimate example of a higher time. Talal Asad similarly observes the "interlinked times (eternity and its moving image, and the irruptions of the former into the latter: Creation, Fall, Christ's life and death, Judgment Day)" that structure "the complex medieval Christian universe."[36]

Taylor suggests that important aspects of medieval European religious belief and practice can best be understood in the context of this complex confluence of times. Since higher time breaks the linear order of secular time, medieval Christians found it easily imaginable that events of eternal significance might be prefigured before their advent (as in the typological interpretation of the Bible, which reverses chronology by reading Old Testament events allegorically in light of New Testament events) and might persist after it (as in Christ's passion, re-presented in the mass).[37] The liturgical calendar brings together each type of higher time, structuring the calendar year around events in the life of Christ and his followers the saints[38] and fortifying this structure by typologically arranged readings from scripture. For the ordinary medieval layperson, the liturgical year constituted a frequent point of contact with higher time.

Whether it is a Catholic or Protestant document as a whole, in its liturgical calendar the Book of Common Prayer carefully preserves the medieval Christian conception of time that Taylor elucidates and the vertically oriented society it assumes. As Alan Jacobs has observed, "Almost uniquely among the leading Reformers of the age, he [Cranmer] insisted on a Kalendar that followed the ancient pattern of the Church Year much as the Roman church kept it."[39] From the first, then, the Book of Common Prayer was concerned with structuring time, and its preservation of a Christian Year was one of the major Puritan objections to the book.[40] The Prayer Book's calendar, like many aspects of the Prayer Book, is an adaptation of the practices of the medieval English Catholic Sarum Rite to the concerns of the Reformation. The *temporale* or seasonal calendar—the progression from Advent to Christmastime, on to Lent, Easter, Pentecost and back again—is structured around major events in the life of Jesus and the early Church and continues unchanged from medieval Catholicism. The Anglican Church also retained the practice of assigning feast days to particular saints throughout the year (the *sanctorale*) but reduced the number of saints celebrated.[41]

Significantly, given the focus of the present study, the historical trajectory of Anglicanism after the Reformation has been to add new feast days rather than remove them, to sacralize rather than disenchant time. The 1549 Prayer Book, which overall stayed closest to pre-Reformation practice, nonetheless removed all saints who lived after the period of the New Testament (as is common in Lutheranism).[42] The 1552 Prayer Book, although typically Calvinist in orientation, restored such popular celebrations as St. George's Day and Lammas Day, and the 1559, 1604, and 1662 Prayer Books restored the celebration of over sixty saints as minor feasts or "Black-Letter Days." The 1662 Prayer Book sanctified additional days by adding vigil days for major holy days and feasts of the saints.[43] The 1662 Prayer Book also broke with previous practice by asserting the possibility of celebrating feast days for post-Reformation figures and ascribing divine meaning to major recent events in national history. The 1662 Prayer Book adds a celebration of King Charles the Martyr (January 30th), the Restoration of the Monarchy (May 29th), and the failure of the Gunpowder Plot (November 5th).[44]

The Prayer Book also includes a lectionary (or "Table of Lessons") that designates which scriptural passages—generally, an Old Testament text and a New Testament text—should be proclaimed during Morning Prayer and Evening Prayer for each day of the liturgical year, following the order of the *temporale* and *sanctorale*. The Anglican lectionary, particularly in its selections from the New Testament epistles, is fundamentally identical with that of the medieval Roman Rite, which had assumed its basic structure by the eighth century, lending the Prayer Book an air of antiquity.[45] The Anglican Psalter also assumes that the entirety of the book of Psalms will be recited over the course of each month, without regard to the liturgical cycle.[46] Cranmer thus combined and popularized the Liturgy of the Hours and the liturgical calendar, causing Anglican worship to move simultaneously according to two different orders of divine time. For most of Anglican history, the daily services were not actually practiced on a daily basis, and Morning and Evening Prayer were reserved for Sundays, or perhaps Sundays, Wednesday, and Fridays.[47] Nineteenth-century Anglo-Catholicism revived the daily service, which it saw as important both for continuity with the medieval past and for the sanctification of time.

The revival of the daily service and the poetic works I study were both part of a larger Anglo-Catholic attempt to resist the nineteenth-century secularization of time (a subject discussed more fully later in this introduction). Most of the authors in this study will draw their understanding of time primarily from the *temporale* and *sanctorale*, but for Christina Rossetti the Psalter is of equal importance in investing time with meaning. Since the Psalter uses the older Miles Coverdale translation of the Psalms (1535), rather than that of the 1611 King James Version,[48] it is possible to distinguish whether an author is referencing the Prayer Book when citing a Psalm; I will indicate throughout when quotations from the Psalms have been taken from the Psalter.

III

Anglo-Catholicism

Keble, Rossetti, Sayers, and Eliot all approach both liturgy and literature not merely through a common experience of Anglican time and a common membership in the Anglican Church, but through a common commitment to the High Church or Anglo-Catholic movement. The term "High Church" was first introduced into general usage as a Whig term of abuse,[49] but has come to indicate broadly that element of historic Anglicanism that emphasizes tradition, ritual, and episcopal authority. The contours of the High Church movement are broad and illusive, however, and have served as the subject of considerable scholarly debate.

Although, as Dominic Janes notes, it too possesses "no foolproof definition,"[50] I will throughout this book typically prefer the term "Anglo-Catholic." I will use the term "Anglo-Catholic" to refer to the belief that the Anglican

Church is one branch of the Catholic Church and that as such its sacraments effect that which they signify. In their ecclesiology, Anglo-Catholics conceive of the church as a vertically ordered hierarchical institution. All of the authors in this study explicitly affirmed a Branch Theory of Christianity, in which the Christian churches that are governed by bishops whose episcopal orders can be traced in a line of succession back to the apostles—which is to say, the Anglican, Roman Catholic, and Eastern Orthodox churches—each constitute the legitimate embodiment of the universal Catholic Church for a particular geographical area. From this perspective, as T. S. Eliot publicly asserted to considerable controversy, the dissenting Protestant churches are not "churches" in the full sense of the term, whereas the Anglican Church is "the Catholic Church in England."[51] The term "Anglo-Catholic," with its implicit rejection of Protestantism and hyphenated tension between the local and the universal, captures this position quite exactly.

As their emphasis on apostolic succession implies, these Anglo-Catholic writers take a high view of the authority of the early Christian church. They believe that the undivided early church was inspired by the Holy Spirit and take the writings of the Apostolic Fathers—the primary theologians and bishops of the undivided first eight centuries of Christianity, the "patristic" period—to be definitive guides for interpreting the teachings of Jesus and the Christian Faith.[52] Consequently, the authors whom I study make no distinction between the human "Jesus of history" who lived in Palestine in the first century C.E. and the divine "Christ of Faith" constructed by the early church. To capture this element of their worldview—which is congruent with their general rejection of disenchantment and affirmation of higher times—I will use the terms "Jesus" and "Christ" interchangeably throughout this book.

The term "Anglo-Catholic" also implies a view of the sacraments typically associated with Roman Catholicism rather than Protestantism, one that emphasizes the objective efficacy of the physical elements (rather than the internal disposition of the recipient or the celebrant). From this point of view, for instance, the reenactment of Christ's passion and death in the Eucharist does not merely cause the members of the congregation to "remember" these events in an internal and subjective manner; rather, this communal act of remembering and reenactment renders the events recalled mystically present, and Christ himself truly present in the elements of bread and wine. Each author in this study held a Platonic or philosophically realist position on the sacraments in which, when properly celebrated by priests who possess apostolic succession, the elements effect what they signify; "the symbol somehow shares in its archetype," and thereby reorders material reality.[53] These shared sacramental and ecclesiological commitments are significant for the liturgical poetry I will analyze, which attempts to create an efficacious symbolic order and thereby to reinstate an organic and divine community.

Each of these authors was also consciously participating not just in a shared theology, but also in a shared Anglo-Catholic subculture and literary tradition. Here are a few examples of their common cultural circles: Keble in 1833 founded and, with John Henry Newman and Edward Pusey, led the Oxford Movement. Christina Rossetti worked with and supported Pusey's Anglican sisterhoods and wrote poetic tributes to Newman. An accomplished amateur vocalist and devout Anglo-Catholic, Dorothy L. Sayers inhabited a cultural world that swayed according to the rhythms of the Oxford Movement production *Hymns Ancient and Modern* (1861); she was also was deeply influenced by Bishop Charles Gore, the former Principal of Pusey House at Oxford. In 1933, as a member of the publications division of the Anglo-Catholic English Church Union, Eliot oversaw the release of many titles celebrating the hundredth anniversary of the Oxford Movement, and in Anglo-Catholic clubs and social organizations (such as St. Anne's, Soho) he shared a physical and cultural space in common with Sayers. In sum, Keble was perhaps the leading High Churchman of his day and, as their letters and biographers attest, Rossetti, Sayers, and Eliot did not simply attend the local Anglican parish, but instead carefully sought out a priest with suitably High Church convictions. While Anglo-Catholicism certainly develops and changes between the high-theological Oxford movement in the mid-nineteenth century, the aesthetically and liturgically oriented Ritualism of the late nineteenth-century, and the mass-audience Eucharist Congresses of the interwar period, all of these authors consciously belonged to an historically continuous subculture.

This cultural relationship could also be expressed in literary terms. Christina Rossetti's poetic debt to John Keble is well known (she personally illustrated her copy of *The Christian Year*), and Dorothy L. Sayers in youth openly admired pre-Raphaelites like Rossetti and in middle age praised T. S. Eliot's verse plays. Until the publication of his letters and uncollected prose, it was impossible to establish T. S. Eliot's relationship to this tradition. But we can now show that T. S. Eliot had read *The Christian Year* and considered its author to possess "a certain gift for verse," and that he valued Christina Rossetti precisely as the first figure in the tradition of the Oxford Movement to compose "great religious poetry."[54] Eliot also befriended and encouraged Anglican clerical poets who in the 1930s were writing books whose very titles (like *Lyra Subapostolica*) marked them as a continuation of the poetic tradition of John Keble (who, with John Henry Newman and others, wrote the poetic volume *Lyra Apostolica*).[55] Each of these authors participated in a common project of reordering time according to the liturgical calendar, and each possessed a knowledge of other Anglo-Catholic poetic projects oriented toward the same end.

This shared religious commitment to Anglo-Catholicism also possesses significant literary implications. For these Anglo-Catholic poets, the Anglican liturgy is more than a social imaginary; it is a transcendent formal structure. In her fine work *Form and Faith in Victorian Poetry and Religion*, Kirstie Blair shows that Victorian arguments about the value (and/or constraints) of poetic form are inextricably linked with similar arguments about the benefits or limitation of external religious forms such as liturgy.[56] Through a thorough analysis of the literature and theology of the period, Blair demonstrates that Low Church or Dissenting poets, such as Robert Browning and Elizabeth Barrett Browning, typically viewed both a perfectly regular poetics and a set order of religious service as cultural straightjackets that confine and oppress the human spirit, keeping it from reaching higher insights and expressions. By contrast, High Anglican or Roman Catholic poets, such as John Henry Newman or Coventry Patmore, typically defended the use of regular, defined structures in both poetry and religious ritual. God, they held, has created a supremely ordered universe, and sin—often identified with impulse or unchecked emotion—amounts to a deviation from this pattern. Hence, both religious ritual and formal poetry are valuable as organic means by which emotion and inclination can be directed into their proper channels and the individual restored to the order of creation.[57] The restrictions of form are then "the only way to access grace and true freedom."[58] Blair's work can be used to explain why English poets seeking to re-enchant the universe and break from the secular order so often drew upon liturgical form in their poetics; it offered them a divine structure.

The intense liturgical mysticism of Anglo-Catholic poetry is typically overlooked or minimized by literary critics, perhaps because of our current cultural assumptions about Anglicanism as a moderate, rationalistic religion or because of the Tractarians' own belief in "reserve," the practice of articulating one's full religious convictions only within the boundaries of a shared community of faith. But for the authors I discuss, the Anglican liturgy possesses a power that might more commonly be associated with the Hindu *Rig Veda*; the order of the liturgy is literally the order of the universe. As I shall explain in more detail in the chapter on John Keble, these high Anglicans held that Jesus had unlocked the meaning of the universe to the Apostles, who passed this understanding on to the Apostolic Fathers, who transposed it on to daily life for the average Christian in the liturgy and liturgical calendar, which liturgy and calendar were providentially preserved by the Anglican Church. As Kirstie Blair alone among literary critics has noted, in the Oxford Movement "the Book of Common Prayer in particular was defended . . . as an inspired volume, less the product of its specific historical context than of pure Christian tradition, approved by God. This meant that in effect its prescriptions, rituals, and linguistic forms could be viewed as divinely ordained."[59] For the Anglo-Catholic liturgical poets as well, the structure of the liturgy is not merely one reflection among many of a structured universe; it is *the* structure of the universe.

IV

Liturgical Time in a Secular Age

The Anglo-Catholic liturgical poets construct their visions of a divinely ordered world that moves according to liturgical time in what might seem the most unlikely of cultural moments: the nineteenth and twentieth centuries. As late as 1800, England was still a nation that conceived of time primarily in liturgical terms. William Gibson asserts in his history of the Anglicanism in the long eighteenth century, "The religious calendar located Britain and her history in the triumph of Anglicanism. It permeated both the poor and elite in sermons and festivals."[60] Throughout the eighteenth century, Holy Days were used as popular points of reference in determining dates and describing seasons, and folk customs such as festivals for harvest, planting, manuring, and the parish's patron saint's feast day remained firmly in place.[61] Many of the most widely celebrated Prayer-Book festivals were national in character, and encouraged an understanding of the social order as vertical and divine and the nation as an organic, unified body.[62] As E. P. Thompson has influentially argued, "until the first decades of the nineteenth century" the liturgical calendar was so widely observed that it precluded the development of a standardized work week; the whole year was punctuated with holy days on which one could not work, and "the people clung tenaciously to their customary wakes and feasts, and may even have enlarged them in both vigor and extent."[63]

Gibbon's and Rosendale's pioneering studies trace the cultural life of the Prayer Book from the sixteenth to the eighteenth centuries, concluding at a moment when English popular culture still moved according to the rhythms of the Anglican calendar. In contrast, the Anglo-Catholic liturgical poetry I analyze in this volume emerges after and grapples with the collapse of a culturally shared sense of liturgical time. A broad scholarly consensus attests to the idea that time was secularized, commodified, and homogenized over the course of the English nineteenth century. Most literary scholars and social historians would explain these changes in economic terms. As E. P. Thompson noted in his classic study of the subject, industrial capitalism required the populace to internalize a new model of time. The nineteenth century is the first era of mass industrialization and, via the railways, mass transit. These developments necessarily entailed the detachment of time from both the cycles of nature and the dictates of regional custom.[64] In order to comply with the exact timetables of the new factories, laborers ceased to orient themselves according to a traditional solar sense of time and began to regulate themselves by the more invariable clock and watch.[65] As E. P. Thompson observes, "the seasonal rhythms of the countryside, *with its festivals and religious holidays*" gave way before the "needs of industrial production" (italics mine).[66] The liturgical calendar yielded to the time clock. As Guy Debord pithily states, abstract, secular time may be best understood as "time-of-production, time-as-commodity."[67]

One might add, "time-as-standardized-mass-market commodity." Wolfgang Schivelbusch notes that Victorian railway transit and shipping schedules—which were themselves linked to the production demands of the factory system—could not be reconciled with the chaotic patchwork of local and regional times that marked early nineteenth-century England.[68] Railway timetables required a uniform national method of measuring time. By the 1840s, each English railroad had developed its own standardized system of time; by the 1880s, a unified system of railroad time had become English "standard general time."[69] Trish Ferguson succinctly summarizes the effects of this altered sense of time on Victorian subjectivity: the Victorians lived in an "increasingly disciplinary industrial world of factories, the mail system, and transport schedules, all of which was facilitated by the strict observance of the newly developed concept of public time kept by the town clock."[70] In this industrialized context, it first became possible for secular, homogenous, clock time to be equated with "time itself."[71]

Although I am indebted to each of these analyses of the nineteenth-century secularization of time, this book relies especially on the model of secularization Charles Taylor has offered in in his landmark study *A Secular Age*. I am aware that *A Secular Age* is only one of many rival accounts of the phenomenon of secularization and that Taylor's theories have been controversial in some quarters.[72] I do not ask readers to accept his narrative absolutely or unreservedly. I turn to Taylor because he most fully analyzes the consequences of the nineteenth-century transformation in the social nature of time for broader cultural conceptions of the self, community, nature, and the transcendent. Unlike other accounts of secularization, Taylor's model provides a theoretical vocabulary that can be used to explain why nineteenth- and twentieth-century poetry that aims to restructure time around the liturgy also inevitably attempts to reshape the self and reimagine both community and world.

Taylor concurs with the scholarly consensus that marks the nineteenth century as the period in which secularity and secular time first became culturally viable in Western Europe and the twentieth century as the period in which secularity becomes firmly established in European mass culture. But Taylor's original understanding of secularity as a concept leads him to perceive consequences for self and society in this cultural shift on which others have not remarked or at which they have only hinted. For Taylor, secularity refers not only or principally to the governmental "emptying of religion from autonomous social spheres" or to the personal or collective decline of religious belief and practice, but especially to the creation of a social order where neither belief nor unbelief can be assumed as axiomatic.[73] Daily life under secularism is experienced in terms of the horizontal and the immanent, though individuals may interpret their experience within this "immanent frame" as being either "open" or "closed" to contact with a transcendent order that lies beyond it; hence, the question of spirituality continues even in a secular age. Taylor asserts that whether people are believers or skeptics, in a secular age their ideas of themselves and ideas about the world experience "fragilization" by their constant awareness of viable alternative possibilities. And he holds that one of the primary means by which individuals have experienced and internalized secularism in their daily lives has been the secularization of time, the loss of the liturgical calendar.

In Taylor's account, the origins of secularization antedate industrial capitalism, which merely accelerates the process. He holds that late-medieval and post-Reformation efforts at cultural and personal reconstruction required and eventually accomplished the disenchantment of world and time and the isolation of the self. To briefly summarize his lengthy and complex argument: An enchanted world is inherently resistant to the notion of progress. Both the political structure (i.e., the monarchy) and the religious structure (i.e., the church) are perceived as vertically ordered and connected to higher times; the order of things as it stands is, in a sense, divine. But in a disenchanted world, the material universe is assumed to be devoid of teleology and can therefore be interpreted in purely instrumental terms; the social world of politics can be subject to a similar analysis.[74] Order does not preexist in the external world, but is, rather, invented or discovered by the individual human mind. Lacking teleology, both human society and the material world comprise inherently pliable materials that can be reconstructed according to what is perceived as an improved model or reoriented toward what are seen as better ends. Taylor cites figures as diverse as Oliver Cromwell's Puritans and the French Revolutionaries as sharing this project in common. A world of homogenous time and linear progress is appealing to reformers of all types because it is more easily remade and managed. Taylor holds that such a disenchanted world is inevitably inhabited by individuals who possess "buffered selves"; they conceive their (meaningful) interior personal identities as radically cut off from the (meaningless) exterior world, a phenomenon which can be experienced as either freedom or isolation.[75] The modern state for Taylor is an amalgam of individual buffered selves, and derives its authority from its promises to protect their individuality and to create an imagined community that allows them to experience some sense of the festive and the collective.

Less obviously, for Taylor the reformist concept of progress also requires the abolishment of higher times. The idea that the nation and the world originated in higher times both assumes the belief that each possesses a fixed, if imperfectly realized, ideal form and contradicts the idea of history as a linear, forward progression. As Taylor puts it, "The dominance of instrumental rationality in our world, and the pervasiveness of secular time go together."[76] In the liturgical calendar, days possess set meanings and fixed cycles that lack instrumental value, stand independent of individual consent, and signify vertically via their connection with higher times; time units are not isolated and interchangeable and can in fact penetrate, reshape, and convert the individual self. Hence, Taylor sees the buffered self that inhabits a disenchanted world as also "deeply anchored in . . . our embedding in secular time."[77] For all these reasons, the creation of linear, "homogenous, empty time" is a key part of the "modern secular outlook."[78] The disenchantment of the world and society both contributes to and depends upon the secularization of time.

Taylor's work can help us to grasp the philosophical and cultural significance of the nineteenth and twentieth-century Anglo-Catholic poetic attempts to order time according to the liturgical calendar. Anglo-Catholic poetry begins its efforts to mediate between the individual self and the collective liturgical calendar precisely at the historical moment when in England liturgical time becomes significantly fragilized and must be consciously chosen as a point of reference in preference to other viable alternatives. Walter Benjamin observed that the "historical consciousness" of calendrical time sets it apart from, and places it to some extent at odds with, clock time.[79] If, as Trish Ferguson has suggested, in industrialized Victorian England, all "narratives that reject the principles of chronological standardized time" constitute a form of "resistance" against the "new disciplinary time culture,"[80] liturgical poetry may be a particularly effective and culturally appropriate site of such resistance. The liturgical calendar in the nineteenth century provides a model of both time and social life that is alternative to that offered by secularism and industrial capitalism, a model that had also been dominant within living memory. The Anglo-Catholic liturgical long poem creatively exploits this difference, as it self-consciously questions the inevitability of both the secular age and secular time, envisioning alternate worlds and measuring alternate times. Taylor's account of secularity can show us why this Anglo-Catholic poetic effort to recover liturgical time must pose a significant challenge not to secular time alone but to the secular world order as a whole. Since all aspects of cultural secularity are mutually interdependent, the resumption of liturgical time inevitably involves the resurrection of the enchanted world, the end of the buffered self, and the reconstruction of society.

In her early poem "The House of the Soul: A Lay" (1918), Dorothy L. Sayers explicates the subversive power of liturgy in a secular age in terms that strangely mirror Taylor's. The speaker of Part VI of this poem longs for a tool by which she could break the sequence of homogenous, empty time. Clock time, she realizes, alienates an individual from his or her experiences, and renders the external world both meaningless and insolid. These sentiments are expressed in what amounts to a metaphysical nursery rhyme:

I hate the clock;
It first says Tick,
It then says Tock;
I hear days flick,
I see years flock,
The whole world rock;
Had I the trick
I'd like to lock
Time with a block
To make it stick. (Sayers, "House of the Soul: Lay," VI, lines 1–10)

The speaker yearns for a "brick" or "stock" that could she "drop" "in the nick" and stop the clock and the progression of linear time (lines 14–15, 17). She finds it (lines 11–12) in the liturgical pronouncements: "Hic, haec, and hoc" ("For this [is the chalice of my blood"]; "May this [mingling together . . . of the body and blood of our Lord Christ, become, to us who receive them, profitable to eternal life]"; "For this [is my body]"). Sayers realizes that the liturgy is a weapon, a brick that could smash the order of clock time, an insight that she embodies most fully in her contributions to the Anglo-Catholic liturgical long poem.

V

I define the Anglo-Catholic liturgical long poem as a book-length work designated by the author as poetry that, using the course of a single year as a synecdoche, employs the liturgy to reorder time—and thereby the world—as a whole. I have chosen the four authors of Anglo-Catholic liturgical long poems included in this study for their importance in the worlds of letters and Anglo-Catholicism, and for the ambition and scope of their poetic projects. John Keble's inclusion is axiomatic, as he both founded the Oxford Movement and in the last years of the Romantic period wrote the first Anglo-Catholic liturgical long poem, *The Christian Year*. As G. B. Tennyson has noted, English literature before Keble contains nothing like *The Christian Year*'s attempt to provide a poetic accompaniment to the entire liturgical calendar; at most, previous poets wrote for a few feasts or a single liturgical season.[81]

John Keble's *Christian Year* constitutes the first book-length poetic sequence structured around the Anglican liturgical calendar and reveals the basic philosophical, political, and theological stakes of this project. The contents of the Anglican lectionary—like those of the Roman Catholic lectionary—are chosen on a largely typological basis. In typology, time runs backward, as events in the Jewish Old Testament are reread in light of the lives of Jesus and the apostles. The Apostolic Fathers of the Christian Church both set the typological pattern of the lectionary and extended this method of reading out onto the natural world; if the earlier Jewish revelation is to be read as a foreshadowing of the life of Christ, then God's original revelation in creation can be similarly interpreted. For Keble, the liturgical calendar both teaches the typological method of reading and bridges the gap between this symbolic world and the ordinary world of daily experience, providing a key to each day. As Keble's speaker moves through the liturgical year, he transforms from being a modern alienated individual possessing a buffered self to living as part of a transcendentally oriented community in an enchanted world.

I have also focused on three very different later authors who took on the same basic literary and theological challenge as Keble. A few mid-Victorian poets performed nearly note-for-note imitations of *The Christian Year*. But the later writers on whom I focus lived in a cultural and literary environment that had greatly altered since Keble's time and recreated the project of *The Christian Year* for their own eras; direct imitation of Keble was for them impossible. The authors whom I study all possess a shared sense that secular modernity entails a profound sense of isolation and meaninglessness, a state of alienation that they feel can be resolved only by returning to a common sacred text and common temporal order. For them, as for Keble, poetry serves a mediating function, connecting the buffered secular self to the collective rhythms of the liturgy. But philosophically and politically these authors differ greatly in both their diagnoses of modern disenchantment and in the re-enchanted worlds they imagine; their works are correspondingly various in both style and form.

Christina Rossetti's poetic career spans the second half of the Victorian period, but she publishes her seventy-poem poetic sequence structured around the Anglican liturgical calendar ("Some Feasts and Fasts") only in her final volume of poetry, *Verses* (1893). *Verses* addresses the apocalyptic skepticism that marked the fin-de-siècle by being more apocalyptic and more skeptical than the era itself. In Rossetti's work, as much as in Oscar Wilde's *Intentions* (1891) or *The Picture of Dorian Gray* (1891), the world viewed in itself is unstable and devoid of inherent meaning, and human life similarly lacks a meaningful trajectory and coherence. Rossetti attempts to find a way past this conundrum by means of the apocalypse. By reading time backward, the muddled present as a typological foreshadowing of an apocalyptic state of ultimate meaning, Rossetti reinscribes purpose and significance upon an empty world. The Anglican liturgical calendar serves for Rossetti as the bridge, both theological and structural, between apocalyptic time and ordinary time; only by means of the Prayer Book can the temporal be seen in light of the eternal. The reader moves from the difficulties of *Verses*' opening section ("Out of the Deep have I called unto Thee, O Lord") to the apocalyptic certainty of its final section ("Songs for Strangers and Pilgrims") precisely by means of the pivotal central section on the liturgy ("Some Feasts and Fasts"). *Verses* reinvents the Anglo-Catholic liturgical long poem for a world Keble could not have imagined, a post-Romantic world intellectually dominated by biological and anthropological materialism. In Rossetti's work, the essentially Platonic conception of the material world as a partial reflection of the ideal world of the liturgy is placed in a productive dialogue with the most nihilistic tendencies in fin-de-siècle thought.

Anglo-Catholicism peaked in terms of both cultural influence and popular appeal during the interwar period. For this reason, I have chosen to address the interwar work of two different English authors, one of whom amply represents the movement's popular appeal and the other of whom exemplifies its cultural influence. Dorothy L. Sayers initially entered a literary scene transitioning from the Georgian to the modernist aesthetic, publishing her first liturgical poetry in *Catholic Tales and Christian Songs* (1918). But Sayers is of course best known as a detective novelist; the creator of Lord Peter Wimsey, she was judged by the British Crime Writers' Association in 1998 to have written the greatest mystery novel of all time.[82] Sayers attempted in her final novels to raise the literary status of Golden Age detective fiction, and insisted that her most famous Wimsey novel, *The Nine Tailors* (1934), should actually be read as a prose poem; throughout this study, I will follow her guidelines and analyze it as a poetic work. In *The Nine Tailors*, a car accident and a murder pull the cosmopolitan agnostic Lord Peter Wimsey into the world of Anglican village life. He solves the crime only by developing an increasing mastery of the Book of Common Prayer and is over the course of the novel interpellated in spite of himself into its understanding of the world and time. When read as a poem, the volume derives its central motif and music from the church bells—the titular *Nine Tailors*—that order Anglican life and time and that are mandated by the Book of Common Prayer. For Sayers, the liturgy and sacraments rescue materiality itself from the simulacrum that dominates secular England and the bells of the Anglican church bring even the traumatic noise of World War I back into musical rhythm. Her final novels, taken collectively, suggest that the Prayer Book alone retains the capacity to reconcile the diverse factions of an increasingly divided England; it is a final hope for an organic society and a meaningful world. She also illustrates the political diversity of Anglo-Catholic uses of liturgical time, constructing a restored England in which gender equity is valued and the excesses of capitalism are curbed.

The last body chapter, on T. S. Eliot, addresses Anglo-Catholic modernism's literary and political aspirations and potential. After his 1927 conversion to Anglicanism, T. S. Eliot maintained a consistent interest in the poetic uses of the liturgy. From "Ash Wednesday" (1930) to "The Cultivation of Christmas Trees" (1954), his work reflects on the feasts and fasts of the church year. But only in his first and most famous verse drama, *Murder in the Cathedral* (1935), does Eliot attempt to use the liturgical calendar to reorder time and remake the world. Eliot held that poetic drama had a potential to make and shape a community that conventional poetry—which exists primarily in a textual rather than oral form and is typically read by solitary individuals—does not. *Murder in the Cathedral* is liturgical interwar assault drama. The chorus, like the audience, lives in a world devoid of meaning, where the only discernible shape or order is that derived from raw power. Both chorus and audience are confronted with the figure of Thomas Becket, who is depicted as a living embodiment of the liturgy, and they are forced to witness his martyrdom. As witnesses, they must determine whether they would testify on Becket's behalf, or whether the liturgical world is better left dead and buried. Eliot is the only author in this study who does not order his liturgical poetry around the Book of Common Prayer. He prefers the Anglo-Catholic liturgy known as the *Anglican* (or *English*) *Missal*, which was not legally approved for public worship in the Anglican Church. Eliot's preference for a dissident liturgy reflects a twentieth-century skepticism about the possibility of a common culture absent in Keble and Sayers. A common culture and a world of meaning have for Eliot both already been lost, and if they were to be reborn would have to rise transfigured from the dead. The move toward re-enchantment begins with the avant-garde and is likely to be resisted by mass culture. Faith belongs to a subculture, and it is up the audience to determine whether it finds the liturgy's dissident vision of life and polity compelling. In this form, the power and challenge of liturgical poetry remain, even as the Prayer Book itself fades. The concluding chapter uses the late work of Dorothy L. Sayers and T. S. Eliot to analyze both the 1940s high water mark of the Anglo-Catholic liturgical long poem, when liturgically derived social change seemed truly possible, and the literary form's postwar struggles and collapse as the Church of England declines and the Book of Common Prayer loses its legal mandate.

The present volume is a study in counter-cultural religious poetics. Each of the Anglo-Catholic authors whom I study felt that through the liturgy the English people possessed access to the basic structure of the universe, but also judged that England was not presently—or perhaps had never fully been—in sync with this divine order. For each of the authors whom I study, poetry serves a mediating function, showing how an individual might be restored to the divine order and the benefits of this restoration. If poetry is, after William Wordsworth, a means of capturing and reflecting upon individual experience,[83] a liturgical poetry might serve to limit the excesses of autonomous individualism and reverse the process of social fragmentation. The Anglican liturgy assumes enormous metaphysical and literary weight for these authors because they construe it as the primary common language and model of community that England possesses or could come to possess, the principal means by which their world could be remade. Individual by individual, the community might be reconstructed and liturgical poetry might reinstitute, or newly create, a liturgical order. For the critic writing in what some have called a "post-secular" age, Anglo-Catholic liturgical poetry provides both an instructive dissident account of the process of secularization and an intriguing vision of a post-secular, post-capitalist England. The cultural project of the Anglo-Catholic liturgical long poem is both deeply traditional and potentially revolutionary; these authors are engaged in the work of reconstructing and reimagining the world.

NOTES

1. Dennis, introduction, vii.
2. For an example of Yonge's characters quoting Keble, see Charlotte Yonge, *The Heir of Redclyffe*, ed. Barbara Dennis (Oxford: Oxford University Press, 1997), 54. Text references are to chapter and page numbers from this edition.
3. Barbara Dennis provides this quotation in her survey of the book's reception in introduction, viii.
4. See Brontë, *Jane Eyre*, 466–67.
5. Taylor, *A Secular Age*, 374.
6. She recites a stanza of Keble's poem for the Second Sunday After the Epiphany from *The Christian Year*.
7. Tennyson, *Victorian Devotional Poetry*, 218.
8. Prickett "Tractarian Poetry," 279.
9. Prickett "Tractarian Poetry," 288–89.
10. Prickett, "Tractarian Poetry," 289. Prickett excepts only Gerard Manley Hopkins from this critique, as the eccentric and individualistic nature of his theology and literary style cause him to stand to some degree apart from Tractarian religious communality.
11. I will develop and support this claim in subsequent sections of the introduction.
12. Rosendale, *Liturgy and Literature,* 5, 35.
13. Rosendale, *Liturgy and Literature*, 7.
14. Gibbon, "Rewriting Spiritual Community," 35.
15. Rappaport, *Ritual and Religion*, 33, 24.

16. Rappaport, *Ritual and Religion*, 27.

17. Althusser, "Ideology," "An Example: The Christian Religious Ideology."

18. Arseneau and Palazzo's insightful works—*Recovering Christina Rossetti: Female Community and Incarnational Poetics* and *Christina Rossetti's Feminist Theology*—deserve fuller treatment and are discussed in more detail in the chapter of Christina Rossetti.

19. See. for instance, Julia Saville's book *A Queer Chivalry: The Homoerotic Asceticism of Gerard Manley Hopkins* (Charlottesville: University Press of Virginia, 2000); Frederick Roden's book *Same-Sex Desire in Victorian Religious Culture* (Basingstoke, England: Palgrave, 2002); Dennis Sobolev's article "Hopkins's 'Bellbright Bodies': The Dialectics of Desire in his Writings" in *Texas Studies in Literature and Language* 45 (Spring 2003): 114–40.

20. Bell, *Ritual Theory, Ritual Practice*, 8, 222.

21. Asad, *Formations of the Secular*, 179.

22. Pickstock, *After Writing*, 40.

23. As multiple critics have observed in the anthology *Varieties of Secularism* (eds. Warner, VanAntwerpen, and Calhoun), both Pickstock's and Asad's theories possess meaningful analogies with Charles Taylor's revisionist analysis of religion and secularity, on which I draw throughout this book. See particularly, John Milbank, "A Closer Walk on the Wild Side," 72–73, and Warner, VanAntwerpen, and Calhoun, editors' introduction, 25.

24. Dieleman, *Religious Imaginaries*, 2.

25. R. Williams, foreword in Hefling and Shattuck, *Oxford Guide*, xiii.

26. See Jacobs, *The Book of Common Prayer*, 24–25.

27. See Gregory, "The Parish Church," in Hefling and Shattuck, *Oxford Guide*, 103.

28. On this point, see Jeanes, "Cranmer," in Hefling and Shattuck, *Oxford Guide*, 28.

29. Buchanan, "Preserving," in Hefling and Shattuck, *Oxford Guide*, 261.

30. On this point, see Alexander, "The Shape," in Hefling and Shattuck, *Oxford Guide*, 65.

31. On this point, see Jacobs, *The Book of Common Prayer*, 58.

32. Sayers, "Worship," 46.

33. See Daniel R. Gibbons's article "Rewriting Spiritual Community" both for a valuable contribution to this discussion and a summary of the discussion to date.

34. Taylor, *A Secular Age*, 59, 54.

35. Taylor, *A Secular Age*, 57.

36. Asad, *Formations of the Secular*, 194.

37. See Taylor, *A Secular Age*, 54, 96.

38. See Taylor, *A Secular Age*, 58, 195.

39. Jacobs, *The Book of Common Prayer*, 52.

40. Mitchell, "Sanctifying Time," in Hefling and Shattuck, *Oxford Guide*, 478.

41. On the Anglican adaptation and revision of the medieval liturgical calendar, see Mitchell, "Sanctifying Time," in Hefling and Shattuck, *Oxford Guide*, 476.

42. See Mitchell, "Sanctifying Time," in Hefling and Shattuck, *Oxford Guide*, 478.

43. See Mitchell, "Sanctifying Time," in Hefling and Shattuck, *Oxford Guide*, 478.

44. On these additions, see Hefling, "State Services," in Hefling and Shattuck, *Oxford Guide*, 73.

45. On this point, see Baldovin, "The Liturgical Movement," in Hefling and Shattuck, *Oxford Guide*, 256.

46. See Alexander, "The Shape," in Hefling and Shattuck, *Oxford Guide*, 70.

47. See Gregory, "The Parish Church," in Hefling and Shattuck, *Oxford Guide*, 97.

48. See Alexander, "The Shape," in Hefling and Shattuck, *Oxford Guide*, 72.

49. See Nockles, *The Oxford Movement*, 28.

50. Janes, *Victorian Reformation*, 7.

51. For the phrase "the Catholic Church in England," see Eliot's essay "Thoughts After Lambeth," 337. For the implications of this position for relations with the dissenting churches, see *Reunion by Destruction* (458), in which Eliot writes, "The Church of England has always regarded itself, as have the Eastern Churches, as a living member of one visible Church. . . . If its members are to enter into a union, on terms of complete parity, with non-conformists, they must acknowledge that they are leaving a church and entering a society." For Dorothy L. Sayers's endorsement of the Branch Theory, and her application of the term "Anglo-Catholic" to herself, see her letters of September 24, 1941, and October 7,1941, to the Rev. Neville Garton and to Count Michael de la Bedayere, respectively (in *The Letters of Dorothy L. Sayers*, ed. Barbara Reynolds, Vol. 2, *1937–1943* (New York: St. Martin's Press, 1998), 298, 306.

52. For a fuller explanation of the Anglo-Catholic approach to the Apostolic Fathers, see my Keble chapter.

53. Janes, *Victorian Reformation,* 7. On the essentially Platonic nature of this position, see Janes, *Victorian Reformation,* 15.

54. Eliot, "Types of Religious Verse," 54.

55. For Eliot's efforts to help the Rev. Geoffrey Curtis's poetic volume *Lyra Subapostolica* achieve publication, see Eliot's letters to The Secretary, Student Christian Movement, February 3, 1932—in *The Letters of T. S. Eliot*, ed. John Haffenden and Valerie Eliot, Vol. 6: *1932–33* (New Haven: Yale University Press, 2016), 79—and to Curtis himself, January 14, 1932 (in *Letters*, 6:31). For Eliot's appreciation for Keble's poetry and his knowledge—at least at second hand—of Keble's poetic theory, see his letter to Charles Harris of September, 15, 1932 (in *Letters* 6:443–44).

56. Blair, *Form and Faith*, 1–2.

57. See Blair, *Form and Faith*, 32–33.

58. Blair, *Form and Faith*, 11.

59. Blair, *Form and Faith*, 25.

60. Gibson, *The Church of England*, 165.

61. Gibson, *The Church of England*, 165–66.

62. Gibson, *The Church of England*, 165.

63. Thompson, "Time, Work-Discipline," 377–78.

64. See Kimaid, *Modernity, Metatheory,* 52–53.

65. On this point, see Taylor, *A Secular Age,* 541–42 and Zemka, *Time and the Moment*, 2–3.

66. Thompson, "Time, Work-Discipline," 397. On this point, see also Kimaid, *Modernity, Metatheory*, 58–59.

67. Debord, *The Society*, 110.

68. Schivelbusch, *The Railway Journey*, 56.

69. Schivelbusch, *The Railway* Journey, 57.

70. Ferguson, introduction, 1.

71. Taylor, *A Secular Age*, 566.

72. For a useful summary of common models of secularization, see Pecora, *Secularization without End*, 21. For a sustained critique of *A Secular Age*, see During, "Completing Secularism," in Warner, VanAntwerpen, and Calhoun, *Varieties of Secularism*, 107–10, 125.

73. Taylor, *A Secular Age*, 2.

74. See Taylor, *A Secular Age*, 541.

75. From a more materialist perspective, Wolfgang Schivelbusch concurs, suggesting that the "Industrialized Consciousness" must be surrounded by a thick "stimulus shield" that detaches the individual from the environment in order to prevent the psyche from being overwhelmed by the bombardment of modernity (*The Railway Journey*, 153–54, cf. 179).

76. Taylor, *A Secular Age*, 542.

77. Taylor, *A Secular Age*, 301–2.

78. Taylor, *A Secular Age*, 124.

79. Benjamin, "Theses," 263–64.

80. Ferguson, introduction, 5–6.

81. Tennyson, *Victorian Devotional Poetry*, 75, 218.

82. Bury, "Agatha Christie," paragraph five.

83. For this definition of poetry by the most influential of Romantic poets, see Wordsworth, "Preface to *Lyrical Ballads*," paragraphs 15 and 26.

Chapter 1

"Tun'd to Hymns of Perfect Love"

The Romantic Prayer Book of John Keble's The Christian Year

John Keble's *The Christian Year* (1827; expanded third edition, 1828) was the bestselling book of poetry in nineteenth-century England. Keble's poetic accompaniment to the Anglican liturgical calendar, with a poem for every Sunday, feast day, and special service, went through ninety-five separate editions during Keble's lifetime, and had sold "half a million copies . . . by 1877."[1] According to Kirstie Blair, the most perceptive recent critic of Keble, "Almost every literate Victorian household would have possessed at least one copy."[2] *The Christian Year* reconfigured Romanticism in terms of orthodox Anglicanism, and in so doing influenced both English poetry and worship for the rest of the century.[3] Keble's poetry has, however, been largely ignored by literary critics, and he is remembered more often as an influence on other Anglo-Catholic writers than as a writer in his own regard.[4] Critics have missed the power and ambition of Keble's poetry because they have typically analyzed only individual poems; as G. B Tennyson notes, *The Christian Year* seems a "highly original poetic document" primarily when considered in terms of its overall structure and "form."[5] Keble first envisions, without any substantive precedent,[6] the poetic experiment that is the subject of the present volume: the Anglo-Catholic liturgical long poem or poetic sequence. While excellent work on Keble's view of nature and theory of poetry have been published in recent decades,[7] no critic has systematically analyzed how Keble's liturgical theories impact his poetic practice. The project of *The Christian Year* is, as its title would suggest, nothing short of a sacralization of time and nature, the reconstruction of Romanticism on a collective, textualist basis.[8]

At first glance, John Keble might seem a rather conventional Romantic. As Stephen Prickett has observed, Keble derives the central assumption of his Romanticism, the belief that the universe is "a living, active organic whole charged with divine meaning inseparably binding men and Nature," from his more famous friend William Wordsworth.[9] Like Wordsworth, Keble feels that though nature is divinely meaningful, he personally inhabits a fundamentally inorganic society and disenchanted world. He blames early nineteenth-century England's scientific empiricism and industrial capitalism for having defaced nature and rendered its meaning illegible. For Keble, as for William Blake in "Mock on, Mock on, Voltaire, Rousseau," empiricism can "on God's works no seal of Godhead find" because empiricism is a faulty method of reading the world.[10] Employing an image from Jesus's rhetorical question about John the Baptist—"What went ye out into the wilderness to see? A reed shaken with the wind?" (Matt. 11:7)—Keble laments that the early nineteenth-century English *do* go out into the wilderness merely "to count the reeds that tremble in the wind," to translate nature into quantifiable terms, rather than to find any divine significance there.[11] Keble envisions the modern British industrial city as a "Babel," where the urban poor live in "Mammon's gloomiest cells" in a "crowded loneliness."[12] Industrial pollution, Keble suggests, is an (unsuccessful) attempt to sever the City of Man from the Creator; the "mist that man may raise" is an effort to "hide the eye of heaven."[13] So far, so Romantic.

But very early in *The Christian Year* Keble begins to sound like a failed Romantic. The speaker of his poem "Fourth Sunday in Advent" longs to feel emotionally connected with nature and the external world, but instead—through no apparent will or intention of his own—finds himself isolated and cut off, his self buffered.[14] He opens the poem with a wistful lament:

Of all the bright things in earth and air
How little can the heart embrace!
(lines 1–2)

In an attempt to cast off the sense of disconnection and meaninglessness that Keble finds typical of secular modernity, the speaker then turns to the Wordsworthian imagination. If he cannot feel an automatic and intuitive connection with the world, perhaps he can cognitively perceive a divine order in nature. But he fails. He "cannot trace" the pattern and finds himself unable and "unworthy" to "read / One page of Nature's beauteous book" (lines 4–6). As a good Romantic, he next appeals to memory. If nature and imagination fail him, perhaps interpersonal connection and memory's gift for imposing order and pattern will restore his sense of a coherent, interconnected world. But memory betrays him and its objects, functioning as a tool of erasure rather than preservation, an attempt at presence that only reinforces absence:

I cannot paint to Memory's eye
The scene, the glance, I dearest love—
Unchang'd themselves, in me they die,
Or faint or false their shadows prove.
(lines 9–12)

Unable to help himself, in desperation he finally implores the ultimate source of Romantic authority, poetry, for aid. But he is not only unable to gain poetic inspiration; he is tone-deaf and cannot follow the notes of those who have come before him. "In vain, with dull and tuneless ear, / I linger by soft Music's cell" (lines 13–14). His lack of emotion, imagination, and memory renders him unable to "hear / What to her [Music's] own she deigns to tell" (lines15–16); he does not belong in the company of the poets.

The Christian Year places this poem precisely at the darkest part of the year, the days immediately preceding the winter solstice (and Christmas). The poem is subtitled "Dimness," and fittingly so, as by the end of the fourth stanza, the speaker has reached an impasse. None of the principal Romantic methods of finding meaning in the world—emotion, imagination, memory, poetry—will work for him. He has an intuition that the world must have meaning, but he finds all things dim and uncertain; he lives in confusion with no solid footing or place to stand.

'Tis misty all, both sight and sound—
I only know 'tis fair and sweet
'Tis wandering on enchanted ground
With dizzy brow and tottering feet.
(lines 17–20)

We are only seven poems into the volume, but we seem to have hit a wall. How can we have a book of Romantic poetry, in which neither the individual's emotion, nor imagination, nor memory, nor poetic inspiration is to be trusted? The answer seems to be the collective liturgical calendar itself. "But patience!" the speaker advises himself and his readers at the start of the next stanza (line 21). The apocalypse is a state of perfect meaning and connection, as the second half of the poem reminds its readers, but neither the speaker nor the readers are as yet apocalyptic. In the "Fourth Sunday in Advent," *The Christian Year* is barely a month into the first season of the liturgical calendar, under whose tutelage both reader and speaker may eventually resolve the poem's basic quandary. The speaker suggests that both he and his readers hope to understand the order, meaning, and poetic beauty of the universe; both "fain / Wouldst thread the maze of harmony" (lines 53–54). But they wish for more than rank beginners at the mystical life can handle. Instead, the speaker advises the reader,

Content thee with one simple strain,
The lowlier, sure, the worthier thee.
(lines 55–56)

Readers will learn, as in music lessons, by attending to the plain music already set before them without their conscious volition: the poetry of the liturgy and the rhythms of daily life. By this method, they will gain new depths of emotion, poetic inspiration, and apocalyptic perception. The poem's concluding lines promise that once speaker and reader are thus "duly trained, and taught / The concord sweet of Love divine; / Then, with that inward Music fraught" they may "For ever rise, and sing, and shine" (lines 57–60).

Keble's *The Christian Year* was the single bestselling piece of poetry written during the Romantic era, and as I have mentioned Keble himself was a friend and admirer of Wordsworth. But this is a surprising sort of Romanticism, in which the collective is more reliable than the individual, and the poet's inspiration, emotion, and identity possess worth only if he has been "duly trained, and taught" by an external authority (line 57). Before moving any farther in *The Christian Year*, before proceeding past Advent, I should back up, and unpack how Keble's Romanticism ends up in the impasse this poem describes and why the collective liturgy seems to resolve it.

I

Despite his essentially Romantic outlook, Keble was deeply skeptical of the individualism typically valorized by nineteenth-century Evangelicalism, Liberalism, and Romanticism.[15] If he shared a Romantic sense that modernity had lost touch with nature's divine meaning, he lacked the Romantic faith that the individual inspiration of the poetic genius might somehow remedy this problem. His poem "Fourth Sunday in Advent" does not merely depict a failed Romanticism; it also forcibly expresses the problems and quandaries of early nineteenth-century subjectivity, the alienation and skepticism that come with the buffered self. In his sermons, he identifies individualism as an unfortunate result of the Fall of Man, complaining that "[t]here is in all mankind, by corrupt nature, a certain proud love of independence, a desire of standing alone, the ill effects of which are seen and felt in a thousand ways every day."[16] He asserts that since even "original genius" is usually "mixed up with so much of error and paradox," it generally causes "more harm than good" to its possessor; a wise person will be sufficiently self-skeptical as to avoid the exercise of "personal judgment in matters of faith" whenever possible.[17] High Anglicans often critiqued Dissenting Protestantism's reliance on private—rather than communal—interpretation of God's revelation in Scripture. Keble is equally skeptical of Romantic interpretations of God's revelation in Nature. He critiques the interpretations of nature proffered by secular poets on the grounds that they are devoid of "certainty, much less any sacredness," since as individual surmises they lack a foundation in an order of meaning "intended [by God] from the beginning."[18] Since for Keble individualism is at the root of modern isolation and alienation, he concludes that an individualistic Romanticism can only exacerbate, rather than remedy, the cultural ailments it diagnoses.

In the writing of the Apostolic Fathers, Keble found a method of reading both scripture and nature that he considered to be free from the dual errors of individual interpretation of scripture and Romantic individualism. Like all traditional Christians, Keble believed that the Apostles were the divinely authorized interpreters of Jesus's life and mission, and that their biblical writings offered an inspired account of his thought. Like all Anglo-Catholics, Keble believed that since the Apostles designated their successors, the first bishops of the Christian church, and those bishops in turn designated their own successors, the writings of the Patristic bishops—or Apostolic Fathers—authentically interpreted the thought of the Apostles.[19] Throughout his work, Keble consistently treats "[t]he constant tradition of the early Church" as the reliable measure of the meaning of Scripture.[20] Keble ascribed a level of authority to this tradition that exceeded even the judgments of most of his High Anglican contemporaries, asserting that the writings of the undivided church of the early Christian centuries provide a "practically infallible" guide to the interpretation of the Christian scriptures and, thereby, of the life and thought of Jesus himself.[21]

The dominant method the "practically infallible" Apostolic Fathers employ to interpret both scripture and nature is typology. As George Landow notes, typology began in the early Christian church as a means of reading the Old Testament. Events, symbols, and rituals in the Old Testament were taken to foreshadow, symbolize, or suggest "Christ and His dispensation"; the Old Testament "type" is fulfilled and transcended by the New Testament or church "antitype."[22] Typology provides Keble with the anti-individualistic method of symbolic interpretation he requires. As George Landow has noted, types are "divinely created symbol[s]"; in order for an object to be a type, the type/antitype relation must be thought to have been designed by God himself and to have been indicated or at least implied in the New Testament.[23] The individual imagination of the poet can make an object a symbol in the conventional sense; personal poetic inspiration, however, cannot make an object a type.[24]

Keble conceptualized his book-length work on biblical typology, *The Jewish Nation, and God's Dealings with Them, Paralleled with Individual Christians, and God's Dealings with Them,* while working on *The Christian Year* and wrote it in the interval between *The Christian Year*'s first edition (1827) and the expanded third edition (1828).[25] The thesis of this work is that typology paradoxically brings together the collective and the individual, as "the conduct of the [Jewish] nation [in the Old Testament is] a continual type of man's conduct towards his God," "God's mercies to them [the Jewish people] are typical of His mercies to us [Christians]; to us individually, to them in their collective and national capacity."[26] Given Keble's obsession with typology in 1827 and 1828, it should not be surprising that typology is in many ways central to *The Christian Year*'s treatment of the Bible, nature, and the Book of Common Prayer.

As Keble observes in *Tract 89: On the Mysticism Attributed to the Early Fathers of the Church*, the Apostolic Fathers extrapolated typological reading out onto the natural world, positing that, like the divine revelation in the Jewish covenant, the divine revelation in creation foreshadowed and suggested God's ultimate revelation in Christ.[27] Keble was an authority on the Fathers, and believed that nature takes on meaning only when one projects a patristic, typological reading method from the Bible out onto nature (and *not* one's reading of nature back onto the Bible.[28] As Keble explains, when Jesus in the Gospels ascribes meaning to a natural object—such as the "lilies of the field" in Matthew 6:28–29—"the CREATOR [is] applying to moral or spiritual uses His own outward and visible works; which work He had created, knowing in His Omniscience that He should so apply them, and therefore (among their other final causes) with the very purpose of doing so."[29] The "material world," Keble insists, is quite literally "constructed" with the "symbolic alphabet of Scripture" in mind, and one can construe its meaning by reference or analogy to scripture.[30] Christ taught this lesson to the Apostles, who passed this knowledge on to the Apostolic Fathers via oral tradition.[31] From the Apostolic Fathers, Keble learned that the "visible world" is "an index or token of the invisible," that the whole physical world is "typical" of the divine.[32]

The Apostolic Fathers, in Keble's words, opened "a window . . . for the lamps lighted within the Church to stream here and there upon the external world."[33] In M. H. Abrams's classic analysis of Romantic literature, *The Mirror and the Lamp,* the "mirror" represents an eighteenth-century claim that the artist simply represents reality as it is; the "lamp" represents a more truly Romantic claim that the artist depicts the world only as illuminated by the artist's consciousness. Since Keble holds the Apostolic Fathers of the Christian church to be "practically infallible," the lamp they hold up to the external world *both* inscribes meaning on and reveals the meaning of the world. As Keble speculates,

> [M]ay it not be affirmed that He [Christ] condescends . . . to have a Poetry of His own, a set of holy and divine associations and meanings, wherewith it is His will to *invest* all material things? And the authentic records of His will, in this, as in all other truths supernatural, are, of course, Holy Scripture, and the consent of ecclesiastical writers [the Apostolic Fathers]. (*Tract 89*, 144, italics mine)

For Keble, the poetry of Christ succeeds where typical Romantic poetry fails. The writings of the Apostolic Fathers provide him with religiously authoritative proof that his Romantic belief in a divinely meaningful natural world is not merely another individualistic delusion. They present a "fixed and regular" set of divine hieroglyphs.[34] In the Book of Common Prayer, Keble found a Rosetta stone that unlocks these "divine hieroglyphs," enabling him to use them to interpret all creation.

II

The Book of Common Prayer, the public liturgy of the Church of England, is a combination of readings from the Old and New Testament with prayers from patristic and medieval liturgies, as translated, edited, and added to by the Anglican bishops of the sixteenth and seventeenth centuries. As I have mentioned, the 1662 edition was formally definitive, and was the only licit Anglican liturgy for over three hundred years.[35] Keble held that the bishops of the Church of England were, by merit of their apostolic succession, the legitimate heirs of the Apostolic Fathers, and the Church of England an organic continuation of the early church.[36] For Keble, the authority of the Book of Common Prayer comes both from the apostolic succession of the bishops who authorized it and from the patristic origins of its liturgical structure and many of its prayers. Keble asserts that the basic order of Scripture readings contained in the Prayer Book goes back to "the early church," and the elements of the liturgy may even originate with the Apostles themselves.[37]

In Keble's thought, the Prayer Book's synthesis of patristic content and apostolic authority serves to legitimate the divine authority and organic character of the church that produced it. The Book of Common Prayer constitutes a basic connection between contemporary Anglicanism and (to use Charles Taylor's term) the "higher time" of the era of Christ and the Apostles. Keble asserts that "[t]he Prayer-book, *taken as it is from the Prayer-books of the first and best times*, teaches everywhere . . . that Christ's Holy Catholic Church is a real outward visible body, having supernatural grace continually communicated through it by succession from the Apostles, *in whose place the bishops are*" (italics mine).[38] For Keble, then, in the Book of Common Prayer the modern Apostles (the bishops of the Church of England) both interpret the ancient Apostles and, via the sacrament of Holy Orders, transmit their gifts; in the Book of Common Prayer, the inspired ancient church speaks with an authoritative, even oracular, modern voice. In Keble's poem "St. Luke," for instance, the speaker assumes that apostolic and Anglican worship are fundamentally identical, addressing the saint:

Thou hast an ear for angels' songs,
A breath the gospel trump to fill,
And taught by thee the Church prolongs
Her hymns of high thanksgiving still.
(lines 69–72)[39]

For Keble, in fact, the Book of Common Prayer preserves and presents the prayers and reading methods of the Apostolic fathers in a divinely guided manner; it is itself in some sense an inspired document. Keble wrote that compiling its "Canons and formularies" (which is to say, the Book of Common Prayer) the Anglican church had been "providentially guided" to preserve the doctrines of the Apostolic Fathers.[40] Charles Wheatly, an eighteenth-century Anglican divine repeatedly cited in Keble's footnotes to *The Christian Year*,[41] pointedly informs his readers that when the original Prayer Book was issued "the king and the three estates in parliament" praised the work as having been produced "BY THE AID OF THE HOLY GHOST" (Wheatly's capitalization).[42] In a similar vein, *The Christian Year* depicts the Anglican church as an angelic singer chanting "heavenly song" and the Anglican liturgy with its annual "round of holy thought" as an inspired teacher.[43]

Significantly, for Keble typology is the key to the Prayer Book's inspired structure.[44] Keble considers the Prayer Book to be a supremely and designedly typological document. By its very nature, the Prayer Book places the Old Testament in typological relation to the New, the New Testament in relation to the writings of the Apostolic Fathers, and all three in relation to the external world and the secular calendar. For many high Anglicans of Keble's time, the Prayer Book was the "authorized interpreter" of scripture; for this reason, many high Anglican divines insisted that the Bible should be available for purchase only when accompanied by the Prayer Book.[45] Keble himself suggests in *Tract 13* that the selection of scripture readings in the Book of Common Prayer was "providentially" arranged so as to serve as "a clue to many Scripture difficulties" and to "the true use of the Old Testament."[46] Read apart from the Prayer Book, Scripture could only be misinterpreted. Keble makes a very original deduction from this common high Anglican premise: for Keble, since the Bible is the interpretive key to the universe, and the Prayer Book the interpretive key to the Bible, the world itself is read correctly only when read in terms of the Book of Common Prayer. As Joshua King has noted, "Keble assumes that every detail of reality acquires typological significance only if read according to a shared text."[47]

Keble's theology of the liturgy might seem to render liturgical poetry superfluous. If each individual believer performs a daily act of enchantment by reading the world by means of the Bible and the Bible by means of the Book of Common Prayer, then no special role in the process of enchantment remains for the poet. There is no need for yet another level of reference in which the individual interprets the Book of Common Prayer by means of *The Christian Year*. Perhaps this is why the Anglican Church of the eighteenth century, which recent historical scholarship has shown to have remained firmly rooted in both the liturgical calendar and the enchanted world, produced so little liturgical poetry. As William Gibson notes, eighteenth-century and early-nineteenth-century Anglicanism was still largely a communal, traditional, rural enterprise that moved according to the rhythms of the liturgical calendar. In farming communities, public penances were still administered by church courts and were accepted by the penitent as a natural part of the moral order.[48] As I have discussed in the introduction to this book, liturgical feasts were still collectively observed, and honored by both employers and employees, to the extent that no standard work week existed. Anglican liturgical time remained essentially time itself, to the extent that "Morning and evening prayer . . . became familiar elements in the collective inner landscape of eighteenth-century society."[49] The omnipresence of the Anglican Church—led by the bishops under the authority of the King—was crucial in maintaining a general belief that English society constituted a unified, organic, vertically ordered whole.[50] During the Napoleonic wars, nationalist sentiment served to reinforce the popular belief that the Anglican Church was a divine institution and that only Anglicans should be trusted to lead the nation. In popular opinion, Protestant Dissent and Roman Catholicism were considered unpatriotic, to say the least, and were not construed as viable religious options worthy of serious consideration. The Test and Corporation Acts restricting government office to Anglican communicants and the Acts of Uniformity requiring the use of the Prayer Book received mass support and were widely popular.[51]

Keble was born in the late eighteenth century, and carefully observed and keenly felt the collapse of both the enchanted world and liturgical time. He publishes *The Christian Year* during the 1827–1828 national debates over whether Catholic Emancipation should be approved and the Test and Corporation Acts repealed, allowing non-Anglican Christians to serve in parliament and on the boards of public organizations. He delivers his Assize Sermon on "National Apostasy" that inaugurates the Oxford Movement only six years later (1833). Both gestures are acts of protest against the rise of a horizontally oriented society in which time lacks inherent meaning. In 1828, the Irish Roman Catholic Daniel O'Connell had initiated a constitutional crisis by gaining election to a parliamentary seat that he could not legally occupy. By this time, Protestant Dissenters had come to play a crucial economic role in the developing industrial north of England. It seems retrospectively inevitable that both Catholics and Dissenters would be allowed to serve in parliament and help guide the direction of the nation. But the fundamental alteration in British society entailed in Catholic Emancipation and the repeal of the Test and Corporation Acts was not missed or minimized by contemporary observers. As John Wolffe notes in *God and Greater Britain*, the repeal "significantly changed the constitutional basis of the British state," taking "a significant step towards constitutional pluralism."[52] An "era of constitutional change" ensued that includes the 1832 Reform Act and the Irish Church Temporalities Act of 1833, which "scaled down the resources of the Church of Ireland" to reflect the proportion of the population it represented.[53] Non-Anglican members of parliament could now pass parliamentary decrees and influence ecclesiastical appointments that would change the shape of Anglicanism as a religion. The church was being legally treated not as a divine institution whose authority derived from Christ and the Apostles, but as a department of the state whose authority was derived only from the level of popular consent it could command.

Both the unity and vertical reference of English society were threatened by these developments—as John Keble well recognized. His "National Apostasy" sermon was occasioned by the Irish Church Temporalities Act, but also addresses the repeal of the Test and Corporation Acts.[54] In the "Advertisement" to the sermon, Keble rants against the collapse of the hierarchical, vertically oriented, religious society he had known. He is one of "those members of the Church who still believe her authority divine,"[55] but knows that English society is moving in the opposite direction:

> the Legislature of England and Ireland, (*the members of which are not even required to profess belief in the Atonement*") . . . . has also ratified, to its full extent, this principle;—that the Apostolical Church in this realm is henceforth only to stand, in eye of the State, as one sect among many, depending, for any preeminence she may still appear to retain, merely upon the accident of her having a strong party in the country. (Keble, "Sermon on National Apostasy," 127, Keble's italics)

Pluralism and popular consent are now the sole determinants of worth and meaning and vertical claims to divine authority have no force. Keble's analysis of the traits of a secular age, and his sense of the exact moment of its rising, corresponds with that later offered by Charles Taylor.

As I have shown above, Keble is also keenly aware of—and in his poetry acutely depicts—the consequences of secularity for the individual psyche:

a buffered self that struggles with a sense of alienation and general meaninglessness. He believes that to live in such a world is to lose any sense of higher times. He praises in his sermon "Shadows and Substance" the parishes in rural England that still acknowledge the primacy of the liturgy and liturgical time, ushering in the calendrical New Year (for instance) with a widely attended daybreak church service. But he knows that he and his hearers no longer belong to such a world. They live in an England busy "beginning the New Year with music and feasting, with in-door or outdoor sports, or with some promising experiment in the way of business," an England that moves in secular time and is oriented around the immediate, the tangible, and the economic.[56] He imagines that his description of a world structured according to liturgical time will strike his hearers as so utterly foreign that they will "draw back . . . as from something very strange, unreal, and uncomfortable."[57] He sardonically notes that for most Englishmen, church would possess real meaning and become a priority in their lives only if someone paid them to attend; promises of heaven and claims about a higher reality no longer possess currency.[58] Keble recognizes that he is part of this secularized world, and does not wholly exempt himself from this critique. As he laments, "we are so used to live in shadows" that if we hear of a world of "substance," one that prioritizes the celebration of the liturgy over secular concerns, our first reaction is to be "amazed, and startled, and almost offended."[59]

The function of Keble's liturgical poetry is to make the world of the liturgy less "strange, unreal, and uncomfortable" to this secularized reader. Keble shares the common Romantic assumption that poetry is a vehicle for the expression of intense individual emotion and perception. Liturgical poetry, then, is particularly suited to mediate between the collective wisdom of the Prayer Book and the isolated psyche of the individual. Like the speaker of the early poems in *The Christian Year* or even Keble himself, the English public of the 1820s and 1830s no longer instinctively experiences time in a liturgical manner and no longer automatically perceives the world sacramentally. Liturgical poetry constitutes a primer by which it might relearn these lost methods of perception. *The Christian Year* will depict the psychological state of the secular subject and the difficulties of a disenchanted world as Keble perceives them, and remedy them not through original poetic vision, but through reference to a common text, a preexistent structure of meaning. The book will train readers in the use of vertical structures of signification and enable them to imagine a self so structured. As Keble writes in the "Advertisement" to the first edition of *The Christian Year*, "The object of the present publication will be attained, if any person find assistance from it in bringing his own thoughts and feelings into more entire unison with those recommended and exemplified in the Prayer Book."

III

The Christian Year treats the Prayer Book as both a model and teacher of a patristic method of typological reading whereby, with divine authority, we can find renewed meaning in the world. Keble asserts that if we are "tun'd" to God's and, by extension, the Prayer Book's, "hymns of perfect love," we will live in a divinely symbolic reality, a divinely ordered world, and nature will become for us a book that "he who runs may read."[60] Over the course of a year, the reader will be gradually brought into and trained to understand an enchanted world, and early nineteenth-century secularity will be reversed.

As in the patristic idea of God's rhetorical economy, in *The Christian Year* divine meaning is always approximate, and unfolds gradually, simultaneously constructed and revealed over the course of the liturgical calendar.[61] Since an analysis of each poem in *The Christian Year* would be impracticable, I will exemplify Keble's method of gradually re-sacralizing the world through intertextual reference by analyzing four key poems: "Morning" (the first poem in the volume), "Septuagesmia Sunday," "King Charles the Martyr," and "Ordination" (the last poem in the volume).

In both *Tract 13* and his work on typology, *The Jewish Nation,* Keble places special emphasis on the role of Psalm 95 in the morning service. He suggests that "[t]hat one Psalm may, on reflection, give the key to the arrangement of the [Scripture] lessons" for the whole Anglican liturgical year.[62] Keble asserts that the Christian typological reading of this Psalm begins with the New Testament writer of the Epistle to the Hebrews. When the author of Hebrews "comment[s] on the words of the ninety-fifth Psalm"—"Today if ye will hear his voice, Harden not your hearts, as in the provocation in the day of temptation in the wilderness: When your fathers tempted me. . . . So I sware in my wrath, They shall not enter into my rest" (Heb. 3:7–9, 11)—his comments imply that "the conduct and fate of the first generation of the Israelites in the wilderness" serve as a type of the temptations and perils individual Christians will face in their attempt to worship God.[63] The Apostolic Fathers then applied this interpretation to the Christians of their own era by making it a rule "from Primitive Times" that Psalm 95 be read as part of the church's daily worship.[64] Finally, the compilers of the Book of Common Prayer providentially placed this Psalm in the center of the first service in the volume to provide a key that shows that the scriptural readings in Prayer Book are arranged on a patristic, typological basis and must be read in a typological register.[65]

As in Keble's analysis of the Book of Common Prayer, in *The Christian Year* the opening selection serves as an interpretive key for the volume as a whole. The poem "Morning" states the basic problem of *The Christian Year* and suggests its solution.[66] Like the Anglican morning service, the poem begins with an act of penitence and a sense of disconnection from God. The speaker is the isolated economic individual living in a disenchanted world whom Keble takes to be now typical of England. He asserts that the "hues of the rich unfolding morn," the "rustling breeze," and "fragrant clouds of dewy steam"—by implication, nature as a whole—only "waste" their "treasures of delight / Upon our thankless, joyless sight," since we are out of step with the divine nature, "awak[ing]" "to sin," but "seldom" "partak[ing]" of "Heaven" (lines 1, 5, 9, 13–14, 15–16). He feels no connection with the exterior natural world that he observes. For Keble, the solution to this problem is to re-enchant the world by rereading and rewriting it so that it reflects the divine. As he writes,

If on our daily course our mind
Be set to hallow all we find,
New treasures still, of countless price
God will provide for sacrifice . . . .

Oh, could we learn that sacrifice,
What lights would all around us rise!
How would our hearts with wisdom talk
Along life's dullest, dreariest walk!
(lines 29–32, 45–48)

If we perform this act of reading, Keble suggests, we will find our lives to be "a road / To bring us daily nearer God"; if we resign ourselves to God's providence, we will find "The secret . . . of Rest below" and prepare ourselves "for perfect Rest above" (lines 55–56, 60, 62). Our worlds and psyches can be remade, and *The Christian Year* will model this process.

As Kirstie Blair has noted, the apparent simplicity of Keble's poetry has led to its current critical devaluation. Keble's "Morning" lyrics may on the surface sound like simplistic inspirational poetry, and indeed are popularly used as a hymn in the Church of England.[67] However, when read in intertextual relation to the Book of Common Prayer, "Morning" proves to be a complicatedly allusive typological reflection on both spiritual life and nature. Read in this register, the key words in Keble's poem are "Sacrifice" and "Rest." Keble's assertion that if we read the world with eyes of faith, God will miraculously provide us with "treasures . . . of countless price," but we in turn must "sacrifice" these treasures back to God recalls the biblical story of Abraham and Isaac. God miraculously provided Abraham in his old age with an heir, his son Isaac, but then insisted that Abraham offer Isaac up to him as a sacrifice; when Abraham complied, God then miraculously provided a ram to take the place of Isaac, and Abraham immediately offered it up to God instead. In the Benediction in Luke 1, recited daily in the Anglican Morning Service and referenced in Keble's footnote to his poem "St. Luke," Zacharias applies the story of Abraham to his own time, asserting that in the miracles surrounding the birth of Christ, God has "performed the oath which he sware to our forefather Abraham: that . . . we . . . might serve him without fear, / In holiness and righteousness before him: all the days of our life."[68] Keble, then, suggests that our mornings will take on meaning if we read them in light of the Book of Common Prayer's recitation of the Gospel of Luke's reference to the Old Testament story of the patriarch Abraham: with this interpretive key, our own lives become allegorical and, as in the case of Abraham, what had seemed like a life of lost wandering becomes really a straight "road to . . . God."

As I have mentioned, Keble considers the Morning Service, and the whole typological framework of the Book of Common Prayer, to revolve around its use of Psalm 95. Psalm 95 ends by pronouncing in the divine first person the doom that befell the rebellious first generation of Israelites out of Egypt, "I sware in my wrath: that they should not enter into my rest"; literally, they will never enter the Promised Land.[69] In Keble's typological reading, this is also the spiritual doom of the individual Christian who fails to live according to the divine order. But, the poem "Morning" suggests, if people are faithful and read through the lens of faith rather than the lens of disenchantment, they *can* live in the divine order, the infinitely meaningful, even allegorical, divine universe, participating in God's divine, seventh day "Rest" while still here "below" and eventually entering Heaven, God's "perfect Rest above." They *can* read nature as the book of God. In the Canticle of the Three Holy Children (or Benedicte, Omnia Opera), read in the Anglican morning service but never explicitly referenced in Keble's poem, the "Sun and Moon," the "Showers and Dew," and the "Winds of God"—each of the natural objects from which the speaker of Keble's poem feels disconnected—are all divine signs that "praise [God], and magnify him for ever."[70]

The final lines of Keble's poem indicate how the world is to be re-sacralized, as the speaker asks God to "Help us, this and every day, / To live more nearly as we pray" (lines 63–64). Here the poem proclaims the interpretive method it enacts and without which it cannot be understood. In "Trinity Sunday," Keble more explicitly asserts that the Book of Common Prayer is the providential means by which the reader is to learn how to live and how to interpret the world. The speaker, echoing the image from "Morning" of life as a "road" to God, reflects:

Along the Church's central space
The sacred weeks, with unfelt pace,

Hath borne us on from grace to grace.
(Keble, "Trinity Sunday," 10–12)

By seeing life as a reflection of the Book of Common Prayer, by performing daily this act of allegorical, intertextual reading, in Keble's revisionist Romanticism we gradually renew ourselves and create the world anew. *The Christian Year* depicts the speaker's progress along this path, his gradual loss of buffered isolation and disenchantment.

In the poem "Septuagesmia Sunday" Keble returns to each of the nature images from which the speaker felt alienated at the beginning of "Morning," and the speaker, trained by the process of the liturgical year, now confidently reads each of them as Christian types. "Septuagesmia Sunday," the third Sunday before Lent, was a particularly important date in Keble's analysis of the liturgical year (and of nature in light of the liturgical year), since on that date the cycle of scripture readings of both the Anglican and early church begin again with the creation of the world in Genesis 1 and 2.[71] In the Anglican liturgy, the second lessons for matins and evensong on this date come from Revelations 21 and 22, and relate God's recreation of the universe in the new heaven and new earth.

Consonant with these themes, Keble devotes "Septuagesmia Sunday" to showing more explicitly and in more detail how a Christian reading of the natural world imaginatively recreates it and transforms it into allegory. As the opening stanza of the poem asserts, the world is "a book, who runs may read, / Which heavenly truth imparts" to readers who have "Pure eyes and Christian hearts."[72] The poem largely consists of a series of examples of this premise, showing how the liturgy should train the devout Anglican to see natural objects as types of the eternal. To relate only the images which Keble repeats from his "Morning" poem, the "Sun," which symbolizes Christ, gives its "radiance" to the "Moon," which symbolizes the Church, glowing with light "borrow[ed]" from the sun (lines 13–16).[73] "The dew of heaven," an image echoing both the Garden of Eden[74] and the baptismal font, paradise and redemption, is a symbol of God's "grace," as "It steals in silence down; / But where it lights, this favoured place / By richest fruits is known" (lines 29–32). In an image going back to the Gospel of John (3:8), The "gentl[e] breeze" represents the Holy "Spirit's viewless way," the power that both created and now recreates the world, hovering over creation,[75] blowing where it will and invisible to the eye of the natural man (lines 39–40).

Sticking closely to his anti-individualist interpretive method, Keble unlocks the divine meaning of nature solely by interpreting nature images that have been given symbolic weight in scripture, then applied to all creation by the Apostolic Fathers,[76] and finally highlighted for his attention on Septuagesmia

Sunday by their presence in the readings for the day in the Book of Common Prayer. He *will* celebrate nature as emblematic of the divine, but he will *not* use his own imagination to identify these emblems. The poem's concluding stanzas assert that both the material universe and the human self possess a mystical significance legible to those who employ the proper interpretive method. The speaker first prophetically declares,

Two worlds are ours: 'tis only Sin
Forbids us to descry
The mystic heaven and earth within,
Plain as sea and sky
(lines 41–44)

He then more humbly begs God to "Give me a heart to find out Thee / And *read* Thee everywhere" (lines 47–48, italics mine). Only thus construed does the world become infinitely meaningful, the line buffering the inner world of the psyche from exterior reality erased.

G. B. Tennyson has provocatively suggested that the failure of modern literary criticism to understand nineteenth-century Britain's fascination with *The Christian Year* "stems from [the critics'] unwillingness or inability" to read the book in its intended intertextual context.[77] It is an unfortunate irony, then, that Rodney Edgecombe, who has performed a valuable service to scholarship by composing the only sustained critical analysis of the entirety of *The Christian Year*, considers "Septuagesmia Sunday" to be an ineffective poem because he as a reader "resist[s] Keble's readiness to offer problematic parallels as if they were transparent."[78] The parallels lack transparency only if the poem is separated from the Book of Common Prayer, and one object of the poem—and the volume as a whole—is to exemplify the premise that the world gains a meaningful order and structure of correspondences only when read in terms of the Prayer Book. If the poem and its interpretation of the world prove unsatisfying when divorced from the Prayer Book, this result simply proves Keble's point.

IV

Keble's Romantic treatment of the Book of Common Prayer as an inspired communal text that reshapes both its readers and the world is heightened, and reaches its logical conclusion, in the six poems he added to *The Christian Year* for its third edition in 1828. His theology of the Prayer Book is perhaps most clearly expressed in his controversial poem "King Charles the Martyr."

In "King Charles the Martyr," the Anglican liturgy possesses supernatural power, especially, the power to inscribe meaning on time. In this poem, King Charles gives his life for the Prayer Book, and God responds by imposing the Prayer Book's divine meaning on time. As I have noted, Keble saw the Book of Common Prayer as a divinely inspired guide to typological interpretation of Scripture and the world. The basic function of a liturgical calendar is to order time and, as George Landow has noted, typology also gives "an order and significance to human time" in the form of type and antitype, before and after.[79] Mirroring the combination of finite and finite that is the Incarnation, the liturgical calendar gives human time eternal meaning by centering it on Christ. As Keble writes in the poem "Easter Day,"

Enthroned in thy sovereign sphere,
Thou [Christ] shedd'st thy light on all the year;
Sundays by thee more glorious break,
An Easter Day in every week:

And week days, following in their train,
The fullness of thy blessing gain
Till all, both resting and employ,
Be one Lord's day of holy joy.
(lines 5–12).[80]

In "King Charles the Martyr" the theory that Keble asserts in "Easter Day" is performed. In "King Charles the Martyr," the Anglican liturgical calendar is supernatural in its functions, ordering and shaping time with prophetic authority.

Keble treats the feast of "King Charles the Martyr" as an authoritative Anglican condemnation of the dissenting Protestants who objected both to his version of typology and his liturgical theology, threatening his attempt to restore a divine meaning to time. Until 1859, the Anglican Church annually observed the death of King Charles I on January 30 as the feast of a saint and martyr. Since Charles was put to death by the Puritans under Oliver Cromwell, the Anglican church, in commemorating his death, offered an annual condemnation of dissenting Protestantism to match its annual condemnation of Roman Catholicism on November 5. Like many high Anglicans, Keble had "a romantic, almost mystical" devotion to King Charles I and a pronounced dislike of Protestant dissent.[81]

In his famous "National Apostasy" sermon, Keble attributes the evils of the Dissenters especially to their failure to read the Old Testament typologically—that is, according to Keble's personal typological theory that "God dealt formerly with the Jewish people in a manner analogous to that in which he deals now . . . with the souls of individual Christians."[82] Literal interpretation of Scripture, Keble suggests, leads either to fanaticism and regicide or to unbelief.[83] Keble's *Tract 13,* which shows that the Book of Common Prayer would have taught a typological reading method to the Dissenters, had they listened, followed less than a year later. Most Dissenters also objected to the idea of a prescribed, common form of prayer and many to the very idea of a liturgical year. Charles Wheatly's work on the Book of Common Prayer, which Keble repeatedly cites in both *The Christian Year* and *Tract 13,* was explicitly written to justify the idea of a "precomposed" national liturgy and liturgical calendar against "the objections urged by the Dissenters."[84] The Dissenters, then, represent for Keble a world devoid of typological meaning, a world where time is a meaningless succession of secular days. For Keble, Dissent—like Byronic Romanticism and the modern age itself—is fundamentally individualistic, and is therefore demystifying and nihilistic in its effects, if not in its intentions.

Keble's poem "King Charles the Martyr," like many of his poems, begins by stating the problem it will attempt to solve: the present age—"our fallen days"—seems to be devoid of divine meaning.[85] Keble enumerates two basic reasons for this problem. Nature no longer openly speaks to us (as it did to Jesus and the Apostles) of its meaning, and the modern age, unlike the Apostolic age, is devoid of the supernatural miracles that serve as transparent, self-interpreting signs of the deity. "The thunders of the deep prophetic sky" are "silent now" and "in our sight no powers of darkness bow / Before th' Apostles' glorious company" (lines 2–4). In the face of such divine silence, Keble finds meaning through the Christian logic of redemptive suffering; if Anglicans cannot produce miracles by the power of Christ, they can still die for him. Even "Far in the North" in "our fallen days," he writes, we have seen that "The Martyrs' noble army is still ours," for King Charles has died for the faith of his people (lines 6, 5). The Feast of King Charles the Martyr serves as a divine sign that the Anglican faith is legitimate and has been accepted by God.

For Keble, King Charles is the symbolic representation of all Anglicans, the "True son of our dear Mother" church, the king who individually represents his collective people (line 21). As a synecdoche for all Anglicans, King Charles is both the product of and now a part of the Prayer Book. King Charles, Keble writes, was "early taught" by mother church to "worship" according to the forms of the Prayer Book and "love[d] to trace her daily lore" (lines 21, 22, 25). He serves as a concrete example of the liturgical subjectivity that *The Christian Year* is attempting to inculcate in its readers. Like the speaker of *The Christian Year* as the work nears its end, his "heart" was one with the sentiments of the Prayer Book, an idea Keble makes explicit by stressing that "where we look for comfort or for calm," Charles "didst love" "Over the self-same lines to bend" (lines 27–28). The Prayer Book, in fact, gives Charles the spirit to die an Anglican martyr. Keble writes that "[w]hen all forsook" Charles, as all forsook Christ, the church "repay[ed]" his "loyal love" by "turn[ing his] dying eye" "straight to the Cross" (lines 29, 30, 32). Seeing meaning in his predicament because of the Prayer Book, seeing himself even as an antitype of Christ, Charles can have the courage to die a martyr in these empty, demythologized "fallen days" marked by a general lack of faith.[86] And as a martyr, Charles can now become part of the Anglican liturgical calendar, the only new saint added to that calendar after the Reformation and before the late twentieth-century era of liturgical experimentation and revision. As Keble writes, "Yearly now . . . she [the Anglican church] offers her maternal tears" for King Charles, calling on all Anglicans to imitate his example (lines 33–35). The Feast of King Charles the Martyr is the epitome of *The Christian Year,* as the Anglican shaped by the Prayer Book dies for the Prayer Book and, subsumed into the Prayer Book, becomes part of the divine order. In a certain sense, the Prayer Book itself—which Cromwell banned—dies with Charles and is resurrected in the institution of his feast.

The Prayer Book's supernatural power both to inscribe meaning on and reveal the meaning of time is most clearly indicated in Keble's footnote to "King Charles the Martyr." In his footnote, Keble relates a story about King Charles also narrated in Charles Wheatly's work on the Book of Common Prayer.[87] On January 30, the day of his execution, King Charles heard Bishop Juxon read the Anglican service for the day. The service included a reading of Matthew 27, in which Jesus is brought before Pilate, and then crucified. The king assumed that the bishop must have personally chosen the text in question as a consolation to him upon his own imminent martyrdom. The bishop assured him that, on the contrary, it was simply the prescribed reading for January 30 in the Anglican liturgical calendar. King Charles is both moved and strengthened by this coincidence, and goes forward to his martyrdom.[88] January 30, of course, later becomes the feast of King Charles the Martyr, assuring that the scripture readings for that day will always include Matthew 27. For Keble, the Table of Lessons in the Book of Common Prayer thus both prophecies many years in advance the date of King Charles's martyrdom (predicting the day's inherent meaning) and proclaims that this day is ever to be remembered as the day of his martyrdom (inscribing meaning on the day). "Forms of Prayer to Be Used at Sea," another of Keble's 1828 additions to *The Christian Year*, applies the same paradox to nature, as "The lonely Ocean *learns*" the "orisons" of the Anglican Church; the Book of Common Prayer, like Christ, speaks divine words that control and reorder the waves (italics mine).[89]

V

The Christian Year closes with Keble's poem "Ordination," which was also the final poem he wrote for the volume. "Ordination" completes the logic of "King Charles the Martyr" as it directly asserts that the Book of Common Prayer has the power to call down the deity and order creation. In this poem, Keble meditates on the ordination service itself, the means by which a priesthood legitimated by apostolic succession is conveyed in the Anglican Church.[90] He takes his epigraph from the Prayer Book's order of service and, following the Prayer Book, invokes the Holy Spirit in a paraphrase of the eighth century hymn "Veni, Creator Spiritus" ("Come, Creator Spirit") as he prays that the apostolic gift would continue in the Anglican church (lines 23–24).

Thus, in Keble's Romantic Anglicanism, the Prayer Book bestows identity with the Apostolic Fathers on its priests by quoting the words of the Apostolic Fathers over them. Taken into the divine sacramental order, these priests in turn bestow typological order and meaning on creation. In "Ordination," the moment of silence prior to the singing of "Veni, Creator Spiritus" in the Anglican ordination service serves as both the antitype of "Israel's prayer" in the "temple" and the type of the silence in heaven as God judges the world in the book of Revelation (lines 4, 2, 5–8). Keble writes that the patristic hymn that breaks this silence "seems not to th' entrancèd ear / Less than Thine [Christ's] own heart-cheering call" (lines 27–28); the language of the Fathers *is* the language of Christ, *is* the divine order, and ushers the Anglican Church into this divine order. The "Veni, Creator Spiritus" serves as Christ's

> earnest given
> That these our prayers are heard, and they [the ordinands],
> Who grasp, this hour the sword of Heaven,
> Shall feel Thee on their weary way.
> (lines 29–32)

The words of the Fathers are the pledge that the gift of the Holy Spirit has been given, and the ordinands now live in a divine, ordered world.

After proclaiming the efficacy of the ordination service, Keble immediately brings the volume back to its beginning. He echoes the titles of *The Christian Year*'s first two poems ("Morning" and "Evening"), depicting the new priest's sacramental labors as taking place at "morn or soothing eve" (line 32). In this sacramental context, Keble revisits for the last time in the volume the basic nature images from which the speaker felt alienated in the poem "Morning." The speaker is no longer alienated, and he now lives in an enchanted world. Keble no longer writes of the light of the morning that typifies God, but now writes directly of the "Spirit of Light" (line 37). Keble no longer writes of the natural wind that typifies the Holy Spirit, but now begs the "Spirit of Christ" to blow, as in Pentecost, directly into the new ordinands, to "fan them with Thine airs serene" (line 36). He no longer writes of the dew that typifies the waters of baptism, but now writes of "the Holy Fount" over which the priest "lean[s]" as he ushers a child into the sacramental economy through baptism (lines 32–36). The sacramental vision that, in Keble's critique of conventional Romanticism, poetry has taken from the divine mysteries has been reconnected to the sanctuary. The patristic logic of apostolic succession that has informed *The Christian Year* ends in ordination; the sacramental picture of reality that has infused the work is consummated by a depiction of the sacrament that confers the power to bestow sacraments. A vertically oriented society—based around apostolic succession—has been restored, and the self, no longer buffered, can be affected and reshaped by exterior objects (such as the waters of the baptism). Keble's book-length mystical meditation on the Book of Common Prayer concludes with the words of the Prayer Book becoming Christ's own.

Keble's belief in the Church as a divinely organic institution has permitted him to resolve in a very original manner a central tension that Stephen Prickett and others have noted in Wordsworthian Romanticism: Wordsworth's seemingly contradictory assertions that the meaning he finds in nature is created by his poetic imagination, and that his poetic imagination is itself the product of his communion with nature.[91] Wordsworth, in short, cannot decide whether the meaning he finds in nature is inherent or ascribed. For Keble, paradoxically, nature's meaning is inherent *because* it is ascribed. God, with divine foreknowledge, creates the natural object at the beginning of time *because* it will later be invested with typological meaning by Christ and the Apostolic Fathers, and *because* still later this typological meaning, enshrined in the Book of Common Prayer, will be read back onto creation by the Anglican faithful. In Keble's revisionist Romanticism, the liturgical precedes the material; the collective text creates our shared world.

Keble has generally been considered a lesser Romantic, a clerical footnote to the movement. But he was as much a Platonist as a Romantic. Keble recognized that his allegorical treatment of nature was basically a Christian application of Plato's theory of the forms,[92] and his treatment of the liturgy has Platonic resonances as well. In her influential work *After Writing: On the Liturgical Consummation of Philosophy*, Catherine Pickstock has perceptively rediscovered and rehabilitated Plato's theory of the liturgy. In Pickstock's interpretation of Plato, liturgical performance is capable of resolving fissures in subjectivity, society, and language—the dilemmas that have marked philosophy and culture as a whole since the Renaissance and Enlightenment. Liturgy, Pickstock asserts, abolishes the binary between (active) subject and (passive) object; as in Keble's rendition of the story of Abraham and Isaac, "liturgy is at once a gift *from* God and a sacrifice *to* God, a reciprocal exchange which shatters all ordinary positions of agency and reception."[93] Liturgy also avoids the sharp dichotomy between self and other, individual and group, that marks modernity and that makes alienation—as Keble laments—a distinguishing characteristic of modernity; in their ritual, dialogical nature, "communal acts of liturgy . . . ensure that subjectivity is both open and interpersonally constituted."[94]

For Pickstock, liturgy is the ultimate enactment of a Platonic metaphysics of participation, in which all material actions and objects gesture toward an ideal plenitude which they cannot fully embody; in this context, linguistic slippage and uncertainty are evidence of fullness rather than lack. The sign points toward ultimate meaning but, being limited, cannot contain it. Similarly, if Keble's speaker cannot always precisely pin down the meaning he intuits in the world ("dizzy" and confused, he proclaims "'Tis misty all"), this difficulty ultimately indicates only the world's plenitude of meaning (he is "dizzy" precisely because he is "wandering on enchanted ground").[95]

For both Pickstock and Keble, to engage in the performative enactment of an ideal world that is the liturgy is also to participate in and become part of the ideal world of heaven or the forms; liturgical poetry thus transcends mimesis.[96] The sacred "round" of the liturgical year reveals the true nature of time; the baptismal font alters the very nature of water. As Pickstock writes of the medieval Roman Catholic liturgy, "it is possible to argue that the theological body [of Christ in the sacrament] turns everything into sign, in such a way that the distinction itself been thing and sign can no longer be sustained."[97]

I am not suggesting that Keble himself—who was emphatically an *ancien régime* figure and in no way democratic or dialogical—consciously reached or shared each of Pickstock's conclusions. But Pickstock's synthesis of liturgy, philosophy, and literary theory puts us in a position as critics to understand the potential value of Keble's achievement. Keble creates a model of the liturgical poem that is also the world, and the liturgical tune that is also the rhythm of time itself. Liturgical poetry offers a vision of an infinitely meaningful universe that is textual, communal, and Platonic in nature, a vision whose force and appeal differs significantly from that of conventional Romanticism. The endeavor to order books of poetry, and to reorder and re-enchant the world, by the means of the Anglican liturgy would continue for over a hundred years after *The Christian Year* and would be shared by major authors who loathed the very word "Romanticism." Like Keble, they turn toward a Platonic "doxological polis and . . . acknowledgement of transcendence" as "the only alternative" to "the sway of capital and linguistic debasement" and see in the liturgy "a model for a genuine consummation of language and subjectivity in and through a radical transformation of space and time."[98] The subsequent chapters of this book tell this critically neglected story.

NOTES

1. Nockles, *The Oxford Movement*, 197. On the editions of Keble's work, see Goodwin, "Keble and Newman," 475.
2. Blair, "John Keble," 129.
3. Many scholars have attested to the influence of Keble's Romantic Anglicanism on Victorian religion. See, for instance, Tennyson, *Victorian Devotional Poetry,* 10–11; Francis, "'Healing Relief," in Blair, *John Keble*, 118; Nockles, *The Oxford Movement*, 197; Fraser, *Beauty and Belief*, 5.
4. On the neglect of Keble in literary criticism, see Kirstie Blair, "John Keble," 130.
5. Tennyson, *Victorian Devotional Poetry,* 75.
6. On the extent to which Keble's experiment was without precedent, see Tennyson, *Victorian Devotional Poetry*, 218.
7. I refer particularly to Gregory Goodwin's and Kirstie Blair's valuable work.
8. Blair has analyzed Keble's use of poetic meter and the Book of Common Prayer as means of regulating individual emotion, and my suggestion that Keble posits a collective Romanticism is indebted to her work.
9. Prickett, *Romanticism and Religion*, 104.
10. Keble, "Third Sunday in Advent," line 30. Keble consistently considers empiricism a theological heresy. Historically, he criticizes Gnosticism as a "low-minded empirical system" (Keble, "Primitive Tradition," 215). Philosophically, he condemns John Locke as "an Arian" (Keble, "Postscript," 380).
11. Keble, "Third Sunday in Advent," 27.
12. Keble, "St. Matthew the Apostle," 5, 57, 22.
13. Keble, "St. Matthew the Apostle," 64, cf. 9–12.
14. John Keble, "Fourth Sunday in Advent." In *The Christian Year, Lyra Innocentium, and Other Poems, Together with His Sermon on "National Apostasy."* (London: Oxford University Press), 1914, 13–15. Text references are to line numbers from this edition.
15. In *Romanticism and Religion*, Stephen Prickett observes that Keble shunned with horror "the fervor and aggressive individualism of the Evangelicals" (93).
16. Keble, Sermon XXX, 355.
17. Keble, "Favour Shewn," 4–5.
18. Keble, *Tract 89*, 166–67. By contrast, Keble writes in "Fifteenth Sunday After Trinity" that, while we are unable to interpret the many natural objects whose divine meaning has not been revealed to us, we can truly know the symbolic meaning of

the lily, since Christ has revealed it in Matthew 6. The speaker addresses the lily, observing, "ye could draw th' admiring gaze / Of Him [Christ] who worlds and hearts surveys: / Your order wild, your fragrant maze, / He taught us how to prize" (lines 36–40).

19. On this point, see Keble, "Primitive Tradition," 195.

20. Keble, *Jewish Nation*, 449. See also Keble, "Primitive Tradition," 202.

21. Keble, "Postscript," 361. See also Keble, "Primitive Tradition," 191.

22. Landow, *Victorian Types, Victorian Shadows*, 3.

23. Landow, *Victorian Types, Victorian Shadows*, 37, 43.

24. On this point, see Bump, "The Victorian Radicals," 38.

25. The earliest preserved textual account of Keble's typological theories is found in a letter he wrote to J. T. Coleridge on June 22, 1827. In this letter, Keble both expounds his typological theory at some length and announces the publication of the first edition of *The Christian Year* (Coleridge, *Memoir*, 151). Keble's book-length work on typology, *The Jewish Nation,* was not published until after his death, but can be precisely dated by its location in his common-place book. The work is placed exactly between the final poems written for the first edition of *The Christian Year* and five of the six poems added to the work's 1828 third edition (Pusey, preface, ix–x). Keble's work on typology can, then, be dated between mid-1827 and early 1828; it is both informed by his composition of *The Christian Year* and informs the new poems in the 1828 third edition. As I discuss, the 1828 poems—especially "Forms of Prayer to be Used at Sea," "King Charles the Martyr," and "Ordination"—exemplify Keble's typological theory in a particularly explicit manner.

26. Keble, *Jewish Nation*, 437, 475. Keble's ideas about typology here seem analogous to S. T. Coleridge's ideas about poetry; for Coleridge, as M. H. Abrams notes in *The Mirror and the Lamp*, poetry is a means of "reconciling the opposites" of the universal and the individual (56).

27. Keble, *Tract* 89, 29, 149.

28. See Keble, *Tract 89* 29, 181. Keble, along with other Anglo-Catholic poets, revived and popularized the patristic typological reading of nature. In *Tract 89: On the Mysticism Attributed to the Early Fathers of the Church,* Keble forcibly argues against evangelical Protestants (who would restrict typological references to Christ or the Church) that the idea of a "Type" can be legitimately "transfer[red]" from scripture out onto "the works of nature" (Keble *Tract 89* 166; cf. Landow 46, Bump 33).

29. Keble, *Tract 89*, 123.

30. Keble, *Tract 89*, 173.

31. On this point, see Keble, *Tract 89* 99, 181; Keble, *Sacred Poetry*, 99–100.

32. Keble, *Tract 89*, 152, 164.

33. Keble, *Tract 89*, 29.

34. Goodwin, "Keble and Newman," 493.

35. Karen Dieleman has asserted that Keble prefers the 1549 Prayer Book to the 1662 Prayer Book. Her grounds are that Keble offers poems for none of the feasts added in the 1662 book (*Religious Imaginaries*, 161). However, in the third edition of *The Christian Year*, Keble does add poems for the 1662 feasts, such as "King Charles the Martyr," which problematizes this assertion. In the version of *The Christian Year*

most widely read, Keble emphasizes the common nature of the *Common Prayer*, and uses the form of the book commonly employed.

36. See Keble, "Primitive Tradition," 209, and Sermon XXX, 365. Keble held to a branch theory of ecclesiology, in which the Anglican Church, Roman Catholic Church, and Eastern Orthodox Church each embody the ancient Catholic Church for the area under its geographical jurisdiction. He asserted that "our visible communion with the Church of England" is "our earnest" of "virtual communion with the One Catholic Church, East and West, as before its separation" ("Endurance of Church Imperfections," *Sermons Academical and Occasional.* 2nd ed. [Oxford: John Henry Parker, 1848], 320).

37. Keble, *Tract 13*, 2; see also Keble, "Postscript," 356. Charles Wheatly, an eighteenth-century Anglican divine whose ideas influenced *The Christian Year*, argues at scholarly length that the liturgies on which the Book of Common Prayer is based may be apostolic in origin, preserved by and developed further by the apostles' successors, the Apostolic Fathers (*Rational Illustration*, 13, 125).

38. Keble, Sermon XXX, 367.

39. One of Keble's footnotes for the poem lists the hymns used in the liturgy that are first found in the Gospel of Luke: "the Magnificat, Benedictus, and Nunc Dimittis."

40. Keble, Letter XXII, in Wilson, *Letters of Spiritual Counsel*, 233–34. Keble's letters were published in the nineteenth century in a volume that typically omits recipient and date.

41. See Keble's footnotes for "St. Stephen's Day" and "The Churching of Women."

42. Wheatly, *Rational Illustration*, 25.

43. Keble, "Trinity Sunday," 42 and "Sunday Next Before Advent," 13. For evidence that Keble's poetic images about the divine nature of the Anglican service are also meant quite literally, see his sermon "Eucharistical Offices," in which he rhetorically asks, "What is there wanting in our altars to make the comers thereunto perfect? Have we not an Apostolical Creed, an Apostolical Ministry, Apostolical yearnings after unity? Have we not the presence of Angels in our hymns, of Saints departed in our holy commemorations?" (271).

44. In *Tract 13: Sunday Lessons. The Principle of Selection*, Keble argues, in language that directly echoes his earlier work on typology, that "the arrangers [of the Book of Common Prayer]" chose their "selection of scriptural readings" in order "to exhibit God's former dealings with His chosen people *collectively* . . . in such manner as best illustrates His dealing with each *individual* chosen now to be in His Church" (2, Keble's italics). In his biography of Keble, J. T. Coleridge notes that *Tract 13* is essentially "an application" of Keble's typological theory (225). No critic has noted the typological content of *Tract 13*, perhaps because it can be recognized as typological only according to Keble's own definitions of Type and Antitype, which, as Rodney Edgecombe notes, "tak[e] considerable license" with traditional conceptions of typology (Edgecombe, *Two Poets*, 117). Keble himself grants that he uses the terms "in a wider sense" than most other authorities on the subject (Keble, *Jewish Nation*, 475).

45. Nockles, *The Oxford Movement*, 107–8.

46. Keble, *Tract* 13, 9.

47. King, "John Keble's *The Christian Year*," 404.

48. Gibson, *The Church of England*, 130–36.

49. Gibson, *The Church of England*, 226.

50. See Gibson, *The Church of England*, 2.

51. See Gibson, *The Church of England*, 57.

52. Wolffe, *God and Greater Britain*, 45, 126.

53. Wolffe, *God and Greater Britain*, 45.

54. On Keble and the repeal of the Test and Corporation Acts, see also Skinner, "The Duty of the State," in Blair, *John Keble*, 33–34.

55. Keble, "Sermon on National Apostasy," 134.

56. Keble, "Shadows and Substance," 210.

57. Keble, "Shadows and Substance," 210.

58. Keble, "Shadows and Substance," 209.

59. Keble, "Shadows and Substance," 210.

60. Keble, "Fourth Sunday After Epiphany," line 56 and "Septuagesmia Sunday," line 1.

61. Keble endorses the principle of the economy in both *The Christian Year* and in his sermons. In the poem "Catechism," Keble uses the religious instruction of children as an analogy to show that our language regarding the divine is always "but cries of babes" compared to the divine reality; Christ graciously accepts and gradually corrects our inadequate language and understanding (line 35). Keble holds that God "condescend[s] to teach us," "by imitating" our "imperfect utterance"; the Bible gradually "lead[s] those who approach it in the right disposition, from one degree of spiritual strength to another" (Keble, "Favour Shewn," 20, 12).

62. Keble, *Tract 13*, 8.

63. Keble, *Jewish Nation*, 489.

64. Keble, *Tract 13*, 8–9. See also Keble, *Jewish Nation*, 489.

65. Keble, *Tract 13*, 8–9.

66. John Keble, "Morning." In *The Christian Year, Lyra Innocentium, and Other Poems, Together with His Sermon on "National Apostasy."* (London: Oxford University Press), 1914. 3–5. Text references are to line numbers from this edition.

67. Tennyson, *Victorian Devotional Poetry*, 90.

68. Church of England, the Book of Common Prayer, 10.

69. Church of England, the Book of Common Prayer, 5.

70. Church of England, the Book of Common Prayer, 8.

71. Keble, *Tract 13*, 2.

72. The quotations are from lines 1–2, 4 of John Keble's poem "Septuagesima Sunday." In *The Christian Year, Lyra Innocentium, and Other Poems, Together with His Sermon on "National Apostasy."* (London: Oxford University Press), 1914. 42–43. Text references are to line numbers from this edition.

73. See Gen. 1:15–16.

74. See Gen. 2:6.

75. See Gen. 1:1.

76. On the Apostolic Fathers' treatment of the sun and moon as symbols, see *Tract 89*, 155–56. On their treatment of dew as a symbol, see *Tract 89,*179–81. On their treatment of wind as a symbol, see *Tract 89*, 179.

77. Tennyson, *Victorian Devotional Poetry*, 75, 80.

78. Edgecombe, *Two Poets*, 82.

79. Landow, *Victorian Types*, 5.

80. On the eschatological import of the liturgical calendar, see also "First Sunday After Christmas," lines 43–48.

81. Nockles, *The Oxford Movement,* 72. See also Keble, "Danger," 119.

82. Keble, "Sermon on National Apostasy," 543–44.

83. Keble, "Sermon on National Apostasy," 543–44; see also, Keble, *Jewish Nation*, 438. Nockles relates that Keble's political use of King Charles I's death was not uncommon in High Church circles at the time: "Even as late as the 1820s, High Churchmen could invoke the cult of the Royal Martyr as a political weapon in defense of Orthodoxy and to discredit Protestant Dissenters who were branded as heirs of the regicides" (*The Oxford Movement*, 52).

84. Wheatly, *Rational Illustration*, 1.

85. The quotation is from line 6 of John Keble's poem "King Charles the Martyr." In *The Christian Year, Lyra Innocentium, and Other Poems, Together with His Sermon on "National Apostasy."* (London: Oxford University Press), 1914. 204–5. Text references are to line numbers from this edition.

86. In relation to Charles I as an antitype, see Landow, *Victorian Types*, 145.

87. Wheatly, *Rational Illustration*, 512–13.

88. See Keble, "King Charles the Martyr," footnote 1.

89. Keble, "Forms of Prayer to Be Used at Sea," line 10.

90. John Keble, "Ordination." In *The Christian Year, Lyra Innocentium, and Other Poems, Together with His Sermon on "National Apostasy."* (London: Oxford University Press), 1914. 209–10. Text references are to line numbers from this edition.

91. Prickett, *Romanticism and Religion*, 76.

92. Keble's preface to his edition of the works of Richard Hooker, page xcii. For a fuller discussion of Keble's (and Rossetti's) Platonism, see my chapter on Christina Rossetti.

93. Pickstock, *After Writing*, 176–77.

94. Pickstock, *After Writing*, 57.

95. Keble, "Fourth Sunday in Advent," 17, 19–20.

96. Pickstock, *After Writing*, 39.

97. Pickstock, *After Writing*, 261.

98. Pickstock, *After Writing*, 169, 48. Pickstock refers in this context to the medieval Roman Rite, but her words aptly describe Keble's vision of the Book of Common Prayer, which Anglo-Catholicism has always insisted stands in continuity with the medieval Roman Rite.

Chapter 2

"Earth cannot bar flame from ascending"

Nature's Apocalyptic Liturgy in Christina Rossetti's Verses

Throughout most of the Victorian period, John Keble's *The Christian Year* had a broad literary influence but produced few direct literary rivals or heirs. As I have mentioned, Keble's poems were present in virtually every literate home, and they popularized the composition of liturgical poetry, especially in Anglo-Catholic circles. A sizable minority of English society began to think self-consciously in terms of the liturgical calendar in a way that had been conceptually impossible prior to the secularization of time, and its cultural productions were many and significant. Anglo-Catholic editors produced many liturgically themed poetic anthologies, most commonly structured around a single liturgical season. They also issued new collections of hymns—some already well known, others previously obscure—selected, arranged, and contextualized to fit the format of the liturgical seasons.[1] Most famously, John Mason Neale translated hundreds of hymns from medieval and patristic liturgical texts, a number of which—such as "All Glory, Laud, and Honour" and "O Come, O Come Emmanuel"—continue to be used in worship throughout the theological spectrum. And the many Advent and Christmas carols newly translated from Latin—Frederick Oakeley's English rendition of "Adeste Fidelis" as "O Come All Ye Faithful" may be the most popular example—encouraged the faithful to perceive the continuity of their worship with that of the medieval church and to ruminate on the mysteries of the liturgical calendar.

But, contrary to some of the most recent scholarship on Keble's poetic legacy, relatively few Victorian poets followed Keble by writing a single-author poetic accompaniment to the Anglican liturgical calendar. Krista Lysack has claimed—citing as proof the appendices to G. B. Tennyson's classic study of Tractarian poetics—that "*The Christian Year* stood out not just for its own sales and longevity but for the many imitators that followed in its wake. . . . Writing a version of *The Christian Year* became almost a rite of passage for ambitious clergymen."[2] But Lysack's analysis assumes that each item on Tennyson's giant list of poetic works whose title begins with the word *Lyra* constitutes a new *Christian Year*. Keble was indeed one of the authors of the Tractarian poetic collection *Lyra Apostolica*, but this work does not share *The Christian Year*'s liturgical structure. Neither do the bulk of titles Tennyson lists. If we are looking at poetry rather than hymnody, of the many texts listed in Tennyson's appendices only one edited collection (*Lyra Sanctorum*)—and no single author text—is structured around more than a single season of the Anglican church year.

Tennyson's appendices list only one single-author poetic text structured around the liturgical year: Frederick Oakeley's *Lyra Liturgica: Reflections in Verse for Holy Days and Seasons* (1865). Oakeley converted to Roman Catholicism with John Henry Newman in 1845, and his work is structured around the Roman Catholic, rather than the Anglican, liturgical calendar. In his preface, Oakeley offers the best contemporary explanation as to why *The Christian Year* has so few Victorian poetic heirs. He admits Keble as an inspiration; his own work is "an attempt to apply to portions of the Catholic Liturgy the method of illustration so beautifully exemplified in *The Christian Year*."[3] But he dramatically disclaims the possibility, and begs the reader not to suspect, that he could possess "any such presumptuous and hopeless design as that of producing a counterpart to a work in so many ways so inimitable" as *The Christian Year*.[4] Both culturally and theologically, Anglo-Catholic poets were the authors most likely to produce book-length poetic works on the Anglican liturgical calendar. But in the mid-Victorian period, the very ubiquity of *The Christian Year*—and of high Anglican veneration for Keble—precludes others from personally producing poetic volumes similarly structured. The attempt seemed both arrogant and, more importantly, unnecessary; the cultural work had already been done. Oakeley thinks his own work can be forgiven only because its differences in rite and structure from Keble limit its redundancy and presumption. Only a different world, with different concerns, could need a new *Christian Year*. Hence, only as the nineteenth century is ending does another major Anglo-Catholic poet, Christina Rossetti, compose another very original poetic rendition of the Anglican liturgical calendar.

Christina Rossetti's final volume of poetry, *Verses* (1893), was also her most popularly successful, selling over fifteen thousand copies in its first four years of release.[5] *Verses*—which includes a pivotal, seventy-poem section on the Anglican liturgical calendar—is a sometimes-baffling mixture of nearly nihilistic despair and apocalyptic hope. The speaker of "Sunday Before Advent" summarizes one of the work's recurring themes when she observes, "Earth shows poor, a slippery rolling ball";[6] we live in a world devoid of fixed points of meaning, ever-changing, ever-shifting, merely part of a game that we do not understand. In such a world, as the speaker explains, no person can achieve stability: our only choice is whether we will live in conscious instability and fear, working out our salvation with trembling, or we will naively imagine ourselves secure—and smash.

We all
Stand in the balance trembling as we stand;
Or if not trembling, tottering to a fall.
(lines 2–4).

To this world of shifting and uncertain meaning, the speaker compares hell, "a gulf unplumbed, unspanned" (line 8), an absolute formless void, in which shape and order are not merely evasive but impossible. Hell is a de-created world, in which one cannot even slip but only plummet, without any determinate points of reference. No wonder the speaker, like so many in the 1890s, expected or desired the apocalypse; for the ordinary person who longs for a coherent world and a meaningful life, the world of this poem is unendurable. The poem begins and ends with the simple declarative sentence, "The end of all things is at hand" (lines 1, 11).

The speaker's primary hope resides with heaven, which she imagines as both earth's reversal and its Platonic fulfillment. If earth pitches humanity toward a fall, "Heaven flings wide its gates to great and small" (line 10). If earth is limited and shifting and hell completely formless, heaven is "the unending land" (line 5), both entirely solid and without limit. In heaven, fixed meaning and stable points of reference *do* exist. In earthly terms, "land" denotes a space that is solid *because* it is limited, to be implicitly contrasted with the vast and insolid oceans and (by the late nineteenth century) the infinite emptiness of space. As an "unending land," heaven thus both Platonically fulfills and violates our conventional conceptions of land. In the poem's most exuberant moment, the speaker exclaims "O hearts of men, covet the unending land!" (line 5). Thanks to the concept of heaven, we need not accept existence on the terms that earth seems to provide; a resistance of yearning and anticipation is possible.

Like so much of Rossetti's late work, this poem situates a nearly nihilistic vision of earth in creative tension with a Platonic picture of heaven. This tension reflects—and is to some degree mediated by—the Anglican liturgy. The "Sunday Before Advent" marks the end of the liturgical year, and, like the poem, the Anglican scripture readings for the day combine earthbound skepticism with apocalyptic hope. The Book of Common Prayer stipulates that for Morning Prayer on this date the final chapters of Ecclesiastes (11 and 12) be read. Here the author, textually designated merely as "the Teacher" or "the Preacher," concludes his skeptical account of human existence with an analysis of the follies of youth and age. "All that cometh is vanity" (Ecc. 11:12), which logically follows from the book's general premise, that "all is vanity" (Ecc. 12:8). One might add: "on this slippery, rolling ball." Malachi 3 and 4, which is read as part of Evening Prayer on the same date, strikes the note of apocalyptic reversal: "For behold, the day cometh, that shall burn as an oven; and all the proud, yea, and all that do wickedly, shall be stubble: and the day that cometh shall burn them up. . . . But unto you that fear my name shall the Sun of righteousness arise with healing in his wings" (4:1–2). At the end of the liturgical year, the end of all things is at hand. What hope can we have, save to "Fear God, and keep his commandments" (Ecc. 12:13)? What can last, but eternity? For Rossetti, the liturgy, which replicates but does not explain away the paradoxes of heaven, provides a way of anticipating eternity in time. Rossetti's speaker exclaims of heaven, "O hearts of men, covet the musical, / Sweet, never-ending waters of that strand!" (lines 6–7). The liturgy transposes the music of heaven into the register of time, just as the waters of the baptismal font both typologically prefigure the waters of heaven and sacramentally sustain the believer in their absence.

In Rossetti's late work, we encounter a liturgical poetry that is influenced by Keble.[7] As a young woman, she annotated and illustrated her personal *Christian Year* and in the last years of her life—the years of *Verses*—she was still reading books by and about Keble.[8] Diane D'Amico and David Kent have suggested that Rossetti draws from Keble her basic poetic "goal": "To awaken our sensibilities to the invisible world made intelligible and tangible through the symbolic use of nature."[9]

But Rossetti's poetry expresses a much darker vision of human existence than *The Christian Year*. Rossetti uses the patterns of the Anglican liturgical calendar and the music of the Anglican Psalter to give shape to an empty and silent earth, to create from the abyss a new world. In her effort to recreate the world, she pushes Keble's model of liturgical re-enchantment almost to the breaking point, flamboyantly extrapolating patristic symbology onto the native flora and fauna of England and using the liturgical calendar to reverse the solar calendar. Her poetic use of the *Common Prayer* is so original and counterintuitive as to prove inaccessible to the general reader. *Verses* was issued by an Anglican book company (the Society for Promoting Christian Knowledge, or S.P.C.K.) and was published for and marketed to an exclusively high Anglican audience. The volume consists almost entirely of poems first printed in Rossetti's S.P.C.K. devotional prose works—*Annus Domini, Seek and Find, Called to be Saints, Time Flies,* and *The Face of the Deep*—and its poems are best understood within the intellectual context that they provide. Perhaps inadvertently, Rossetti creates a truly *fin-de-siècle* liturgical poetry, in which—as in much of the literature of the 1890s—spiritual meaning survives in a materialistic and indifferent world by becoming privatized, the coded possession of a coterie.

I

Unlike the Romantic Keble (who was dead by 1866), Rossetti writes in a post-Darwinian intellectual world in which dreams of the Book of Nature which "he who runs may read" have vanished and a religiously skeptical materialism has become dominant. If, as Isobel Armstrong has asserted, Rossetti did not write in ignorance of but as "a deliberate challenge to the *fin de siècle*," a brief overview of this cultural transformation may be necessary to contextualize her thought and poetry.[10] I will focus primarily on the ramifications of late Victorian materialism for two issues that inherently concern her as a religious writer and that she directly addresses in her devotional prose: the nature of language and the nature of religion.

As Marjorie Wheeler-Barclay notes, the period between 1860 and World War I witnessed "the first attempts . . . to create a coherent field of study that would treat religion purely as an element in human cultures."[11] Sociology and anthropology were just emerging as independent disciplines, and were dominated by influence of Auguste Comte and Edward Tylor.[12] As he explained in his *Positive Philosophy,* Comte believed that human society progressed from a theological stage, in which supernatural beings were seen as the causes of events and the world order; to a metaphysical stage, in which abstract principles and ideas served as the primary explanatory model; to the scientific or positive stage, in which causes were taken to be material.[13] For Comte and positivism, traditional religion represents a primitive or mistaken explanatory model, destined to be superseded, while the scientific or positive stage of development constitutes, the "fixed and definitive state" of "human understanding."[14] Most Victorian anthropologists shared this assumption.[15] As I have explained in the introduction, the linear model of time employed in such a narrative of progress is itself characteristic of secular modernity, and marks an abandonment of the cyclical and typological approaches to time embodied in the liturgical calendar.

For Tylor, religion is rooted in humanity's tendency to animism, which he defines as "the doctrine of souls and other spiritual beings in general."[16] He considers the animistic idea of the soul to stem from the primitive inability to separate the external object as it exists in the material world from the word or idea representing that object as it is held in the mind.[17] Tylor treats all believers in any form of soul as animists and holds that the real religious divide is not that between "the savage fetish-worshiper and the civilized Christian"—which is illusory—but "that which divides Animism from Materialism."[18]

For Tylor as for Comte, progress consists in recognizing that events have external, material causes and recognizing the psyche's severance from external reality. To restate the matter in Charles Taylor's terms, progress consists in the creation of a buffered self.

In such an extremely empiricist epistemology, only what is material and what is concrete can ultimately count as knowledge. This judgment influences much of late Victorian linguistics and comparative religion. For the linguistic materialist, words themselves have meaning only insofar as they possess a direct referent in the material world.[19] Things are the ultimate reality, and words possesses value only as a way of denoting and organizing things.[20] For these Victorians, language becomes corrupted or diseased when it becomes "metaphysical" or "mythological," as abstract concepts meant to describe material phenomena instead come to be taken as realities in themselves.[21] Although "metaphysical" was for Comte an inevitable if ultimately mistaken stage of human thought, here it becomes a term of abuse. In the linguist Max Müller's influential narrative, religious language was itself originally an attempt to describe material phenomena—particularly the solar cycles—and translate them into conceptual terms. As he asserts, "the very name of deva in Sanskrit of *deus* in Latin which afterwards became the name of God meant originally bright and no more. It came to mean God after a long process of evolution."[22] In this early, earthy stage, religious language and ritual serve as organic means of celebrating the cycles of day and night and of the seasons, in which the sun seems to be defeated and is later reborn.[23] According to this model, the death and resurrection of Jesus are simply another variant of the solar myth. The problem with traditional Christianity from this perspective is its failure to recognize its material origins and its tendency to cling to its metaphysical dogmas—like the Trinity, justification, or transubstantiation—in what should be a positivistic age.[24] As a deliberately metaphysical and neo-medieval movement in the most scientifically advanced of countries, the Anglican High Church party was a particular bête noir for many Victorian scholars of comparative religion.[25]

This master narrative of religious history received its last, and probably most famous, major presentation in James Frazer's *The Golden Bough*, which did not receive its final form until 1915, but which was originally issued in 1890, prior to Rossetti's *The Face of the Deep* or *Verses*. In the work's first edition, Frazer traces what he feels is a general pattern in religious history, in which fertility and the harvest are celebrated when "the corn-spirit is killed in the person of his representative and eaten sacramentally," "the worshippers partaking of the body of the god."[26] As cultures develop, this ritual may take the shape of eating cakes of new corn rather than human or animal flesh, but these cakes are still "partaken of sacramentally, that is, as the body of the corn-spirit."[27] As his word choice suggests, Frazer considers "the Christian communion" to be an unconscious performance of this ancient harvest ritual, "a sacrament which is doubtless far older than Christianity."[28] Similarly, he asserts that "Christmas is nothing but an old heathen celebration of the winter solstice."[29] Frazer's controversial "note on the crucifixion of Christ," in which the story of Jesus is explicitly identified as yet another example of the dying and rising of a fertility god associated with the sun and the harvest, does not appear until the 1900 second edition, but in 1890 the point is already clearly implied.

Rossetti carefully followed these developments in Victorian comparative religion, which as I have noted were often explicitly formulated as a threat or challenge to her religious position. In a decision that would shape her late poetry, she responded by starkly inverting both the materialist account of religion and the materialist account of language. In her apocalyptic work *The Face of the Deep*, Rossetti quite accurately summarizes (without resorting to names) the thought of James Frazer and his fellow anthropologists. For them, the Christian story, like the "heathen myths," merely "symbolize[s] various processes, phases of nature"; the spiritual merely restates the material, as Christ is a resurrection myth, and resurrection myths symbolize the cycle of the seasons.[30] It would be more just, Rossetti suggests, to read the world in exactly the opposite register, and take the seasons themselves as dim reflections of the Christian story. As she tersely sums up her point, "The antitype [God] determines the type [nature], not this that," and to say otherwise "is to deny the faith."[31] Taking the point to the level of hyperbole, she sometimes goes so far as to suggest that the liturgical calendar does not so much reflect as transcend natural seasons, constituting an "alternate" order in which "Christmas hath a chillness / Warmer than the heat of June," in which "winter bestow[s] and summer take[s] away."[32] The material universe is but a distant echo of an infinite idea.

Rossetti can make these assertions because she ascribes not to the weak version of Platonism common among late Romantics—which holds to a logocentric belief in "a language of power and plentitude" yet rejects the theory of the forms[33]—but to a consistent Platonic idealism. Rossetti identified Plato as her favorite philosopher,[34] and her mature philosophical position was a Christian Platonism, in which every object of the material universe seems meaningless and illusory when viewed in and of itself, but becomes invested with ultimate meaning and significance when viewed as a partial embodiment of a divine type or form.[35] Endorsing Plato, and reversing the materialist philosophy increasingly dominant in the second half of the nineteenth century, Rossetti asserts in *Time Flies* that "spiritual" things are "the reality" of which "literal" or material objects are only the "symbol."[36]

Similarly, time gains meaning for Rossetti by Platonically participating in eternity. Rossetti was a critic of "the automated time of nineteenth century modernity" and for her Darwin's error is precisely his belief in linear, progressive time.[37] If the universe is contingent on God for its existence, then the universe is in a continual state of coming to be that cannot be meaningfully related in linear narrative. As she writes with a deliberate echo of Darwin's title and terminology, "the Origin not of species only but of genera" is "[t]he Beginning without beginning, the Beginning that endeth not."[38] All development is contained in God's infinite beginning. Hence, time is not a linear sequence of interchangeable moments, but is, rather, "that condition or aspect of eternity which consists with the possibility of probation."[39] In sum, as Rossetti writes, "'All things are double one against another.' . . . [E]verything cognizable by the senses may be utilized as symbol or parable. . . . matter suggests the immaterial; time eternity."[40] To read the world Platonically is to read the world symbolically, as all temporal objects are shadows cast by the timeless forms.

Rossetti interprets the material world as a symbol of God particularly by applying a typological method of reading to nature. As I have discussed in the previous chapter, typology begins early in Christian history as a method of interpreting the Jewish scriptures. Old Testament events, objects, and religious rites were interpreted as predicting or symbolizing "Christ and His dispensation," the New Testament "antitype" fulfilling and superseding the Old Testament "type."[41] The Apostolic Fathers then projected this interpretive method out from scripture onto nature, reasoning that, since both the creation of the world and the Mosaic covenant were acts of divine revelation, each must prefigure God's ultimate revelation in the Christ event.[42] In this way, typology came to be not just a method of scriptural interpretation, but a way of reading the world as a symbolic text. Like Keble, Rossetti believed that the typological interpretation of nature was invented by Christ himself; Christ, she thought, interpreted his creation to the apostles, who in turn passed this interpretive method on to their successors, the Apostolic Fathers. As Rossetti writes, "Our gracious Master's speech . . . made the earth bring forth spiritual food for our nourishment"; "By analogy of things visible He has shown us things invisible."[43] Since the Apostolic Fathers were highly influenced by Platonic and neo-Platonic thought in developing their typological reading of nature, it is not surprising that Rossetti tends to use Platonic and typological methods of interpreting material existence more or less interchangeably. John Keble himself suggested in a volume that Rossetti read and referenced that the Apostolic Fathers' typological interpretations of nature "realized, though in an infinitely higher sense, the system of Plato."[44]

Rossetti's fascination with the apocalypse, most fully expressed in *The Face of the Deep: A Devotional Commentary on the Apocalypse* (1892; second edition, 1893), is entirely consistent with, and perhaps derived from, her Platonism and her commitment to typological interpretation. If as Mary

Arseneau observes, typological interpretation moves "not just forward in time, but upward to a higher plane transcending time itself,"[45] then typology implicitly points both forward and upward toward the timeless world of ultimate meaning depicted in St. John's Apocalypse as its final end. Rossetti fully recognizes and poetically exploits this implication of typological thought, treating (in Dinah Roe's words) "the world" as "a type to the antitype of heaven."[46] Rossetti's Platonism leads to and justifies the same conclusion. For Plato, the ultimate forms—of which the material creation is an imperfect copy and in which the material creation partially participates—reside in the mind of God. Rossetti assumes a Christianized version of this theory, imagining heaven (often pictured as the New Jerusalem) as the storehouse of forms that give the world meaning. As she explains in a passage ripe with both Platonism and eschatology,

> [T]hose ancients who felt that all forms of beauty cannot be but partial expressions of beauty's very self . . . by clue of what they saw groped after Him they saw not. Beauty essential is the archetype of imparted beauty; Life essential, of imparted life; Goodness essential of imparted Goodness; but such objects good, living beautiful, as we now behold are not that very Goodness, Life, and Beauty which (please God) we shall one day contemplate in beatific vision. (Rossetti, *Seek and Find*, 14)

For Rossetti, famous as much as a poet of despair as a poet of faith, existence becomes legible only if we read the frustratingly ambiguous phenomena we encounter in daily life in light of their apocalyptic termini, the ultimate ends toward which they tend. *Verses* closes with the poem "Looking back upon life's trodden way," in which the speaker, who seems to be a soul already deceased, rereads her life on earth from the perspective of heaven and for the first time gets it right; a life and world that had seemed "black" is actually full of color and light, but this picture can be perceived only when, as the poem repeats three times, "Looking back."[47] Similarly, in *The Face of the Deep* Rossetti suggests that the misery and pain—the "chastisements"—of human life may be read as "mercies," but only if we are systematically interpreting the daily events of our lives as prefiguring the Apocalypse.[48] As she instructs her readers in the same passage, "If I desire the consummation [the Apocalypse], it is in my power to practice its antecedents and to rehearse it day by day."[49]

One principal means by which Rossetti rehearsed the apocalypse day by day was the Anglican liturgical calendar. Since material existence for Rossetti is a combination of faithful anticipation and present lack, the "songs of heaven" alone giving shape to the "silence" of earth,[50] she frequently envisions life itself in terms of the penitential seasons of Advent and Lent.

The Advent lectionary readings situate Anglicans between two moments of superabundant meaning—Jesus's first coming in the Incarnation and second coming at the end of time—but define the present season as a time of lack, a period of penitent waiting. Rossetti extrapolates from this pattern to conclude that all existence is a long Advent, a penitential state apparently devoid of meaning that gains significance only through the terminal point revealed to the eyes of faith. As she writes, "From our Lord's Ascension to the end of time is holy Church's season of Advent. Each Christian's whole life then is one continuous Advent season."[51] Fittingly, Rossetti uses her poem "The Sunday Before Advent," which I analyzed at the beginning of this chapter, to explain that form and structure ultimately reside only in heaven.

Rossetti's fascination with the apocalypse was shared by many in fin-de-siècle England. As Ailise Bulfin notes, the late nineteenth-century sense that technology was accelerating the speed of time resulted in the popularity of secular "end of time narratives" in versions ranging from the heat death of the universe, to biological decline, to Max Nordau's degeneration.[52] "Fin de siècle, fin du globe," Oscar Wilde's characters despairingly quip in *The Picture of Dorian Gray*.[53] In *Verses* (1893), Christina Rossetti does Wilde one better, reading the fin de siècle backward from the perspective of the end of the world.

II

Rossetti's apocalyptic reinscription of meaning upon an empty world obviously possesses its own difficulties and dark side. If for Rossetti earth is a place of silence and uncertain meaning, how *can* an earthbound individual really hear "celestial music"[54] and interpret divine signs? Dinah Roe has observed that for Rossetti "[w]ords in the absence of God are words without meaning," but "[t]he word of God, unlike the word of man . . . has power to make a world over the face of the deep."[55] But how *can* a human being speak anything other than human language? The title and contents of the opening section of *Verses*, "Out of the Deep have I called unto Thee, O Lord,"[56] reflect a fear of a world devoid of both meaning and divinity.

Like the late-century nihilists Friedrich Nietzsche and Oscar Wilde, Rossetti grapples with the uncertainty of human knowledge and the impoverishment of human language, which may be nothing more than a series of empty signifiers. Nietzsche reasons that if—as materialist philosophy would have it—only the particular and the tangible are truly real, then human thought, which is constructed of immaterial linguistic abstractions, is incapable of describing reality.[57] As Linda Dowling has noted, Oscar Wilde and the

Decadent Movement construct a literature that accepts such a critique, and enjoys signs merely as signs, devoid of meaningful reference.[58] Wilde's Dorian Gray recognizes that human life possesses coherent order only in the sphere of language, which "seemed to be able to give a plastic form to formless things," and he doubts that there is "anything so real as words."[59] In a more comic register, in *The Importance of Being Earnest* baptism is important not as a sacrament that effects that which it signifies but as a farcical (and repeatable) naming ritual, a generator of empty signs (such as the term Ernest/earnest). Isobel Armstrong may overstate the case—and underestimate Rossetti's Platonism—in deeming her theology a "Christian nihilism," but she does have a point.[60] Like Wilde, Rossetti refuses the consolations of the materialist view of language dominant in Victorian culture and as a consequence grapples with a world that may fail to signify.

In the opening poem of *Verses*, the speaker depicts an uncertain world prone to constant change, in which the passage of time tends generally toward decay. She laments

> this transitory scope
> Of earth, these pleasures that begin and cease,
> This moon which wanes, these seasons which decrease.
> (Rossetti, "Alone Lord God," lines 3–5)

Rossetti finds in the liturgy—her answer to chronological time—a language capable of referring the impermanent things of earth to eternal referents, of mediating between divine and human speech.

The influences on Rossetti's liturgical thought include the Tractarian poet Isaac Williams, the sixteenth-century Anglican divine Richard Hooker, and especially, the central figure in Anglo-Catholic liturgical poetry, John Keble.[61] Rossetti takes the epigraph to one of her own books on the liturgical year—her analysis of the saints of the Anglican calendar, *Called to Be Saints: The Minor Festivals Devotionally Studied*—from an edition of Hooker's works that Keble edited and for which he provided a lengthy preface.[62] Much of Rossetti's liturgical thought seems to be based on her original synthesis of Keble's and Hooker's work, which emphasizes especially the apocalyptic elements of liturgy.

For Keble and other Anglo-Catholics, the contents of the Book of Common Prayer constitute a divinely authorized proof of the fundamental identity between the faith of the Anglican Church and that of the apostles and Apostolic Fathers. Through "God's providence," Keble explains, the founders of the Anglican Communion retained "fragments of the primitive ritual" in their liturgy.[63] As Hooker explains more fully,

> No doubt from God it hath proceeded, and by us it must be acknowledged a work of his singular care and providence, that the Church hath evermore held a prescript form of common prayer. . . . So that if the liturgies of all ancient churches through the world be compared amongst themselves it may be easily perceived they all had one original mould. (*Of the Laws*, 110–11)

When they perform this "primitive ritual," Anglicans worship with one voice with the "original" liturgy of the apostles and the early church.

To worship with the Apostolic Fathers, Keble believes, is to interpret the world typologically. Keble asserts that for the Apostolic Fathers, "the whole scheme of material things, and especially those objects in it which are consecrated by scriptural allusion, assume . . . a sacramental or symbolic character"; this method of interpretation forms "a real part of the very Apostolical system."[64] Keble asserts that, when designing the Christian liturgy, the Apostolic Fathers both assumed and intended to teach this method of typological interpretation. He suggests that "[t]he Ceremonials of the Church," are structured on this basis. Principally, the liturgical use of material objects as sacraments and sacramentals transforms common objects into divine symbols and the liturgical combination of Old Testament, gospel, and epistle texts frequently assumes a typological relationship between these passages.[65]

Most transparently, of course, the liturgical calendar functions as an alternate reading of time, an interpretation of each day as part of a divine movement from Advent to Easter to Pentecost to the Second Coming. As Esther Hu notes, Rossetti depicts the incarnate Christ as seeing "the possibilities in eternal time visually and aurally superimposed onto the limitations of human temporality."[66] The liturgical year is the church's performative enactment of this Christic vision, a vision at once incarnational and apocalyptic. The apocalypse is an explicit theme in the liturgical year, particularly in the penitential seasons of Advent and Lent. Hooker even suggests that the underlying reasoning behind such basic choices as the movement of Christian worship from Saturday to Sunday is apocalyptic.[67] In Christian thought going back to Paul's epistle to the Colossians, Christ, "the first born of the new creation," is seen as inaugurating the final eschatological era. For Hooker, the alteration in the day of worship from Saturday in the Jewish religion to Sunday in the Christian religion symbolizes this fundamental change in perspective. Whereas the Jewish day of worship commemorates the origin of the world (whose completion was followed by the Sabbath), the Christian day of worship anticipates the world to come (it is a "perpetual remembrance of a far better world begun by him which came to restore all things, to make heaven and earth new").[68] The Saints Days so central to Rossetti's own analysis of the liturgy honor and reflect later citizens of this kingdom, most often those who have already joined it radically and permanently through martyrdom.

If the liturgy is a teacher of typological reading, Rossetti was a very willing student. Her devotional prose works, themselves often structured around the Anglican liturgical calendar, frequently offer typological interpretations of scriptural texts on the basis of the juxtapositions suggested by the liturgy for the day.[69] It is fitting, then, that the liturgical year also resides at the heart of the structure of *Verses,* the poetic volume in which Rossetti aims to transpose eternal time and the eternal order onto temporality.[70] The work moves from the emptiness of the mournful opening section ("Out of the Deep have I called unto Thee, O Lord") to the interpretive certainty of the final section ("Songs for Strangers and Pilgrims") precisely by way of its intermediate sections on the Anglican liturgical year and the Apocalypse ("Some Feasts and Fasts," "The World. Self-Destruction," "Divers Worlds. Time and Eternity," and "New Jerusalem and Its Citizens").

The liturgically derived symbolic patterns that *Verses* typically employs to interpret the temporal in light of the eternal are philosophically justified and explicated in Rossetti's devotional prose works *Called to be Saints: The Minor Festivals Devotionally Studied* and *Seek and Find: A Double Series of Short Studies of the Benedicte.* In the epigraph to her lengthy reflection on the saints of the Anglican calendar, Rossetti quotes Hooker's assertion that Saints' Days are "witnesses of ancient truth, provocations to . . . piety, shadows of our endless felicity in heaven," a quotation which best prefigures the volume if the term "shadows" is taken in its full, Platonic sense. As Rossetti writes in *Verses*, in the Apocalypse, "that morrow / Which makes an end of sorrow," "all saints are / On holyday," an image which clearly positions our present holy days as anticipations of that final day of rest.[71]

Rossetti goes so far as to collapse the worship of "that earthly Jerusalem, which is Thy [God's] Holy Catholic Church" with that of "the New Jerusalem,"[72] poetically envisioning the saints in heaven worshipping exactly according to the pattern of the Book of Common Prayer. Although the worship of the church in the New Jerusalem takes place outside of time and does not "belong" to "day or night," this worship is still best understood as the church's eternal "matins and . . . evensong."[73] The Anglican morning service (or "matins") includes, after the Psalms and scriptures for the day have been read and before Zechariah's Benediction has been prayed, the recitation of either the ancient hymn "Te Deum Laudamus" (traditionally attributed to St. Ambrose) or the "Benedicte, Omnia Opera" (the Song of the Three Holy Children from the Septuagint's version of the third chapter of Daniel). In *Verses*, the saints in heaven pray in precisely this order, "chanting psalms, / Endless Te Deum for the ended fight."[74]

Since in the form of worship recorded in the Book of Common Prayer heaven and earth meet, the liturgical text also possesses a potent ability to reinscribe the world with divine meaning. As the speaker of the poem "Earth has clear call of daily bells" explains, the world is best understood when read as a divine liturgy. In keeping with the rest of Rossetti's treatment of the Book of Common Prayer, in this poem nature's liturgy is depicted as fundamentally identical with that of the Church of England. The Book of Common Prayer stipulates that in all parishes in the Church of England, the curate "shall cause a Bell to be tolled" at "a convenient time before" the start of each service, "that the people may come to hear God's Word, and to pray with him."[75] Rossetti's speaker asserts that, correspondingly, "Earth has clear call of daily bells" to summon all creation to the matins and evensong that are morning and evening.[76] The entire universe is the church in which this service is held; the night sky, for instance, is "A chancel-vault of gloom and star" (line 2).

Everything in heaven and earth, it is suggested, plays some role in these services if we could only see and hear it, if only "man's daily life" were not "out of tune with daily bells" (lines 5–6). The poem's primary concrete example is that of thunder. In both the Anglican Morning and Evening Service, the Third Collect is followed by the solemn religious song known as the "anthem."[77] To Rossetti's speaker, "thunder" is the "organ swell[ing]" as it plays "the anthems" in creation's morning and evening liturgical services (lines 3–4). Ultimately, in the liturgy of nature, "Earth and Heaven" come together, as both play "the chimes" that "Paradise accords" to them (lines 7–8).

By mystically rereading the world as liturgy, Rossetti's speaker is able to interpret even the evidence against God's existence that so troubled many writers of the 1890s—his silence and absence from his creation—in theological terms. In the second half of the poem, Rossetti's speaker grapples with the silence of heaven, humanity's apparent disconnect from any source of transcendental significance. She recasts the frequent silences of heaven, the moments when life seems absent of divine meaning, as "rest fulfilling music's laws," perhaps a dramatic stop or pause in the organ's anthem (lines 8–9). The speaker asserts that the saints know heaven's music well enough to envision and hear, at least in imagination, the darkness ceasing and the music resuming: "Saints sit and gaze, where oftentimes / Precursive flush of morning climbs / And air vibrates with coming chimes" (lines 10–12). The speaker can neither see nor hear this restoration, but still transforms the meaning of the darkness, silence, and lack that she acknowledges in the material world by envisioning them in liturgical terms.

III

Perhaps the most poetically important aspect of Rossetti's liturgical thought is her use of the Book of Common Prayer to invest natural objects with typological meaning. In her devotional prose works Rossetti explains the logic behind the typological reading of nature that she poetically enacts in *Verses.* To each of the feasts of the Anglican calendar that she discusses in *Called to be Saints*, Rossetti assigns a plant (usually a flower), assigning also to the feasts of the Apostles the gemstones of the New Jerusalem and to the feasts of the Four Evangelists the Living Creature traditionally associated with each.[78] Each object is chosen as a fitting symbol or type of the saint for the day.

Sometimes Rossetti chooses as her emblems plants that already possess a conventional symbolic significance, whether from scriptural usage or patristic and medieval tradition. In her devotional prose works, Rossetti particularly cites John Mason Neale's *Medieval Preachers and Medieval Preaching* and the Reverend S. Baring-Gould's *Lives of the Saints* as sources for some of her traditional symbolism.[79] As per tradition, in writing about the Annunciation (March 25), she assigns the violet (elsewhere also the lily and the rose) to Mary, explaining that it is "clothed with humility"; "not sufficed by a lowly nature, [it] crooks downward also the neck of its slender flower stalk."[80] At other times Rossetti chooses English plants—obviously absent from scripture or patristic tradition—as her emblems, reconfiguring the flora of her native land as symbols for the saints in a very original manner.[81] However, the symbolic significance she ascribes even to English plants (such as the daisy) is in most cases ultimately derived from her typological interpretation of liturgical texts, principally the Psalms recited on saint days and the prayer "Benedicte, Omnia Opera" recited in the morning service. Keble would likely have objected to her loose and extrapolative use of the typological method; unlike Keble, she does not simply employ a received symbol system, and her symbology may display a certain amount of individualism. But Rossetti's idiosyncratic revision of Keble's liturgical typology allows her to re-enchant and find divine meaning in important portions of the world that his more literalistic and directly citational liturgical poetry necessarily omits—such as any plant native neither to the biblical Middle East nor the patristic Roman Empire.

Much of *Called to be Saints* is devoted to a typological exposition of each of the Psalms whose recitation falls on an Anglican saint's day. Without any precedent of which I am aware, Rossetti asserts that these Psalms typologically prefigure the lives of the saints commemorated on the day on which they are read. Rossetti is aware that her idea is unusual and counterintuitive. The Anglican monthly round of Psalms does not alter for saint days; on holy days the congregation simply recites the Psalms usually designated for that day of the month. Consequently, the compilers of the Prayer Book could not possibly have intended the parallels between Psalm and saint she is asserting. But Rossetti, like the Oxford Movement as a whole,[82] refuses to allow the concept of authorial or editorial intention to restrict or delimit the plentitude of meaning she perceives in both the Prayer Book and the Bible. As Rossetti explains with characteristically false modesty, her "Memorials," or interpretations of the Psalms in light of the lives of the saints

> took their rise from my own observation of appropriate verses when I joined in our Church Service: once such association succeeded another, until it appeared to me that the Psalms of each feast might be arranged in more or less apt connection with its special history. In the Scripture texts . . . I have observed or imagined some bearing on the subject at hand, at the least either *typical* or suggestive. (*Called to Be Saints*, xvi, italics mine)

Since much of the imagery found in the Psalms is zoological or botanical, this typological interpretation sometimes has an important secondary effect. When an animal or plant is taken to prefigure or represent a saint, it receives a symbolic signification which it then retains outside of an explicitly religious context. As Catherine Cantapulo notes, much of Rossetti's late poetry assumes an elaborate "subtext" in "Scripture and tradition" that the poems themselves neither supply nor indicate through direct reference.[83] *Verses* throughout will assume the liturgically derived symbology of *Called to Be Saints* in poems that on the surface seem to be mere studies in zoology or botany. Lynda Palazzo, who performs the only extended scholarly reading of *Called to Be Saints*, reduces the work's liturgical structure to a mere "precaution" on Rossetti's part designed to render the volume "an acceptable Tractarian publication."[84] I would argue instead that Rossetti employs the liturgical year in unique and original ways to re-enchant a disenchanted world. To illustrate this point, I will offer two primary examples, the first concerned with fauna, the second with flora.

As befits her fascination with the apocalypse, Rossetti cherished a particular devotion to the traditional author of the Book of Revelation, St. John the Apostle. She follows both ancient tradition and the Book of Common Prayer in assigning one of the Four Living Creatures from the book of Ezekiel to each of the Four Evangelists; to St. John, as per tradition, she assigns the figure of the Eagle.[85] St. John's feast day is December 27, and Rossetti finds in the Psalms for that day a typological justification of this symbolic association. On the twenty-seventh of each month, the Anglican round of Psalms is nearing its end; the readings for this day include Psalm 124:5-6: "But praised be the Lord: who hath not given us over for a prey unto their teeth. / Our soul is escaped even as a bird out of the snare of the fowler."

Rossetti's "memorial" for the day, connecting the Psalms with the life of the saint, parses this passage as prefiguring one of St. John's miraculous escapes from martyrdom. According to tradition, St. John was boiled in oil as a punishment for his faith but emerged unharmed. "The Cauldron hurts him not"; the bird that is the saint flies free.[86]

Types, as George Landow notes, are by definition "divinely created symbol[s]" whose meaning is considered to be foreordained by God.[87] As the previous chapter explained, Keble believed that God, when creating the world, foresaw the typological significance that objects would later receive and deliberately designed them to be fit to receive this signification.[88] Correspondingly, Rossetti believes that the association of the saint with the eagle she has discovered in tradition and the Book of Common Prayer extends to, and creates a symbolic meaning for, the eagle as it appears in nature as well. As she writes, "let us consider the natural eagle, if so we may ascribe glory unto Him who formed the eagle, and by whose inspiration each Evangelist wrote down his own proper notes of the divine melody in harmony."[89] As with each of the animals, plants, and stones that she employs as emblems, Rossetti finds symbolic significance in the eagle's physical traits. The eagle's beauty, strength, and speed of flight reflect and prefigure St. John's spiritual perfection and apocalyptic raptures. Still more importantly, the eagle, unlike many birds, prefers day to night, and even possesses a unique ability to stare directly at "the blaze of the noontide sun," which makes it a fitting emblem for the seer who could bear the vision of God unveiled in the apocalypse.[90] Rossetti likely derives her emphasis on the eagle's acute vision from medieval Christian symbology; Neale's anthology of medieval preaching—referenced by Rossetti in *Time Flies*—contains a sermon by St. Anthony of Padua that asserts, "The eagle is so called . . . because she can behold the sun with unflinching eyes."[91] Rossetti also sees the eagle's care for its young as an image for the self-denying Christian love so often commended in the epistles traditionally ascribed to St. John.

The eagle becomes Rossetti's favorite figure of the saintly mystic, who can look at God by whom all things subsist—and in whom reside the Platonic forms of all things—without flinching.[92] This figure applies especially to St. John, but secondarily to all Christians, as Rossetti's treatment of birds as a type in *Seek and Find* reveals. *Seek and Find* is Rossetti's book-length analysis of the "Benedicte, Omnia Opera," the "Song of the Three Holy Children" from the third chapter of Daniel in the Apocrypha. The Benedicte—recited by the faithful Jews Shadrach, Meshach, and Abednego in the midst of the fiery furnace into which the Babylonian King Nebuchadnezzar has thrown them—is one of the most extended poetic tributes to nature in biblical literature. Seemingly destined for immanent death, they defiantly chant a prayer of thanksgiving for each item of material creation. Rossetti studies the text particularly as a prayer recited in the Anglican morning service and uses the translation found in the Book of Common Prayer. She parses the verse, "O all ye Fowls of the Air, bless ye the Lord: praise him and magnify him forever," as symbolically representing the souls of the faithful who, empowered by the Holy Ghost, fly like birds in their ascent to God.[93] As should be apparent, the eagle of *Called to Be Saints* possesses the same traits and signification possessed by birds as a whole in *Seek and Find*, just to an unusually large degree. One might say that the eagle simply actualizes the primary aspects of the Platonic form of bird in a particularly powerful way, just as St. John the Apostle was a Christian who "became Christ" to an unusually heroic extent.

Rossetti assumes and employs the signification for eagles and birds that she has exposited in *Called to Be Saints* and *Seek and Find* in many of the poems in *Verses*. Fittingly, her fullest use of the trope occurs in the two poems dedicated to the liturgical feast day of "St. John, Apostle." In the first of these poems, "Earth cannot bar flame from ascending," apocalyptic vision and the eye of the eagle are synonymous. Rossetti pictures St. John in his exile on the island of Patmos, "with chains for thy wages."[94] However, spiritually John cannot be confined. Like the sacrificial fire of the Jewish temple or the incense burned in many fin-de-siècle Anglo-Catholic liturgies, his spirit must of its very nature rise to the heavens. In vision, he flies forward to the Apocalypse, in which "Heaven shall pass away with a noise" and up to Christ enthroned in glory.[95] Since

Earth cannot bar flame from ascending,
Hell cannot bind light from descending. . . .

Eagle and sun gaze at each other,
Eagle at sun, brother at Brother.
(Rossetti, "Earth cannot," lines 1–2, 4–5)

The poem ends with a prayer calling on Jesus to descend and enable ordinary Christians as well to fly to heaven and enjoy the beatific vision. Recalling and reversing the motion of ascent and descent from the poem's opening, the speaker prays that "Jesus, in love looking down hither" would "by love draw us up thither."[96] The implication is that, as in *Seek and Find*, the Christian soul is also a bird, but one that does not fly as freely as St. John's eagle.

This idea is made explicit in the poem that immediately follows, "'Beloved let us love one another,' says St. John." This poem imagines the saint as the caring "Eagle of eagles calling from above," kindly feeding his flock below with the "Words of strong nourishment," "'Beloved, let us love.'"[97] Moreover, since many of the later poems in *Verses*—such as "Easter Day," "Of each sad word which is more sorrowful," "The Flowers appear on the Earth," and "Yea, the sparrow hath found her a house"—employ a symbolism in which birds represent Christian souls, the typological associations that

Rossetti has developed through her analysis of the "Benedicte, Omnia Opera" and the Psalms for St. John's feast day are retained when both Prayer Book and saint are nowhere in sight.

IV

The eagle is a traditional Christian symbol that becomes a central poetic symbol for Rossetti in part as a result of her unconventional interpretation of the Book of Common Prayer. As my example of Rossetti's treatment of flora, I will offer an example less commonly employed in Christian art. Rossetti offers a symbolic interpretation of the least exotic of all plants, grass, that is both original and literarily important, as it serves as a basis for most of her other botanical symbolism. As far as I can determine, Rossetti's fascination with grass owes nothing to the work of Walt Whitman, the nineteenth-century poet most commonly associated with the plant. In *Called to Be Saints,* she attributes the emblem of grass to the Feast of All Saints (November 1). In assigning this emblem, Rossetti assumes a typological significance for grass that she has already developed in *Seek and Find.* In *Seek and Find,* she explicates verse 53 of the "Benedicte"—"O all ye Green Things upon the Earth, bless ye the Lord: praise him, and magnify him forever"—by explaining, "The first vegetable production mentioned in the Bible is grass," which thereby serves as an image for life itself and, by extension, as a type for all human life.[98] For Rossetti grass typologically represents the varying spiritual potentialities of human life, referring either to human frailty, sin, and death or to "a flourishing human fertility indicative of spiritual vitality."[99] In *Called to Be Saints*, she relates the lives of several saints to the Psalms recited on their feast days by interpreting grass in each of these three typological senses: as a figure for all humanity without distinction, as a figure for all human evil, and as a figure for all human goodness, the "spiritual vitality" of the saints.[100] In the last of these senses, grass is a fit emblem for the feast of "All Saints."

As with her ruminations on the eagle, Rossetti extends the typological interpretations of grass she has developed in reference to the Prayer Book out onto the natural world as well. She finds symbolic significance in many of the physical traits of grass. As she writes, the "grasses" are "trodden at all seasons by all feet," but "stripped" of them "earth would lack half her refreshing charm."[101] "Most precious of all their charms seems to us their inexhaustible verdure," which is easily restored after drought, persists beneath the snow, and survives storms and winds that fell trees.[102] Although the grasses are hardy toward adversity, they are sensitive to both wind and sun; they "clothe the ground with a living carpet which snow cannot nip or tempest destroy, yet which a breeze can break up into a sea of ripples, and of which each component blade is straight-veined pointing skywards."[103] The lowly grasses, like the masses of saints known and unknown, triumph over the world that seems to defeat them, as they move with the wind of the Holy Spirit and point toward God in heaven. Like the saints, grass as a trope receives its final meaning in the apocalypse. When discussing the twelve semiprecious stones that serve as the foundations for the city walls of the apocalyptic New Jerusalem in Revelation chapter 21, Rossetti explains that "the emerald arrayed in *grass-green of earth* symbolizes hope" (italics mine).[104] This heavenly emerald standing at the entrance to the city of the saints is perhaps the Platonic form of grass as Rossetti envisions it, an eternal picture of life, vitality, and hope that is immune to alteration or diminishment.

Rossetti's symbolic reading of grass is employed throughout *Verses*, perhaps most prominently in the poem "Thou knewest . . . thou oughtest therefore." This poem opens with the speaker "Behold[ing] in heaven a floating dazzling cloud" emblematic of the glories of eternity.[105] Somewhat surprisingly, the speaker's reaction is not devotion but despondency. The cloud is "So dazzling that I could but cry Alas! / Alas, because I felt how low I was."[106] The heights of heaven possess no inspirational value if they exist only as totally Other, as a divine foil whose relation to humanity can only be ironic. Faith without hope is crushing.[107] The poem's title is a quotation from Matthew 25:26–27, the master's reproach to the servant who had been given least in Jesus's Parable of the Talents, for burying his one talent instead of using it in his master's service. Like the servant, the speaker is struggling with reconciling her sense of her own insignificance with her fear of and duties toward God. The speaker finds a solution for this dilemma when she

> glanced downward on the grass
> And the grass bowed when the airs of heaven would pass,
> Lifting itself when it had bowed.
> ("Rossetti, "'Thou knewest,'" lines 6–8).

"That grass spake comfort," the speaker asserts, and it teaches the lesson of grass Rossetti associates with All Saints.[108] Although the grass is "weak . . . and low," it is still "strong enough and high enough to bend / In homage at a message from the sky" and as a result "prosper[s]"; no person is too insignificant to sway under the breath of the Holy Spirit.[109] Fortified with this vision, the speaker resolves to be "strong in patient weakness till the end," to endure like the lowly grass, to become one of the lowly saints whose names are never known until the end of time.[110]

More importantly, Rossetti derives her symbolic treatment of many other plants from her typological reading of grass. In her rumination on grass in

Called to Be Saints, she reminds her readers that the "corn of wheat" that Jesus offered as an image of his own sacrifice, and therefore as a model of the Christian life, belongs to the grass family.[111] Rossetti also depicts wheat as being, like grass, a symbol for the souls of the Christian faithful in the opening poem of *Verses*. In an extended metaphor that first raises the volume's primary thematic concerns, she pictures Christian souls struggling against the temporal order that constrains them as a field of wheat. She writes of those who believe:

We turn to Thee [God]; as on an eastern slope
Wheat feels the dawn beneath night's lingering cope,
Bending and stretching sunward ere it sees.
(Rossetti, "Alone Lord God," 6–8)

In this poem, wheat represents the unknown Christian faithful who yearn to see past the shades of time into eternity, resisting the apparently natural order of light and shadow.

As I have mentioned, in *Seek and Find*, grass becomes a synecdoche for all "green things" and, by extrapolation, for life itself. Hence many of Rossetti's symbolic uses of plants partake of the elements she identifies with grass, particularly its lowliness and its ability to resist weather. As Rossetti tends to emphasize the moments when the liturgical calendar is thematically at odds with the natural cycle of the seasons, she also often selects as spiritual symbols plants—beginning with grass—that she perceives as resisting this cycle. For instance, Rossetti associates the daisy with a number of different saints whose feasts she commemorates, including St. Andrew and St. Margaret.[112] The daisy, Rossetti stresses, is common, but beautiful and hardy, surviving even into the frosts of November.[113] Similarly, the violets associated with the Virgin Mary come out in March, in spite of "frost" and "boisterous wind," because they see the sun.[114] The daisy is like the souls of the saints in that it cranes toward the sun and "closes against darkness."[115] The daisy is a small plant, spreading among the grasses, and is hardy, resisting the attempts of animals to uproot it. It spreads its beauty rapidly, as the saints do with evangelization.[116] In *Called to Be Saints,* even as unlikely a plant as the rose bush becomes indirectly associated with grass, as some grasses possess a "thick rose-tinted plume."[117] Since the Virgin Mary, symbolically a rose, is the chief of "All Saints," this improbable association is perhaps less surprising that it would seem to be at first glance.

The liturgically inspired zoological and, more frequently, botanical symbolism of works like *Called to Be Saints* and *Seek and Find* provides a needed interpretive key for many of the poems in *Verses*. Grass, wheat, roses, violets, and daisies alone serve as key images at least thirty-nine times in *Verses*, and they often assume a symbolic significance that the poems do not explicate. Perhaps the best example of this phenomenon is the short poem "'Who hath despised the day of small things?'" Karen Dieleman has noted that "*Verses* remains insufficiently considered" by critics, who have been prone to dismiss it as conventional devotional ephemera.[118] On a first reading, this poem could seem to be sufficiently superficial and saccharine as to justify that conclusion, the stuff of inspirational wall plaques or floral calendars:

As violets so be I recluse and sweet,
    Cheerful as daisies unaccounted rare,
Still sunward-gazing from a lowly seat,
    Still sweetening wintry air.

While half-awakened Spring lags incomplete
    While lofty forest trees tower bleak and bare,
Daisies and violets own remotest heat
    And bloom and make them fair.
(Rossetti, "'Who hath despised,'" lines 1–8)

However, Rossetti's personal symbol system suggests a much deeper meaning. If violets are the Virgin Mary, and daisies stand both for St. Andrew, the first of the Apostles in the Anglican liturgical year and as a broader symbol for all saints, then we have a poem that resembles medieval lyrics in its apparent simplicity and deep mysticism.[119] By imitating Mary's quiet, self-sacrificing piety and willingness to be overlooked, the common English saints can grow in grace, spread their faith, and conquer time and earth, producing, like the liturgical year itself, summer in the midst of winter, life in the midst of death. The poem's title, "Who hath despised the day of small things?" transposes these ruminations into an apocalyptic register. The title is a quotation from the book of the prophet Zechariah, chapter 4, verse 10. In this verse, as Rossetti reads it, those who despise "the day of small things" (in this case, the beginning of the rebuilding of the temple), are witnessed against by "the eyes of the Lord, which run to and fro through the whole earth." The gaze of what seems a sweet nature poem is quite literally apocalyptic. The trees will fall; empires will crumble. The true "day" is not in the calendar; it is the day of God's visitation.

V

As the achievement of *Verses* attests, the complexity of Rossetti's poetry and the originality of her theology increase as the challenges to a typological reading of nature—and to any reading of the world as a unified and meaningful whole—mount in late Victorian England. Rossetti held to the Tractarian doctrines of analogy and reserve in which every object in the world possesses a divine meaning, but this meaning can be revealed only gradually, to the sympathetic reader who has been properly trained to perceive it.[120] One of the most controversial aspects of the Tractarian movement was this insistence that divine truth could never be communicated simply and directly to the masses; it required a tight-knit community possessed with an allusive language of expression. Emma Mason and Catherine Cantalupo, among others, have seen in Tractarian reserve the logical justification of Rossetti's late poetic style.[121] And, alone among the authors in this study, Rossetti writes a liturgical poetry that possesses no vision for England as a whole, no hope of a restored organic social order beyond that represented on a local scale by the devout Anglo-Catholic communities and sisterhoods with which she was affiliated.

Verses has typically been dismissed by critics as excessively simplistic, even trite. We can start to see the significance of the work in Rossetti's oeuvre if we consider the possibility that the volume, like Jesus's parables, is sufficiently complicated as to seem simple to the hearer who misses the point. As its publication history suggests, *Verses* is written for the initiate, for a community of Anglo-Catholic devotees who share Rossetti's interpretation of the world and frame of textual reference. Isobel Armstrong has similarly deduced that *Verses* is written "to an avowedly ecclesiastical readership committed to religious verse" who will "presuppose the revolutionary sacramentalism of her poems,"[122] a subculture sufficiently sizable in late Victorian England to render the volume a significant commercial success. Critics have typically made no attempt to enter into this community. They have failed to ascend to the speculative heights of Anglo-Catholic Platonism or even, more basically, to enter into Rossetti's liturgical community, to entertain the mystical reading of the Book of Common Prayer that serves as the foundation for so much of Anglo-Catholic thought and practice. By ignoring Rossetti's religious influences and community—and her own devotional prose works—critics have placed themselves outside Rossetti's rhetorical economy; *Verses* in its "reserve" will not speak to them, and critics have historically blamed the work rather than themselves. The work's achievement, paradoxically, is the cause of its critical neglect.

The novelist Virginia Woolf treats Rossetti as a precursor in *A Room of One's Own*, but Rossetti has rarely been seen as a precursor of modernist poetics. Karen Dieleman has called for "a cross-century reading of Christina Rossetti alongside Anglo-Catholic poet T. S. Eliot," arguing that, despite their obvious differences in style, their shared theological convictions should result in meaningful literary similarities.[123] *Verses* serves as a meaningful test case for Dieleman's hypothesis. For it is in her last, liturgically inflected poems that Rossetti's stylistics and poetics most foreshadow the innovations of that later liturgical experimentalist, T. S. Eliot. In *Verses*, Rossetti innovatively pushes her Tractarian logic out toward the borders of modernism, writing densely allusive, intertextual poems which reinscribe meaning on an empty world by employing a symbol system accessible only to a limited audience. On these terms alone, she was able to articulate, against the deeply skeptical intellectual culture of the 1890s and its entropic vision of a world running out of time, her vision of an enchanted universe that moves according to divine time.

NOTES

1. For a list of these collections of hymns, see G. B. Tennyson's appendices in *Victorian Devotional Poetry*. For a summary of the ritualist contributions to hymnody, see Reed, *Glorious Battle*, 73–74.
2. Lysack, "The Productions of Time," 456–57.
3. Oakeley, *Lyra Liturgica*, vii.
4. Oakeley, *Lyra Liturgica*, vii.
5. Westerholm, "In Defense of Verses," 192.
6. The quotation is from line 7 of Christina Rossetti, "The Sunday Before Advent." In *The Complete Poems of Christina Rossetti*, Vol. II, ed. R. W. Crump (Baton Rouge: Louisiana State University Press, 1986), 247. Text references are to line numbers from this edition.
7. On Keble's influence on Rossetti and her knowledge of his works, see D'Amico and Kent, "Rossetti and the Tractarians," 93, and Hu, "Christina Rossetti, John Keble," 175.
8. In her article, "Christina Rossetti's *Christian Year*: Comfort for the 'weary heart,'" Diane D'Amico both reproduces and meditates on Rossetti's illustrations to the volume. Rossetti's letters to William Michael Rossetti from January 28, 1890, and April 9, 1894, refer to receiving, respectively, a book by and a biography of Keble (in Harrison, *The Letters of Christina Rossetti: A Digital Edition,* Letters 1720 and 2040).
9. D'Amico and Kent, "Rossetti and the Tractarians," 95.
10. Armstrong, "Christina Rossetti," 21.
11. Wheeler-Barclay, *The Science of Religion*, 2.
12. Wheeler-Barclay, *The Science of Religion*, 9.
13. Comte, *Positive Philosophy*, 2–3.
14. Comte, *Positive Philosophy*, 2.
15. See Wheeler-Barclay, *The Science of Religion*, 9, 28.
16. Tylor, *Primitive Culture*, 23. See also Wheeler-Barclay, *The Science of Religion*, 87.
17. Wheeler-Barclay, *The Science of Religion* 87, 94–95.

18. Tylor, *Primitive Culture*, 501–2.

19. See Riede, *Matthew Arnold*, 18.

20. See Riede, *Matthew Arnold*, 7–8.

21. See Müller, *Natural Religion*, 416.

22. Müller, *Physical Religion*, 120.

23. For an example of this approach, see Arnold, *Literature and Dogma*, 10. For an analysis of this approach, see Wheeler-Barclay, *The Science of Religion*, 47, 55.

24. For an example of this approach, see Arnold, *Literature and Dogma*, 44–46.

25. Wheeler-Barclay, *The Science of Religion*, 62.

26. Frazer, *The Golden Bough*, 68, 47.

27. Frazer, *The Golden Bough*, 69.

28. Frazer, *The Golden Bough*, 71.

29. Frazer, *The Golden Bough*, 366.

30. Rossetti, *The Face of the Deep*, 380.

31. Rossetti, *The Face of the Deep*, 380.

32. Rossetti, "Time seems not short," line 9; Rossetti, "Christmas Eve," lines 3–4; Rossetti, *Seek and Find*, 213.

33. See Riede, *Matthew Arnold*, 9, 16.

34. Arseneau, *Recovering Christina Rossetti*, 142.

35. On this point, see Roe, *Christina Rossetti's Faithful Imagination*, 19.

36. Rossetti, *Time Flies*, 261.

37. Armstrong, "Christina Rossetti," 25–26, 29–30.

38. Rossetti, *Times Flies*, 23–24.

39. Rossetti, *The Face of the Deep*, 278.

40. Rossetti, *The Face of the Deep*, 215. Rossetti's quotation is from the Book of Sirach (also called Ecclesiasticus), chapter 42, verse 24. Although Sirach is not formally considered canonical by the Anglican church, the Book of Common Prayer includes the text as part of its daily scripture readings.

41. Landow, *Victorian Types*, 3.

42. See Keble, *Tract 89*, 29, 149.

43. Rossetti, *Seek and Find*, 246–47, 273. See also Palazzo, *Christina Rossetti's Feminist Theology*, 97.

44. Keble, preface, xcii.

45. Arseneau, *Recovering Christina Rossetti*, 132.

46. Roe, *Christina Rossetti's Faithful Imagination*, 166.

47. Rossetti, "Looking Back," lines 6, 4, 8, 12. As Mary Arseneau has observed about *Goblin Market and Other Poems*, "retrospective appraisal is the definitive gaze" in Rossetti's work (*Recovering Christina Rossetti* 130).

48. Rossetti, *The Face of the Deep*, 495.

49. Rossetti, *The Face of the Deep*, 495.

50. Rossetti, *The Face of the Deep* 241, 242. As Diane D'Amico notes, Rossetti often draws on "biblical texts that describe heaven as a place of song"; for her, "silence was a characteristic of a fallen earth" (D'Amico, *Christina Rossetti*, 153).

51. Rossetti, The *Face of the Deep*, 289; see also Rossetti, *Annus Domini*, 201.

52. Bulfin, "The End of Time," in Ferguson, *Victorian Time*, 154–55.

53. Wilde, *The Picture*, 198.

54. Rossetti, *The Face of the Deep*, 241.

55. Roe, *Christina Rossetti's Faithful Imagination*, 189.

56. The section title quotes Psalm 130:1, in the translation employed by the Book of Common Prayer.

57. Nietzsche, "On Truth and Lying," 249.

58. Dowling, *Language and Decadence*, 148,173.

59. Wilde, *The Picture*, 215.

60. Armstrong, "Christina Rossetti," 37.

61. On Rossetti's knowledge of the work of Isaac Williams, especially his *Tract 80* and *Tract 87*, see Mason, "Christina Rossetti," 197, 201.

62. See Stanwood, "Christina Rossetti's Devotional Prose," 237 for the precise evidence (a transcription error in the text of Hooker) that shows that Rossetti's epigraph for *Called to Be Saints* is taken particularly from Keble's edition of Hooker.

63. Keble, preface, xciii. See also I. Williams, *Tract 80*, 46.

64. Keble, preface, xci; xcii.

65. Keble, preface, xci–xciii.

66. Hu, "Christina Rossetti, John Keble," 179.

67. Hooker, *Of the Laws*, 356.

68. Hooker, *Of the Laws*, 356.

69. See, for instance, Rossetti's ruminations in *Seek and Find*, which often reinterpret biblical texts in light of the combinations of Old Testament reading, Gospel, and Epistle offered in the liturgy (for a particularly explicit example, see 206).

70. As Dinah Roe has noted, Rossetti took the arrangement and order of her poetic volumes seriously and made many changes in content, title, and placement to her late poems when re-presenting them as *Verses* (*Christina Rossetti's Faithful Imagination*, 132).

71. Rossetti, "And now why tarriest thou?" lines 14–16. Rossetti envisions the same scenario from the opposite angle in the poem "Christmas Eve," in which when Earth "strike[s] up" its "music, / Birds that sing and bells that ring; / Heaven hath answering music / For all Angels soon to sing" (lines 9–13).

72. Rossetti, *Annus Domini*, 360.

73. Rossetti, "'The Holy City,'" lines 12–13.

74. Rossetti, "What are these lovely ones," lines 12–13.

75. The Church of England, The Book of Common Prayer, x. The connection between church bells and the Prayer Book receives a more extensive treatment in the chapter on Dorothy L. Sayers.

76. The quotation is from line one of Christina Rossetti's poem "Earth has clear call of daily bells." In *The Complete Poems of Christina Rossetti*, Vol. II, ed. R. W. Crump (Baton Rouge: Louisiana State University Press, 1986), 265. Text references are to line numbers from this edition.

77. See The Church of England, The Book of Common Prayer, 14, 24.

78. On the Living Creatures, see Rossetti, *Called to Be Saints*, xiv. Rossetti's association of the gemstones of the New Jerusalem with the apostles receives an implicit authorization from the Book of Common Prayer. The first lesson for

matins on St. Andrew's Day includes Isaiah 54:11–12, "O thou afflicted, tossed with tempest . . . behold, I will lay thy stones with fair colours, and lay thy foundations with sapphires. And I will make . . . all thy gates of carbuncles, and all thy borders of pleasant stones." and the first lesson for evensong includes Isaiah 65:17, "Behold, I create a new heaven and a new earth."

79. See Rossetti, *Time Flies*, 229, 43.

80. Rossetti, *Called to Be Saints*, 181, 193, 191.

81. Gisela Hönninghausen is an insightful reader of Rossetti's botanical symbolism and gives proper credit to the originality of many of Rossetti's symbolic usages. However, she overstates the case when she asserts that while "[t]he linking of certain plants with certain Saints' Days goes back to the Middle Ages," Rossetti most often "deliberately turns away from accepted emblems and biblical parables" (Hönninghausen, "Emblematic Tendencies," 4).

82. The Oxford Movement's refusal to privilege authorial intention was perhaps most famously expressed in John Henry Newman's assertion in *Tract 90* that the present Anglicans "owe no duties to th[e] framers" when interpreting the Thirty-Nine Articles (83).

83. Cantapulo, "Christian Rossetti," 278.

84. Palazzo, *Christina Rossetti's Feminist Theology,* 63.

85. See Rossetti, *Called to Be Saints*, 85. The general association of the Four Evangelists with the Four Living Creatures from Ezekiel is both assumed and authorized by the readings from the Book of Common Prayer for St. Mark's Day, in which the first lesson for evensong includes Ezekiel 1:1–15, Ezekiel's vision of the Four Living Creatures.

86. Rossetti, *Called to Be Saints*, 82.

87. Landow, *Victorian Types*, 37, 43.

88. See John Keble, *Tract 89*, 123, 173.

89. Rossetti, *Called to Be Saints*, 86.

90. Rossetti, *Called to Be Saints*, 86.

91. Neale, *Medieval Preachers*, 235.

92. See, for example, Rossetti's comment that the Roman centurion who believed in Christ "became in matters spiritual as a Roman eagle gazing upon the unveiled sun" (*Seek and Find*, 295).

93. The Church of England, The Book of Common Prayer, 9; Rossetti, *Seek and Find*, 117.

94. Rossetti, "Earth cannot," line 7.

95. Rossetti, "Earth cannot," line 12.

96. Rossetti, "Earth cannot," lines 16, 17.

97. Rossetti, "Beloved," lines 2–4. Rossetti's image of the Christian church as a flock of eagles may betray a debt to Dante Alighieri's *Divine Comedy*. In canto XVIII of the *Paradiso*, over one thousand saints arrange themselves into the shape of a single eagle, which then teaches Dante in the two cantos following. Rossetti's sister, Maria, comments on this image on page 243 of her work *A Shadow of Dante* (London: Rivingtons, 1871).

98. Rossetti, *Seek and Find*, 97–98.

99. Rossetti, *Seek and Find*, 97–98.

100. Rossetti, *Called to Be Saints*, 456–57, 77–78, 10. A full analysis of Rossetti's treatment of grass in *Called to Be Saints* is beside my purpose, and so is not provided in the body of the chapter, as it might detract from the forward movement of the argument as a whole. For any reader interested in or skeptical about the topic, such an analysis follows.

Rossetti uses grass as a figure for all humanity, irrespective of vice or virtue, in her typological analysis of the Psalms for the feast day of St. Luke (October 18th). St. Luke is traditionally identified as a medical doctor, the author of the third gospel, and a friend of St. Paul. The Anglican Psalm readings for the eighteenth of the month include Psalm 90:5–6: "As soon as thou scatterest them they are even as a sleep: and fade suddenly like the grass. In the morning it is green, and growth up: in the evening it is cut down, dried up, and withered" (The Book of Common Prayer, 462–63). Rossetti parses these verses in reference to St. Luke's life: "As a physician, he learns wisdom"; in studying the human frame (figured as grass), St. Luke also comes to know God, "in Whose hand is the soul of every living thing, and the breath of all mankind" (*Called to Be Saints*, 456–57; Rossetti is quoting Job 12:10).

Rossetti sees grass as a figure for human vice when explicating the Psalms for the feast day of St. John the Apostle (December 27th). The Anglican Psalms for the twenty-seventh of the month include Psalm 129:5–6, "Let them be confounded and turned backward: as many as have evil will at Sion. Let them be even as the grass growing upon the house-tops: which withereth afore it be plucked up" (The Book of Common Prayer, 517–18). Rossetti interprets this verse as prefiguring Jesus's title for St. John and his brother; each is "a Son of Thunder" (*Called to Be Saints*, 77–78). Jesus gives this title to St. John as a reflection of John's hot-tempered anger at the ungodly, which Jesus finds at times excessive (John at one point wishes to call fire from heaven down on a town that has disrespected Jesus and the Apostles). The prayer in this passage is one that Rossetti then imagines as prefiguring the sentiments of the young St. John, wishing for the wicked to be consumed as the grass.

Grass receives a more positive typological treatment in Rossetti's analysis of the Psalms for St. Andrew's feast day (November 30th). The Anglican Psalms for the thirtieth of the month include Psalm 147:7–8, "O sing unto the Lord with thanksgiving: sing praises upon the harp unto our God; Who covereth the heaven with clouds, and prepareth rain for the earth: and maketh the grass to grow upon the mountains, and herb for the use of men" (The Book of Common Prayer, 534–35). Rossetti sees this verse as prefiguring St. Andrew, when he "seats the multitude on the grass" (*Called to Be Saints*, 10). As Rossetti indicates, she is thinking of the gospel of Matthew 14:15–21, the feeding of the five thousand. Here grass is associated both metonymically and metaphorically with faithful souls who are willing to sit at the feet of Jesus and receive provision from him.

101. Rossetti, *Called to Be Saints*, 516.

102. Rossetti, *Called to Be Saints*, 517.

103. Rossetti, *Called to Be Saints*, 517.

104. Rossetti, *Called to Be Saints*, 168.

105. Rossetti, "Thou knewest," line 1.

106. Rossetti, "'Thou knewest,'" lines 2–3.

107. On the sky as a symbol of the virtue of faith, see Rossetti, *Called to Be Saints*, 168.

108. Rossetti, "Thou knewest," line 9.

109. Rossetti, "Thou knewest," lines 9–12.

110. Rossetti, "Thou knewest," 14.

111. Rossetti, *Called to Be Saints*, 518.

112. See Rossetti, *Called to Be Saints*, 20; *Time Flies*, 139.

113. See Rossetti, *Called to Be Saints*, 20. As Constance Hassett notes, Rossetti has many "images for the hopefulness that persists despite (and in part *because of*) all that is numbing, frightful, or dire" (*Christina Rossetti*, 212, Hassett's italics).

114. Rossetti, *Time Flies*, 58.

115. Rossetti, *Called to Be* Saints, 20–21.

116. Rossetti, *Called to Be Saints*, 22.

117. Rossetti, *Called to Be Saints*, 517.

118. Dieleman, "Christina Rossetti," 27.

119. Isobel Armstrong similarly observes of the poems contained in Rossetti's second-to-last book, *A Pageant*: "They are written with a cryptic simplicity, simplicity to the point of being arcane, as a riddle or a proverb is simple and arcane at once" ("Christina Rossetti," 22).

120. For an explanation of analogy and reserve by an author whose work Rossetti knew and admired, see Isaac Williams's *Tract 80* (esp. pp. 19 and 41) and *Tract 87* (esp. p. 27). For an example of Rossetti herself employing the concept of reserve, see *The Face of the Deep*, 23.

121. On the effects of the Tractarian ideas of analogy and reserve on Rossetti's poetic style, see especially Cantalupo, "Christina Rossetti," in Kent, *The Achievement*, 275–78. See also Mason, "Christina Rossetti," 197, 201–2; and Hu, "Christina Rossetti, John Keble," 182.

122. Armstrong, "Christina Rossetti," 22.

123. Dieleman, *Religious Imaginaries*, 262.

Chapter 3

"The Old, Coarse Prayerbook Form"

Liturgy, Materiality, and Community in the Works of Dorothy L. Sayers

As G. B. Tennyson has persuasively shown, Anglo-Catholic devotional poetry constituted one of the most popular literary movements of the nineteenth century. Often self-consciously neo-medieval in imagery, Anglo-Catholic poets attempted to help their readers to see time in light of eternity and to read nature as a collection of divine symbols all the way to the very end of the increasingly skeptical Victorian era. As the previous two chapters have shown, the two most influential Anglo-Catholic poets, John Keble and Christina Rossetti, both wrote lengthy poetic sequences that treat the Book of Common Prayer as the divine key that unlocks the meaning of time and the temporal world and that invite readers to reread their lives as part of a cosmic liturgy. Keble and Rossetti's liturgical sequences were well known in their own time and were included in or themselves constituted their most popular works. Many Victorian religious poets—including major figures like Gerard Manley Hopkins and important minor authors like Isaac Williams—shared their sacramental interpretation of the world, if not their emphasis on the church calendar.

Like many aspects of Victorianism, this poetic tradition was already under fire when Rossetti made her own contributions to it in the 1890s. By 1886, Oscar Wilde was warning his readers that *The Christian Year* possessed a deleterious effect on literary taste and should be removed from the literary canon—to be replaced by the French decadent Charles Baudelaire's *Les Fleurs du Mal*. Wilde insisted, "No doubt . . . in *The Christian Year* there are poetic qualities of a certain kind, but absolute catholicity of taste is not without its dangers. It is only an auctioneer who should admire all schools of art."[1] After 1918, Anglo-Catholic liturgical poetry would seem to have disappeared almost without a trace; after this point, Keble's *The Christian Year* and Rossetti's *Verses* remain for the most part out of print. One need not look far for likely causes. If late Victorian science and anthropology had begun the dismantling of the intellectual credibility of both conventional Christianity and a mystical, Romantic view of nature, then World War I and the rise of modernism might seem to have finished the job.

We can trace what seems the last gasp of a dying poetic tradition in Dorothy L. Sayers's second book of poetry, the 1918 volume *Catholic Tales and Christian Songs*. Her first book of poetry, published when she was fresh out of Oxford and audaciously entitled *Opus I* (1916), had included an explicit homage to the pre-Raphaelite movement;[2] *Catholic Tales and Christian Songs* uses a neo-medieval block print of Christ as a cover illustration and poetically interweaves Christian imagery with flights of fancy from fairy tales in a manner reminiscent of Christina Rossetti. The volume also includes a number of complex poetic ruminations on the Anglican liturgical year, most originally in the poem "Epiphany Hymn."

"Epiphany Hymn" both reflects and transcends the conventions of Anglo-Catholic liturgical poetry.[3] The Feast of the Epiphany (January 6) commemorates the moment when the first Gentiles (the Magi or Wise Men) found Jesus, using clues from both their own cultural heritage (astrology, following the star) and Judaism (consulting Herod's biblical scholars). This incident is the first hint in Matthew's Gospel that Jesus is the culmination of not just Israel's narrative, but the world's. The speaker of "Epiphany Hymn" takes the occasion of the feast to assert the broader point that since Christ is the "Desire of all the ages," his life story fulfills the stories and aspirations of all preexisting religions and mythologies, all "dreams of holiness" whether those of "Jove" or "Osiris" (lines 1, 11, 8). In the speaker's existential Christianity, all those who have lived in authenticity—those who "lov[ing] and look[ing] for no rewarding" were "faithful to the best they were, and were not bought nor sold" (lines 9–10)—have been implicit followers of Jesus. They "bare Thy [Christ's] pain, and knew not what they bare"; they too "hammered out Thy kingly crown of gold" (lines 14, 12). Further, the speaker believes that the ritual "sacrifice"—the symbolic destruction of the material as a tribute to the spiritual—of all cultures ultimately points toward and is given redemptive significance through the culminating self-sacrifice of Jesus upon the cross (line 6).[4] The story of Jesus is culturally specific (his is an "Orient Splendour"), but universal in its implications; he will "rise and shine to all men living" (line 17). For the speaker, the epiphany offers a logical (and theological) justification of the often scandalous and paradoxical life of Jesus; through the universality of his story, Jesus is "justified in Thine epiphany" (line 20). The epiphany reveals that God is continually active throughout the world, even outside the limitations of monotheistic cultural forms.

The "Epiphany Hymn" uses the occasion of the feast and the language of the liturgy to authorize its daring suggestion that all legitimate faith offered up in any religion is redeemed by Jesus. Its originality consists especially in turning Anglo-Catholic theology and poetics into modes by which the provincialism of English Christianity might be critiqued. The First Lesson for Matins for the Feast of the Epiphany in the Book of Common Prayer is Isaiah chapter 60, and the poem uses Isaiah 60:3 ("Nations shall come to Thy light and kings to the brightness of Thy rising") as an epigraph authorizing its focus on all the world's cultures. The poem summarizes its interpretation of the Epiphany—that the culturally particular story of Jesus both reflects and perfects the stories of all world religions—in line 17, the first line of the last stanza: "Arise, O Orient Splendour, rise and shine to all men living." This line derives its wording, grammatical structure, and logical justification from Isaiah 60:1, "Arise, shine, for thy light is come." Intriguingly, the poem presents its most original and possibly subversive ideas as reflections on ideas and images derived from the Book of Common Prayer.

As one might expect from her poetry's combination of innovation and tradition, the young Sayers has been linked to Bishop Charles Gore's *Lux Mundi* group, the principal progressive movement in early twentieth-century Anglo-Catholicism.[5] While retaining a belief in the divinity and miracles of Jesus and the value of tradition and ritual, the *Lux Mundi* group accepted many of the results of the Higher Criticism of the Bible and strongly emphasized social justice. Like the late nineteenth-century "slum priests" who imported Anglo-Catholic "smells and bells" ritualism into impoverished areas of London and a strong social conscience into the Anglo-Catholic movement as a whole, Sayers's early poems insist that a failure to recognize Christ in other people (especially the poor) is equivalent with a failure to recognize Christ in the Blessed Sacrament.[6] Each lapse in recognition implicitly denies that reality is sacramental, that God infuses and interpenetrates the material world; each act of recognition helps to build a community and world of love.[7] *Catholic Tales and Christian Songs* shows that liturgically inflected Anglo-Catholic poetry could strike readers as original and even shocking as late as World War I.[8]

But although *Catholic Tales* was well received by the popular press, which was still largely Georgian in poetic sentiment,[9] it probably will not surprise a modern critic that there was no *Opus III*; Sayers published no more books of original poetry in her lifetime. Despite her innovative theology and creative interpretation of the liturgy, her poetic forms are rigidly metrical and her imagery for the most part strictly conventional. As Ralph E. Hone notes, "the tone of the poems reflects sympathy with what remained of the Oxford Movement" rather than the experiments with imagery, rhythm, and form associated with the rising modernist movement.[10] Modernism may make her whole poetic project seem retrospectively belated. *Catholic Tales* seems an interesting footnote in literary history—a tantalizing suggestion as to what could have come next, in an alternate world in which Anglo-Catholic liturgical poetry continued to develop without the disruption of modernism—but nothing more. For all its potential, the volume seems to serve as a case study confirming the common critical account of the fate of the Tractarian literary tradition in the twentieth century.

However, when she ceased to publish poetry, Dorothy L. Sayers did not simply disappear from the literary scene; instead, she transformed herself into one of the most dominant novelists of the Golden Age of Detective Fiction. *The Nine Tailors* (1934)—an immediate bestseller, which in 1998 was selected by the British Crime Writers' Association as the best mystery novel of all time—is perhaps her most popularly and critically acclaimed novel.[11] In this her tenth novel, Sayers both reflects upon her transformation from liturgical poet to popular novelist and—I would argue—erases the distinction between the liturgical long poem and the popular novel. In the aspirations of the minor character Hilary Thorpe, Sayers reprises her own career trajectory. A teenaged future Oxonian, Hilary loves the Anglican church and writes ecclesiastical poetry about church bells but accepts that she should grow up to write "novels . . . [b]est-sellers," instead since the times are economically tough and poetry doesn't "pa[y] very well."[12]

The novel itself is more literarily ambitious, however, and refuses these simple categorical distinctions. In an essay reflecting on her own work, Sayers asserts that alone among her works *The Nine Tailors* should be read as a prose poem; it is "a shot at combining detection with poetic romance."[13] One might go further: *The Nine Tailors* is the text that Hilary Thorpe thought impossible: the bestselling-novel-liturgical-poem. In this novel—titled after and structured around the movements of church bells, themselves auditory markers of liturgical time—the detective solves the crime and restores the metaphysical and social order only through his intimate knowledge of the Book of Common Prayer. Sayers's late novels depict an interwar England that she considers to have become a mere aggregation of consumers but that would transform into a community once more the moment it began to move in liturgical time.

I

Dorothy L. Sayers's early detective novels depict the cultural chaos of interwar England but do not really attempt to resolve it. For most of the series, Lord Peter Wimsey is a broadly agnostic figure who is comically skeptical about all ultimate solutions and possible futures. As Ina Haberman observes, English society in the 1920s and 1930s was increasingly divided, to the extent that even the reading public and the "discourse of national identity" were becoming "fragmented" and factionalized.[14] Sayers's criminals, suspects, and victims—a parade of modernist poets, post-impressionist painters, behaviorist psychologists, advertisement writers, Bolsheviks, British Nazis, war veterans with PTSD, women-hating men, men-hating women, and women-hating women—vividly embody the forces pushing interwar Britain toward cultural disintegration. One of the enduring charms of the detective series of which Wimsey is the centerpiece is how fully he inhabits and embodies the rapidly changing culture(s) of England between the wars. He is a World War I veteran who suffers from PTSD. He is a philanderer, famous for his flings with opera singers, and like the era of which he is part, traces his sexual cynicism to his disenchanting experiences in the war. Although he is an aristocrat with such highbrow hobbies as rare book collection, he knows that the aristocracy will soon vanish as a social force and he spends more time in the art world, partying with modernists, than with his own class. Sayers said that Wimsey was essentially "an eighteenth-century Whig gentleman," and he is as socially adaptable as Lord Chesterfield himself;[15] his success as a detective derives from his ability to fit into any social situation and to talk with anyone, from Communists to the Archbishop of Canterbury.

Precisely because he is the affable, even comic, mirror of his age, Wimsey is also a cradle Anglican turned agnostic—so agnostic, in fact, that he professes to be unaware what his own religious opinions are.[16] Despite the skepticism of the era's dominant intellectuals, the Anglican Church had retained its popular strength throughout the Edwardian period.[17] But it ended World War I considerably weakened as a cultural force. Edwardian popular Anglicanism had often conflated faith with nationalism, Christian self-sacrifice with imperial military service, muscular Christianity with aggressive masculinity; at the outset of World War I, the Army had been more Anglican than the general populace.[18] Consequently, the slaughter of the Great War led to widespread disaffection with the Anglican social order; between the wars religious and metaphysical skepticism became increasingly common, the percentage of the population that affiliated with the Anglican Church declined, and Anglicanism suffered an internal crisis of morale.[19] Wimsey is yet another disaffected ex-Anglican who following the war can no longer imagine conceiving of the world in religious terms.

Like the protagonists of many other novels of the period, Wimsey knows that he inhabits a doomed world, and that despite the victories he achieves (by catching criminals, by righting immediate wrongs) he can only delay, not prevent, the crash that is coming. Sayers's affably anarchic, darkly comic vision of interwar culture intensifies as the series continues and culminates with *Murder Must Advertise* (1933), the novel published immediately preceding *The Nine Tailors* and written simultaneously with it.[20] *Murder Must Advertise*, which Sayers calls her first conscious attempt at "a criticism of life,"[21] depicts interwar England as a charming dystopia, a glittering simulacrum. In its devastating critique of post-Anglican England, *Murder Must Advertise* provides a logical justification for the liturgical turn that her work takes in *The Nine Tailors*.

Murder Must Advertise depicts contemporary England through a surrealistic, dystopian lens; it is a fragmented society lost in the simulacrum of capitalist advertising culture, thoroughly detached from material reality. Lord Peter Wimsey spends the novel working undercover in an advertising agency to solve a murder committed there, though previously he had been so privileged that he "never" had "paid any attention to advertisements."[22] The world of advertisement strikes the neophyte Wimsey as a "Phantasmagoria—a city of dreadful day, of crude shapes and colours piled Babel-like in a heaven of harsh cobalt and rocking over a void of bankruptcy" (188). Wimsey recognizes with some horror that the overstated figures of advertisement have displaced material reality for much of the populace. As in Guy Debord's theory of the spectacle, hère too "the perceptible world is replaced by a set of images that are superior to that world yet at the same time impose themselves as eminently perceptible."[23] As an ad-man, Wimsey is now condemned to live among such "dim platonic archetypes, bearing a scarcely recognizable relationship to anything in the living world" as "the Thrifty Housewife, the Man of Discrimination, the Keen Buyer and the Good Judge, for ever young, for ever handsome, for ever virtuous, economical and inquisitive"; the rest of his life seems equally dreamlike (188).

Through its setting in an advertising agency, the novel explores the social and psychic toll of this capitalist attempt to one-up and displace the physical world. The employees of Pym's Publicity are in no sense a community and feel no loyalty to or connection with each other beyond the cash-payment nexus. As Sayers writes in her social criticism, in contemporary, horizontal, "contract" society all people and groups "are valued and their relations ordered in virtue of what bargain they are able to strike."[24] Sayers feared that the Western democracies were being weakened by "an excess of liberal individualism," and argued that to function, communities need "some principle of unity,"[25] a principle that Pym's Publicity obviously lacks. The advertising employees who populate the novel are constantly feuding, particularly about issues connected to social class, and are not above blackmailing or betraying each other. They are bound together only by the creation of advertisements for dubious products like the nerve pill Nutrax; their only collective language is the exploitative and distorted language of advertisement.

Likewise, the only unified communities depicted in the novel are the momentary and illusory communities imagined and invoked by advertisement: "EVERY ONE EVERYWHERE ALWAYS AGREES ON THE

FLAVOUR AND VALUE OF TWENTYMAN'S TEAS" (293, Sayers's emphasis). Wimsey ponders this slogan and concludes that

> [n]o doubt it was because agreement on any point was so rare in a quarrelsome world, that the fantastical announcements of advertisers asserted it so strongly and so absurdly. Actually, there was no agreement, either on trivialities like tea or on greater issues. In this place, where from morning till night a staff of over a hundred people hymned the praises of thrift, virtue, harmony, eupepsia and domestic contentment, the spiritual atmosphere was clamorous with financial storm, intrigue, dissension, indigestion and marital infidelity. (293)

Pym's Publicity could stand for England as a whole. In the era when the working class resorts to the General Strike—and the middle-class forms a volunteer force to help break the strike—only in the simulacrum providing by advertising culture does England form a unified community.[26]

The plot of *Murder Must Advertise* encapsulates this critique of the capitalist society of interwar England. Wimsey discovers that an employee of Pym's Publicity (Mr. Tallboy) has been using the text of the firm's weekly advertisement for the nerve pill Nutrax in the newspaper *The Morning Star* to send a signal on behalf of a drug syndicate that would indicate to their dealers the present point of distribution for their wares. The employee murdered (Victor Dean) had discovered the secret and had been blackmailing Tallboy, who killed him when the amount of blackmail demanded grew to be beyond his means. Sayers's satire is effective but broad in its strokes: Nutrax is itself a psychoactive drug of dubious medical value, pushed on the public through an enormous advertisement and distribution system, which promote dependency on the chemical in order to produce profit for the manufacturer. There is no functional difference between the Nutrax advertisement as a legal uncoded sign and a criminal coded sign, between advertisement and exploitation, between capitalism and the underworld. As Wimsey's brother in-law Inspector Charles Parker sums it up, "As far as I can make out, all advertisers are dope-merchants" (251).

Sayers's critics and Sayers herself have noted *Murder Must Advertise* as the point at which the author becomes dissatisfied with the conventions of detective fiction and begins to remake the form. In this novel, her "criticism of life," Sayers uses surrealistic imagery, literary allusion, and narrative intrusion to push her critique of English culture further than the detective plot alone would allow. Sayers's narrator ends a chapter by explicitly identifying advertisement as a form of interpellation that disrupts the continuity of individual identity and ultimately consumes the individual subject. As Wimsey "went home and slept," the voice of advertisement hailed the populace all night long:

> All over London the lights flicked in and out, calling on the public to save its body and purse. . . . The presses, thundering and growling, ground out the same appeal by the million. . . . Whatever you're doing, stop it and do something else! Whatever you're buying, pause and buy something different! Be hectored into health and prosperity! Never let up! Never go to sleep! Never be satisfied! If you are satisfied, all our wheels will run down. Keep going—and if you can't, Try Nutrax for Nerves. (91)

Sayers leaves no doubt that the populace of England has heard this call and has become fully interpellated. The employees of Pym's Publicity "thin[k] in capital letters" and advertising slogans even in their deepest internal monologues (132). As Crystal Downing observes, in their case the subject/object or author/work binaries are reversed, as "advertising starts to perform them, scripting their thoughts and directing their actions."[27] Even the novel's characters engaged in other lines of work are thoroughly interpellated by advertisement, for instance spontaneously ordering a round of beers because they just thought of a Guinness advertising slogan (207).

In this novel, the human subjects hailed by advertisement also live in a temporal order determined by advertisement, thoroughly detached from the ecclesiastical time and solar time that had structured experience in pre-industrial England. The morning begins not with the morning star, Venus, becoming visible just before sunrise, but with the first copy of the popular newspaper *The Morning Star*—complete with its Nutrax advertisement—rolling off the presses prior to 3 a.m. (204–5). The evening is marked not by the appearance of the moon or stars but rather by the profusion of neon signs. This displacement takes on theological significance, as Sayers's narrator parodies God's division of light from darkness in Genesis 1:14–16. The neon-lit advertisements, these "twinkling sky-signs," receive the designation applied in Genesis to the moon: they are the "lesser lights" that "rule the night" (107).

In the novel's jarring ending, advertisements take over the narrative, and all alternatives to the capitalist culture of advertisement seem to collapse. On the final page, the narrator's voice falls largely silent, and is replaced with a barrage of advertising slogans. This litany of slogans seems to dismiss the idea that a political or religious liberation from capitalist advertising culture is even conceivable; politics and religion are merely different sectors of advertisement. The great political hope of the 1930s, "No More War," soon turns into "Whoosh the Dust Away," and the grim Fundamentalist exhortation "Prepare to Meet Thy God" is interchangeable with "Shine Your Shoes with Shino" (356). As in Jean Baudrillard's criticism, in Sayers's novel we witness "the absorption of all virtual modes of expression into that of advertising"; which can absorb "all original cultural forms, all determined language" precisely because it has "has no depth."[28] *Murder Must Advertise* shows us an interwar England in which there seems to be no escape from interpellation by advertisement, no possibility of creating a community on a higher basis than economic self-interest, no language more real than sloganeering, no chance of recovering reality from the simulacrum. Wimsey solves the individual crime but has no solution to the social problem—which he exacerbates during his time at Pym's by devising the most successful cigarette advertising campaign in English history ("Whiffling Round Britain") (265).

II

The Nine Tailors begins by abruptly dismantling the world of *Murder Must Advertise*. Repeatedly, *Murder Must Advertise* raises the question of what would happen "if all the advertising in the world were to shut down" (188, cf. 283) and people ceased to be interpellated by industrial capitalism. Would people, having already internalized the identities given them by advertisement, automatically continue the "hell's dance" of conspicuous consumption "[o]r would the whole desperate whirligig slow down," returning people to the basic realities of "plain grub and elbow grease" (188)? Can reality be recovered from the simulacrum or is the simulacrum the only reality? Wimsey "did not know" (188).

As *The Nine Tailors* opens, Wimsey still inhabits the same world as in his earlier novels; the conspicuously consuming bon vivant has been hurling through the countryside in his luxury car, apparently on the way to a New Year's party.[29] But the whirligig has come to a sudden and surprisingly literal stop. Wimsey's car has crashed in a ditch in the fens, and he is cut off from modern England (3). Seeking shelter and help with his car, Wimsey enters a world that belongs to a different metaphysical order than the London he has just left. As Wimsey and his servant Bunter attempt to locate the nearest town, Wimsey hears "the sound of a church clock . . . chim[ing] the first quarter" (4). "'Thank God!' sa[ys] Wimsey. 'Where there is a church, there is civilization'" (4), and he sets off toward the sound of the bells. From the narrative's opening pages on, Wimsey and the reader will be inhabiting a world in many ways foreign to them, one in which the church—not capitalist advertising culture—hails and interpellates subjects and orders time.[30] Fenchurch St. Paul is a town dominated physically and culturally by the "grey, gigantic bulk" of the church after which it is named (7). The community's very collective faith, of which the harvest festival is a high point,[31] and traditional, hierarchical social order, mark it as (to use Charles Taylor's terms) an *ancien régime* society surviving into the twentieth century.[32] In this agricultural community, where formal education is still the subject of some suspicion,[33] the church remains the primary social institution, and the local economy functions largely on a feudal basis. The parishioners of Fenchurch St. Paul think in the language of the Book of Common Prayer as naturally as the copywriters of Pym's Publicity thought in the language of advertisement. The elderly quote the Prayer Book from memory and children squabble over which Prayer Book is whose.[34]

Although newspaper and radio are not entirely unknown in Fenchurch St. Paul, the village seems to have little interest in mass media; both young and old are effectively immune from interpellation by advertisement. The Reverend Theodore Venables, the parish priest who puts the stranded Wimsey and Bunter up for the night, is so far removed from the world of the popular press that he welcomes Wimsey not as a headline-making detective but as a fellow amateur academic (the author of the "very scholarly little monograph" about book collection called *Notes on the Collection of Incunabula*) (7). Later in the novel the murder plot begins in earnest as an unidentified extra corpse is discovered in a relatively fresh grave. Since such lurid sensationalism is bound to attract readers, a reporter from the *Morning Star* shows up at the unidentified corpse's reburial service; the world of *Murder Must Advertise* attempts to invade Fenchurch St. Paul. But Wimsey and the Rector's wife together evict him from both the town and the novel (132); he never reappears. "How tiresome newspapers are!" the rector's wife remarks, to which Wimsey adds "Curse the Press!" (132–33); the novel's remaining characters would seem to agree.

The ever-adaptable Wimsey is conscripted into this ecclesiastical world as quickly as he was into the world of advertisement. The very High Church (and bell-obsessed) Rev. Theodore Venables is short a bell ringer in his attempt "to ring the New Year in" with a record peal in the distinctively English style of change-ringing (12–13, 36). Sayers's earlier stories establish Wimsey as a child "of the [religious] Establishment" and expert on all things Anglican; he, for instance, can quote the Prayer Book extensively from memory and deduce precise dates from the details of church décor.[35] Although Wimsey's knowledge of Anglicanism is not internalized as belief (he is explicitly agnostic and is no churchgoer), it forms an important part of his gentlemanly ability to be at home in all parts of English society and, thus, is a useful detective tool. Hence, the reader is not entirely unprepared to discover Wimsey has rung church bells in his youth and is able to repay the reverend's hospitality by serving as a substitute bell ringer. He spends a mostly sleepless night attending an evening New Year's vigil service and then ringing bells for nine hours (16). Sayers was the daughter of an Anglican priest, and had, like Wimsey, thoroughly internalized the Anglican calendar and ritual by the end of her adolescence. As a secondary school student, she wrote an essay on "The Origin of the English Prayer-book" and as a teen, she sometimes dated her letters off of the liturgical rather than the secular calendar.[36] The liturgical calendar is never far from her thoughts, and her uses of it are always careful. In the Anglican calendar, New Year's is the Feast of the Circumcision, which commemorates the day Jesus was formally initiated into the Jewish community. Fittingly, the peal of bells on this vigil marks Wimsey's own reinitiation into Anglican life and worship.

The church bells of Fenchurch St. Paul, collectively dubbed *The Nine Tailors*, give the novel both its title and its key plot device. If the novel is, as Sayers suggests, to be read as a poem, the bells provide both the poem's central reoccurring motif and its dominant music. Sayers's section titles—"A Short Touch of Kent Treble Bob Major," "A Full Peal of Grandshire Triples," "A Short Touch of Stedman's Triples," and "A Full Peal of Kent Treble Bob Major"—also suggest that the book is, like a traditional poem, dependent on its dominant music for its structure.

The bells of Fenchurch St. Paul serve primarily as auditory representations of liturgical time, hailing the community to the world order of Anglicanism. The motto on the parish bell tower—a slightly altered quotation from the Book of Common Prayer's translation of Psalm 19:3–4—summarizes the bells' functions of both hailing human subjects and ordering time: "They Have Neither Speech nor Language but their Voices are Heard Among Them, their Sound is Gone Forth into All Lands" (Sayers *Nine Tailors*, 27). The bells' hailing function is explicit in this motto and, as Sayers's narrator observes, all people in Fenchurch St. Paul, even those "on the extreme outskirts of the parish" (*Nine Tailors*, 85), do indeed hear the bells and invariably respond to their summons. Repeatedly, the novel's characters recollect hearing the bells from their homes and having their thoughts stirred and changed by them (cf. Sayers *Nine Tailors*, 172).

More subtly, the bell tower motto alters the referent of the pronoun "they" in Psalm 19:3. In the biblical text, "they" refers to the celestial bodies we employ to mark time: the sun and the stars in the "firmament" of "the heavens" (Psalm 19:1), by means of which "One day telleth another: and one night certifieth another" (Psalm 19:2). The bell tower motto thus reveals that Fenchurch St. Paul's church bells have displaced the natural markers of time just as thoroughly as have London's neon advertisements and newspapers. As Guy Debord notes, human time is always and inevitably socially mediated (92); church bells do not merely call believers to worship but transpose the norms and values of a given social order into temporal form.

Long before Debord, the nineteenth-century Anglo-Catholic priest George Tyack, on whose work Sayers drew extensively when writing *The Nine Tailors*,[37] explicitly identified and connected the bells' twin functions of liturgically ordering time for the community and hailing individuals as believing subjects. Tyack summarizes the earlier portions and forecasts the later portions of *A Book about Bells*: "We have seen how the bells follow the course of the Christian year, tolling or pealing as the various mysteries commemorated seem to demand. We turn now to the life of the individual Christian, and we shall find that, with equal fidelity, the bells accompany him from the cradle to the grave, and even beyond.[38] Tyack supports his thesis by explaining in obsessive detail how church bells have been used to call the community to work as well as to prayer and to shelter from natural disaster; how they have commemorated the collective harvest, as well as individuals' births and deaths, marriages and funerals; and how they mark the movements of the liturgical year, being sounded and employed differently on every major feast and liturgical season.[39] Over the course of *The Nine Tailors*, the bells ring in Fenchurch St. Paul for all of these reasons;[40] this is a community that runs on liturgical time.

The bell-obsessed rector's continual inability to function according to clock time, always "los[ing] count of time" and running off schedule, is the source of much light comedy in the novel; appropriately, the rectory clock gives the right time only one day a week (30, 120–21). But in a real sense Wimsey's polite comment that the rector's problem comes of being "continually in and about this church" which "brings eternity too close" is true (30, 120–21). Henri Bergson, with whose ideas Sayers was familiar, suggests that an individual's experience of time can vary from at one extreme "the pure homogeneous, the pure repetition by which we shall define materiality" to at the other extreme "duration which stretches, tightens, and becomes more and more intensified: at the limit would be eternity."[41] The rector exists solely on ecclesiastical time, not commodified time, and presses toward eternity. He is, perhaps unconsciously, a passive aggressive passive resister to the capitalist and secular world order that runs on homogenous, empty clock time.

In the novel, church bells function as a metonym for the alternate, Anglican world order embodied in the Prayer Book, and for Anglicanism itself. This association is not unique to Sayers, and rests on a broad cultural foundation. The 1662 Book of Common Prayer, which determined the nature of Anglican worship for over three hundred years, highlights the role of bells in establishing a shared communal worship. In fact, the Book of Common Prayer explicitly mandates that churches *must* possess bells to hail believers to participation in the liturgical order—"the Curate . . . shall cause a Bell to be tolled . . . that the people may come to hear God's Word, and to pray with him."[42] In her lecture on the Anglican liturgy, Sayers asserts that the Book of Common Prayer, which is rooted in the liturgies of the Apostolic Fathers and shared in "common" by contemporary Anglicans of all theological stripes, both constructs a community and roots it in antiquity.[43] These are precisely the functions Lionel Basney has noted for the church bells in *The*

Nine Tailors; they "act as factors of order in village life, marking years and lives" and "for[m] a palpable continuity with the far past."[44] The New Year's Eve opening of the novel allows the Reverend Venables to connect the church bells explicitly with the Anglican liturgical order they represent, speaking in his sermon of the bells as a contemporary extension of Psalm 150, in which God is praised on a wide variety of percussive instruments, and which is read on the thirty-first of the month in the Anglican calendar (36).

Further, as Wimsey later discovers, the history of the bells of Fenchurch St. Paul is that of the entire Anglican Church, as that history might be conceived by a devout early twentieth-century Anglo-Catholic such as the Reverend Venables or Dorothy L. Sayers. Like the Church of England in the Anglo-Catholic reckoning, the church bells were initially constructed during the Middle Ages and then refined during the Reformation era. The oldest bell was ordered by the fourteenth-century abbot Thomas, and the bells were supplemented and reshaped during the reigns of Elizabeth I and James I, the monarchs who did most to form the Anglican Church. The bells (and Anglican Church) were nearly destroyed by Cromwell's men, slowly decayed during the putatively rationalistic eighteenth century, and then were triumphantly restored in the Victorian era by "an energetic High-Church" clergy and laity (78, 116–18). Like other Anglo-Catholics, Sayers insists that the Reformation-era alterations to English faith and worship do not amount to "a break with tradition so violent as to destroy altogether the liturgical framework which preserved continuity of form between the pre-Reformation and post-Reformation worship of the Church";[45] the medieval bells may be altered, recast, and restored, but they remain.

When Wimsey rings these bells to mark the end of the old year, he is also unconsciously tolling the death of his existence as a cosmopolitan agnostic (29).[46] His reentry into Anglican life and time does not prove to be an easy process, however. Anglican life has come to seem ironically foreign and provincial to Wimsey (and to the reader). Although by the novel's conclusion, Wimsey will become part of the Anglican community and begin to see the world in liturgical terms—a process that, significantly, takes him almost exactly a single year—he initially resists the liturgy's attempts to hail him.

The Nine Tailors repeatedly narrates the Anglican service (and Wimsey's response to it) in great detail, down to ruminations on the specific prayers and readings for the day.[47] The account of the novel's first liturgical service (Evening Prayer on New Year's Eve) primarily emphasizes Wimsey's resistance to interpellation. Hours after undergoing a dramatic car wreck, Wimsey arrives at the service utterly exhausted. Half-asleep, he stumbles into a pew and finds "a prayer-book" "thrust . . . under his nose" by the elderly and pious bell ringer Hezekiah Lavender (34). Distracted by the magnificent artwork on the medieval church's ceiling, Wimsey ceases to follow the service, and is left standing "alone and agape," staring at the ceiling when everyone else has knelt for the General Confession of sin and promise of absolution. Quite literally, Wimsey fails to respond to the definition of humanity offered by the church (35), and is not hailed; he does not see himself as one of those who has "erred and strayed," who can truly say "there is no health in us" without restoration through Christ.[48] If, as Sayers asserts in her theological works, the Christian "creed purports to tell us the essential facts, not only about God, but also about the true nature of man," then Wimsey has implicitly denied the creed.[49] The offended Hezekiah Lavender, who finds the later readings for Wimsey under the assumption that he has never seen a Prayer Book or darkened a church door before, is not wholly wrong when he decides that Wimsey must be "a heathen" (35). Although Wimsey has virtually memorized the Prayer Book, he is not yet hailed by it; he remains the erect twentieth-century cosmopolitan and rejects—or simply does not recognize—the Christian account of human nature, marked as it is by emphasis on human frailty and propensity to evil.

The morning after the bell-ringing, Wimsey leaves the village, hoping never to return. He remarks to Bunter, "As Stevenson says, we shall pass this way but once—and I devoutly hope he's right" (64). A few months later, however, he is called back by a recently discovered and relatively fresh corpse. Both the corpse's identity and manner of death remain unknown through most of the novel, as its hands are cut off and face bashed in. But the corpse proves to be that of Jeff Deacon, a former butler for the Thorpe family (and bell-ringer for Revered Venables) turned jewel thief and convict, who had been thought to have died in a jail break almost twenty years before.

The crimes around which the novel revolves also encapsulate the key threats to the social order of Fenchurch St. Paul: the economic collapse of the landowning aristocracy and the First World War.[50] The collective cultural trauma of World War I is well known, and need not be related in detail here, but it may be less commonly remembered that the interwar period was an era of massive agricultural depression, affecting farmers of all scales and destabilizing English rural life. In 1921, the government abandoned agricultural subsidies in favor of international free trade; consequently, in England during the 1920s and 1930s, the vast majority of food was imported, the prices of most key agricultural products fell by about half, and the "total area of agricultural land" fell by "roughly 10 per cent."[51] Especially in the eastern counties, the "breadbasket of England," farmers fell into massive debt and abandoned their property.[52] Many of the "local gentry and aristocracy" resorted to selling their property and giving up farming altogether, a development that agricultural communities as a whole found unsettling; Alun Howkins dates the end of the traditional English rural social order of "landlord, farmer, and laborer" at approximately the time of Sayers's novel: "somewhere around 1930."[53]

The traditional English social order remains in place at Fenchurch St. Paul, although its foundations are shaking. The Thorpe family, the local gentry of Fenchurch St. Paul, are depicted as ideal patricians who care more for the village's welfare than for their own. Their ancestors were responsible for the draining of the fens to make them habitable, and they still "farm" their "land well" and do "a lot of good" (48). They are also devoutly Anglican, and are pillars of the church. However, the Thorpes have been on a steady downward economic slide ever since April 1914 (47). That April, Mrs. Wilbraham, a rich relation, attended Henry Thorpe's wedding, bringing with her an uninsured emerald necklace worth thousands of pounds. The necklace shortly went missing, apparently stolen by a conspiracy including the Thorpes' butler, Jeff Deacon. As Wimsey discovers, World War I provided the cover under which Deacon was able to evade the law and assume a new identity. After Deacon broke jail, he killed a soldier, stole that soldier's identity, was mistakenly shipped to the battlefields in France, deserted the army, claimed amnesia, and under yet another name bigamously remarried to start a life in France (210 ff., 311 ff.). Back in England, Deacon's "widow" Mary dealt with her husband's apparent death by marrying the devoutly religious farmer Will Thoday. And the Thorpes financially ruined themselves by reimbursing Mrs. Wilbraham for her never-recovered emeralds, lost under their roof (48). Henry Thorpe, a wounded World War I veteran, dies early in the novel in an influenza epidemic, as does his wife, leaving their teenage daughter Hilary heir to an impoverished and heavily mortgaged estate that seems destined to be sold off. The emeralds represent a world of fixed value and stable social order, one that perishes when World War I begins in the spring of 1914; as Bob Russell observes, since the theft of the emeralds and the war "we been all topsy-turvy like" (126). Like the London of *Murder Must Advertise*, Fenchurch St. Paul turns out to be a superficially stable world actually hovering over an abyss; if these crimes remain unsolved, the village cannot constitute a viable alternate social order.

III

When Wimsey returns to the village just after Easter, he comes prepared to meet this liturgical world on its own terms. Bunter stands at his side carrying "leather-bound" copies of the Book of Common Prayer and (the Anglo-Catholic) *Hymns Ancient and Modern* "on a small salver" (121). Shortly after his return to Fenchurch St. Paul, Wimsey attends the funeral of the as-yet-unidentified Deacon. Here, for the first time, the Book of Common Prayer penetrates him as more than just a cultural artifact. Notably, although he is tentative and guessing a bit, Wimsey this time manages to stand and sit at the appropriate times in the service (129). The liturgy speaks to him when it begins to address the subject which, as an investigator of homicide, is closest to him: death. He is both stirred by and resists the liturgy's call to grapple with his ethics and his mortality. He rejects Psalm 39:5's frank reminder of the finitude of human life: "'That I may be certified how long I have to live'—what a terrifying prayer! Lord, let me never be certified of anything of the kind" (129). He tries skeptically to turn St. Paul's treatise on the resurrection of the body (1 Corinthians 15) into an occasion for wonderment as to whether he or anyone else present really believes that the dead are raised, but his ever-allusive mind slips into a series of quotations on the subject from Donne and Hopkins, whom he can't dismiss easily (129, 130). He is particularly troubled by Psalm 90:9, which reminds him of the morally ambiguous status of his hobby of detection. "'Thou hast set our misdeeds before Thee' . . . very likely, and why should I, Peter Wimsey, busy myself with digging them up? I haven't got so very much to boast about myself, if it comes to that" (129). Overall, he is justified in thinking with a new respect, "People may say what they like about the services of the Church of England, but there was a certain genius in the choosing of . . . psalms" 39 and 90 for the funeral service (129).

But then, suddenly, unexpectedly, as the Rev. Venables intones the prayer "suffer us not, at our last hour, for any pains of death, to fall from thee,"[54] Wimsey thinks, "Damn it! that goes home" (130). For a moment at least, he recognizes himself in the picture of humanity offered by the Book of Common Prayer and is moved by its hope that the pains of death might be given a meaning through life in God. But then he recovers and resists the impulse to deal with God and death in so direct a manner. He wonders "why" that particular prayer penetrated him and reassures himself that he was caught up in the "mere splendor of [the] rhythm, I expect" (130). Then the Reverend Venables's prayer for "our dear brother here departed" reminds Wimsey that no one has yet uncovered the rope used to tie "our brother" up, and he ceases to follow the service and even significantly forgets "to join in the Lord's Prayer" (Sayers *Nine Tailors* 130–31). Wimsey still does not recognize God as Father, desire God's kingdom on earth or in heaven, or believe in the forgiveness of sins. But just for a moment, as the liturgy speaks unflinching words about death that he himself would tremble to say, Wimsey has been interpellated and brought into the Anglican world of the novel. And he is never quite the same character afterward.[55]

Wimsey also must adjust his methods of detection to fit the Anglican order of Fenchurch St. Paul. As many critics have observed, detective novels typically first narrate a fundamentally chaotic universe in which both meaning and justice have both been disrupted, and then restore both sense and order by renarrating the same story from a perspective of more complete understanding.[56] Hence, detective novels are epistemological in nature. In most detective novels, the dominant epistemology is that of scientific empiricism. In the Sherlock Holmes stories and their many imitators, truth reveals itself when the proper scientific tool, such as the lie detector or the magnifying glass, is applied by the proper specialist to the material body or the material world.[57] Peter Wimsey is not above using the tools of scientific detection. Throughout the series, he runs experiments, collects fingerprints and employs Bunter's skills as an expert crime photographer. But scientific empiricism is a fundamentally materialistic means of understanding the universe, appropriate, as many postmodern thinkers have observed, only for the secular, industrialized West. Unsurprisingly, when Wimsey tries to employ this method of detection, he finds that it simply does not work in Fenchurch St. Paul. The only attempt to use scientific detection in the novel fails. Wimsey retrieves a bottle from the bell tower bearing the fingerprints of the probable culprit, but the rector's diligent servant Emily unknowingly cleans the bottle before it can be properly analyzed (266 ff.).

During Deacon's funeral, Wimsey begins slowly to realize what epistemological key *will* unlock the world of Fenchurch St. Paul: the Book of Common Prayer. During the funeral, Wimsey interprets the congregation's responses to the Book of Common Prayer as clues to their possible involvement in the crime. As Rev. Venables intones, "though after my skin worms destroy this body," the virtuous bell-ringing farmer Will Thoday looks sick, making Wimsey think "something wrong there, I shouldn't wonder" (129). At the prayer "Thou knowest, Lord, the secrets of our hearts," Thoday nearly passes out, causing Wimsey to conclude "I shall have to have a word with that gentleman before long" (130). Wimsey later deduces that the Thodays are undergoing a personal and marital crisis because they have correctly guessed that Jeff Deacon is the relatively fresh corpse being buried at the funeral—which would mean that their own marriage was invalid and bigamous. When they later disappear, only Wimsey realizes the reason why they have fled (to try to get validly married in secret, out of town) (289). He comes to this conclusion not through scientific detection but through observing the Thodays' sacramental habits; they have been abstaining from communion out of a fear that they are in mortal sin (303, 328–29). He finds them not by calling Scotland Yard but (quite literally) by calling the Archbishop of Canterbury, not by sending the police on a manhunt but by sending them to check "all church registrars" (304–5). In the world of Fenchurch St. Paul, the Anglican liturgy is a more effective means of detection than conventional interrogation; as Wimsey remarks to Superintendent Blundell, if a policeman wants to know if any of the villages have committed murder, he should just "[g]o read the [Anglican] Burial Service to them and watch their reactions" (180). The bewildered Blundell, himself unable to understand a detective novel that breaks the conventions of the police procedural, replies with some confusion, "Religion's a bit out of my line, except on Sundays" (180).

Wimsey's entrance into the Anglican world order proves to be the key to unlocking the novel's mystery. Through an intricate series of events, Wimsey obtains a bizarre note that turns out not to be (as was originally thought) the ravings of the village idiot, but a coded message written by Jeff Deacon that identifies the location of the missing emeralds. Wimsey simply cannot make out the cipher, though he is something of an expert at code breaking. The code had been found in the bell tower and "particularly mentioned" the bells "Batty Thomas and Taylor Paul," so he realizes that in some way he cannot fathom the bells hold the key not just to the novel's temporal structure but also to its central crime (120). As Wimsey becomes more and more unhinged by the case, he finds himself actually talking to the bells, "but try as he would for him they had neither speech nor language" and they neither literally nor figuratively answer back (120, 256). In a dozen novels, Wimsey charmingly chats his way to a solution to the crime. In *The Nine Tailors* he recognizes that the solution to the crime once again lies within the novel's dominant linguistic structure, but this sacramental language is too foreign for him—or for the reader—to speak fluidly. He, like the reader, gets tantalizing hints of meaning, but nothing that will really hold.[58] He needs an interpreter.

Fittingly, it falls to the Reverend Venables, who ticks entirely in ecclesiastical time and is obsessed with church bells almost to the point of imbalance, to unlock the cipher, which he shortsightedly mistakes for notation for a bell peal (259). Since the code was found in the bell tower the Reverend Venables conjectures that they could be dealing with a bell-based code, and then guides Wimsey through interpreting the cipher using the principles of change-ringing (261 ff.) As the Reverend realizes, the language of the bells is the language of scripture in the Book of Common Prayer's translation; the code turns out to be verses from the Psalms: "'He sitteth between the cherubims'; that's Ps. XCIX. 1. Then 'The isles may be glad thereof'; that's Ps. XCVII. 1. . . . Then we get, 'as the rivers in the south.' That's Ps. CXXVI. 5" (263). Of course, the relevance of these verses to the crime is by no means obviously apparent and to some degree the mystery remains unsolved, waiting for a more liturgically astute Wimsey to crack it.

Fittingly, Wimsey uncovers the emeralds' location by interpreting the enigmatic solution to the bell code in light of the Anglican liturgy. On the Sunday after Ascension Wimsey sits during the sermon gazing at the beautiful ceiling of the church. The Reverend Venables begins by analyzing both "the collect for the day" and the collect for the Feast of the Ascension (282). The former asserts that God "hast exalted thine only Son with great triumph into the Heavens," while the latter prays that the worshippers "may also [like Christ] with heart and mind thither [heavenward] ascend."[59] Reverend

Venables challenges his hearers to imagine heaven as a real place to which they too shall go, joining their songs to those of the "cherubim and seraphim" depicted above their heads on the church ceiling (283). He sees the church building as an extension of the logic of the liturgy, which itself both mirrors the Bible and anticipates eternity: "It is a beautiful description that the Bible gives us—the crystal sea and the Lord sitting between the cherubims, and the angels with their harps and crowns of gold, as the old craftsmen imagined them when they built this beautiful roof that we are so proud of—but do we, do you and I really believe—?" (283). Hearing this connection between the physical space of the building and the logic of the liturgy suddenly enables Wimsey to realize the meaning of the bell code, and thus where the emeralds are hidden. All Thorpe family servants were required to attend the parish church. Deacon was arrested right after coming out of church and—to the police's astonishment—he did not have the emeralds on his person. During the service, he had hidden them in a concealed cubbyhole "Between the cherubims in the south aisle" (283). On this Sunday after the Ascension, the answer to the mystery is to be found literally by looking up.

As Stacey Gillis has noted, the role of post–World War I detective fiction is "to place a pattern of signs behind a corpse," and thereby to restore a sense of causality and ontological order to a world that had seemed to lose both.[60] The corpse of the mystery novel functions as a synecdoche for the millions of war dead, and the identification of "whodunit" is "a form of recuperation" that allows the trauma of the war to receive coherent narrative form and to be accounted for within accepted models of causality.[61] Thus, if the Prayer Book unlocks the mysteries of Sayers's most famous novel—here, the location of the stolen emeralds; later, how Deacon was murdered—then it also serves as the means of Britain's metaphysical and social recuperation.[62] On a metaphysical level, Sayers's similarly asserts in her theological works that the sacramental worship "embodied" in the "liturgy" of the Church of England "gives meaning to the whole" of the universe.[63] On a social level, the finding of the emeralds (298) leads to the economic restoration of the Thorpe family, who no longer need to sell their estate; thus, Wimsey's increasing mastery of the liturgy leads directly to the restoration of the traditional English social order. First, Mrs. Wilbraham "restore[s] the money paid in compensation" by the Thorpes for the loss of her emeralds; then, shortly thereafter, she dies, leaving them "the whole of her very considerable estate" on the grounds that they are "the only honest" people she knows (305, 339).

Unlike the urban England dominated by capitalist advertising culture, the rural England dominated by the aristocratic country estates no longer seems destined to collapse. With the emeralds regained, the claims of the aristocracy no longer comprise a linguistic performance without referent or (to vary the metaphor) a bad check bound to bounce. The restoration of the emeralds means the restoration of a world of fixed value, and Wimsey plays a large and ongoing role in this restoration. Mrs. Wilbraham's will designates Lord Peter as trustee for the Thorpes' young female heir, Hilary. Wimsey takes his role as trustee unexpectedly seriously. He not only (against her uncle's wishes) ensures that she receives a college education, but also persuades her to accept, at least for the time being, her place in the landowning aristocracy on the grounds that she could use her money to help people (340). Hilary later develops a "strong determination to stick to the family estate" (370), and as her trustee Wimsey helps her preserve the familial lands, against the wishes of her uncle, who would rather profit from their lease or sale (370). He thus ushers in a new generation of aristocrats—forward-thinking, feminist, and beneficent—who will be capable of preserving the social order of Fenchurch St. Paul. Wimsey himself as the novel progresses begins to behave for the first time in the series like a rural English Lord, making sure that both he and his brother the Duke are present to ceremonially open the new cut on the fens (194, 339). And these responsibilities to Hilary, this new willingness of the previously escapist Wimsey to accept his social role, also render him unable to break free of the world of Fenchurch St. Paul. Feeling guilty about the difficulties he has caused the Thodays and depressed about his failure to solve Deacon's murder, "Wimsey had determined that he would never go back to Fenchurch St. Paul" (369). But when Hilary "begged him to come and see her during her Christmas holidays, he felt bound to go" (370).

IV

Wimsey returns to the village on Christmas Eve. Chronologically, *The Nine Tailors* is dominated by the Christmas season; most of the action of the novel takes place during Advent or Christmastide. For Sayers, the incarnation was "the central dogma" of the Christian faith.[64] Since Jesus, as God made flesh, reconciles "time and eternity" in his person, his incarnate life confers meaning on all matter and all human history.[65] The liturgy, liturgical calendar, and Christian community are all for Sayers expressions of this basic principle, which she dubs "sacramentalism" or "Catholicism." Sayers suggests that each of the Anglican services—including daily Morning and Evening Prayer ("The Divine Office")—derives from the attempts of the early monks to structure the hours of the day around Christ's passion. The liturgical calendar projects the story of Christ out over the year, as for instance "Passiontide and Easter" tell "the story" of Christ's "victory over the evils of time."[66] Each of the earthy sacraments of Baptism, marriage, and Communion sanctify the material and unite the whole of the community across time and space in light of the incarnation.[67]

For Sayers, as well as the whole *Lux Mundi* school of socially conscious Anglo-Catholicism to which she has been linked, the incarnation provides not only metaphysical but also social meaning, offering the logical basis for a just society. In his contribution to the essay collection that inaugurated the *Lux Mundi* movement, the Rev. R. C. Moberly asserts that "to drop out of communion with the Incarnation of Christ is to drop out of communion with the inner realities and possibilities of humanity."[68] For Sayers as well, the incarnation—God taking material form and thus giving infinite significance to the most difficult and obscure human lives and the most mundane of material objects—logically requires both immediate social action and a more long-range effort to build a just community in which each individual materially actualizes his or her whole spiritual and creative potential.[69] As she writes, "The [Anglo-]Catholic kind of religion . . . aims at Christianizing the *whole* of humanity—body and soul, reason and intuition, individual and society, secular and spiritual vocations and activities, and making them *all* a part of man's sacramental sacrifice."[70] Consequently, Sayers also holds that in its instrumentalist use of people and material objects, unbridled capitalism is a violation of sacramentalism.[71]

The Christmastide setting of the beginning and end of *The Nine Tailors* is then not simply a quaint touch designed to give seasonal appeal; it is thematically crucial to a book whose purpose is to usher the secular Wimsey into the liturgical world order. The collect recited at both the service for the Sunday After Christmas (which is retrospectively narrated to Wimsey by a possible suspect) and on Christmas itself (a service Wimsey attends twice in a single day) explicitly explains that a holy community of God's "children by adoption and grace" becomes possible only through Christ's assumption of "our nature."[72]

The sacrament of baptism also plays a central role in structuring the conclusion of *The Nine Tailors*. In the final section of the novel, four children receive Anglican baptism (374, 377, 395). When Wimsey returns to Fenchurch St. Paul on Christmas Eve, the first person he meets is the rector on the way to baptize an infant (374). As the sacrament by which one is initiated into the sacramental system—the means by which one may be "received into Christ's holy Church, and be made a lively member of the same"—baptism naturally occupies a prominent place in Sayers's restoration of the Anglican world order.[73] Charles Gore (1853–1932), the socially conscious Anglo-Catholic Bishop of Oxford who was a key influence on Sayers, argues that since the Church is "the picture of . . . what the common human life is meant to be and can become," it follows that "the ordained instruments of grace," sacraments, must be "*social* ceremonies—of incorporation" (baptism), for instance (Gore's italics).[74] As Gore's *Lux Mundi* associate Francis Pagett insists, baptism both "effect[s] and involv[es] the communion of saints," taking people "out of the narrowness and isolation of their own lives . . . into . . . the unselfish hope of the City of God."[75]

If *The Nine Tailors*' Christmas setting implies the incarnational logic that for Sayers makes legitimate community possible, baptism is the liturgical rite by which that community becomes actualized. Fittingly, then, the logic of the sacrament of baptism structures the events of the novel's final section. As I have mentioned, for Keble, Rossetti, and the whole Anglo-Catholic tradition, one of the liturgy's primary functions is to teach the individual believer to read the world both sacramentally and typologically. The Anglican baptismal service includes a typological pattern that dates back to the Apostolic Fathers, whereby the waters of baptism are equated with the waters of Noah's Flood, and "Christ's Church" with the "Ark" whereby one survives and overcomes a world of chaos.[76]

The final section of Sayers's novel literalizes this typological pattern, as the sluices and floodgates holding back the fens are overwhelmed, the whole area floods, and the population of town has to retreat to and for several weeks live in the church, the building located on the highest ground. The flooding starts on December 27, and the rector mutters to himself as he works on the preparations, "Out of the deep, O Lord, out of the deep," a verse from Psalm 130 (De Profundis), which is read on the twenty-seventh of the month in Anglican liturgical cycle (379). As the novel moves from a conventional detective plot into a typological world, the language of the Book of Common Prayer now seems to have the power to actuate its utterances, to effect what it signifies, to predict the plot.

The Reverend Venables and his wife have foreseen the possibility of a flood and employ a prearranged signal—the church bells, naturally—to summon the villagers to gather at the church for safety (379, 382). The church now "*is* the community" and, in a quite literal sense, *is* the ark that preserves its inhabitants (italics mine).[77] For weeks, the healthy men, women, and children sleep in the church, "the sick and aged people in the rectory," and the "[a]nimals in the churchyard" (384, 380). The church is a self-sustaining "desert-island" (393), the only refuge in a hostile environment. Folding this baptismal typology back into its sacramental origins, and connecting the ideal community with the actual community, "a baby, which happened to fall due" during the flood is "baptized" and named "'Paul' (for the church)" (395).

For the period of the flood at least, the village and church of Fenchurch St. Paul become an idyllic picture of Anglican England, functioning almost like a monastery or religious commune. During the flood, "each morning was ushered in by a short and cheerful flourish of bells," followed by milking, washing, "a brief service of hymns and prayer," breakfast, school for the children and work for the adults during the day, and concerts, lectures, and comic performances for the evening's entertainment (394). On Sundays, Anglican worship is celebrated, along with "an undenominational service conducted by the two Church of England priests and the two nonconformist ministers" (394). Fenchurch St. Paul is now the physical embodiment of Wimsey's despairing hope in *Murder Must Advertise* for a community that could shut out the hum of capitalist ad culture, and return to the basic realities of "plain grub and elbow grease."[78] Restoration to the liturgical order is also restoration to materiality; to be sacramental (in Sayers's sense) is to be "coarse," even earthy or "vulgar."[79] Life in the church "in course of time, assumed a rhythm of its own" (394) akin to the rhythm of a monastic life or the rhythms of nature itself, and the community becomes unified to such an extent that the Dissenters are literally worshipping in the Church of England.

As the novel's temporal structure and plot are coming to be increasingly dominated by the Prayer Book, Wimsey is also becoming fully interpellated in the Anglican world order. As Lionel Basney notes, Wimsey has gone from being a cosmopolitan outside observer to being a real participant, "absorbed" in this community.[80] Broadly speaking, Wimsey's transformation corresponds with a pattern that Ina Haberman has noted is common in interwar popular fiction: a disenchanted young or middle-aged man returns to the countryside, which constitutes a "'mythical present' of the symbolic form of Englishness," and finds his faith in England or Englishness and his sense of identity restored.[81] This phenomenon is sometimes called "[t]he thirties craze for 'discovering England.'"[82] But in Sayers's novel the Anglican liturgy takes on the role of restoring Englishness and identity assumed elsewhere by the rural landscape itself. The Anglican Church is England.

As Wimsey begins to move according to the liturgical calendar and its higher order of time, he is also restored to festive community. He organizes "games and drill" to keep the children entertained and happy during the flood and Bunter oversees the preparation of their meals (394). Fittingly, Christmas is the novel's final Anglican feast, and Wimsey—far from the man who a year before failed to kneel for the General Confession—both "attended Church twice" that day and "assisted Mrs. Venables to tie wet bunches of holly and ivy to the [baptismal] font" for the occasion (377). After underscoring the font's significance by decorating it, Wimsey himself becomes the means of both literal and figurative baptism. The automobile that he crashed into the fen in the novel's opening pages is now used to usher "two infants and their mothers" from a distant part of the parish "to be churched and christened" and later to bring one of the final men left out fighting the flood to safety in the church (377, 387). In characteristically self-conscious fashion, Wimsey makes the connection between the events of the novel and Noah's flood himself, singing "[t]he animals went in two by two" as he races the flood in his car (385). He also becomes himself the dove bringing back the sign that the flood has subsided. "On the fourteenth day" of the flood, Wimsey swims down the flooded village street, and "notice[s] that the level of the water had shrunk by an inch"; he "return[s], waving a handful of laurels from somebody's front garden, as the nearest substitute for an olive-branch" (395). Then "[a] merry peal of Kent Treble Bob Major" from the church bell tower announces to all that the flood waters have begun to recede (395). We are now in a fully liturgical universe. The novel's sense of time has become that of the Prayer Book—as it cyclically ends almost exactly where it began—and its plot progression has been subsumed into typology.[83]

This transformation lends credence to Sayers's assertion that the novel was intended as a kind of poem. *The Nine Tailors* quietly and gradually shifts readers out of the linear, horizontal time employed by empirical science and industrial capitalism—the mode of time that typically marks the detective novel—into the higher time of the liturgy, where the sacred past breaks into the mundane present and events are connected not by simultaneity but by shared motifs. The poetic character of the liturgy and the liturgical calendar was an Anglo-Catholic commonplace, and the overlap between poetry and liturgy is in this context clear. By reorienting itself around the liturgy, the novel transforms into a kind of prose poem.

In the context of the liturgy, symbols also possess the thaumaturgic properties that W. B. Yeats assigned to them in poetry. Wimsey's solution to the final mystery of the novel—how, exactly, Jeff Deacon died—implies a sacramental understanding of the concept of symbol. The church bells that have featured so prominently in the novel are sacramentals, material objects that aid in sacramental worship and partake to a lesser degree in the nature of a sacrament. At the novel's conclusion, Wimsey comes to realize that the bells have assumed sacramental status, they are (in Augustine's classic definition) "signs that effect that which they signify." The most famous symbolic function of church bells in English literature is to signify the death of an individual: "for whom the bell tolls." The peal of bells to mark the death of the old year that opens the novel also killed Jeff Deacon, who unbeknownst to the ringers was tied up and gagged in the bell tower at the time (he had returned to the city in secret but had been caught and detained without murderous intent by Will Thoday). Sayers believed, and some scientific evidence suggests, that excessive and prolonged exposure to extreme noise can be fatal. The "murderers," Wimsey says, listing the bells, are the bells themselves ("Gaude, Saboath, John, Jericho, Jubilee, Dimity, Batty Thomas, and Taylor Paul"); they have effected that which they signify (396). The sacramental status of the bells resolves a critical debate about whether the bells are active agents in the text—either as in themselves in some Gothic sense alive, or as the hand of God—or merely symbols.[84] In sacramental Christianity, as I have discussed in the introduction, symbols *are* active agents, as they participate in the realities that they represent. The bells are active agents *because* they are symbols, and Wimsey's ability to understand the nature of the crime completes the novel's progression from a prosaic secular economy to a poetic sacramental economy.

Many critics have noted that Sayers at the end of the novel departs from a key convention of detective fiction, as the novel identifies no single culprit who can be blamed for the murder; there is no scapegoat and the community's innocence is not restored.[85] Wimsey's recognition of collective guilt—as he points out, he himself was one of the bell ringers (Sayers *Nine Tailors*, 396)—suggests that he no longer stands aloof from the General Confession; in recognizing collective guilt, he is coming to accept the Christian view of human nature. Significantly, he solves the crime in a scene heavy with Christological imagery; he deduces, identifies with, and in some sense participates in Deacon's excruciating death when he is himself nearly fatally stuck in the bell tower during a peal (389).[86] Since Wimsey and Deacon are both shell-shocked World War I veterans, Wimsey's ability to repeat Deacon's trauma while inscribing it with meaning also signifies a recovery of the social order from the war.[87] The Christian concepts of collective guilt and redemptive suffering are then the foundations on which society is restored.

V

Now that Wimsey has been hailed by the Christian view of human nature, he remains an interpellated Anglican subject for rest of Sayers's detective series. This transformation has escaped critical notice, perhaps because critics tend to assume an individualistic definition of faith which Sayers—who was convinced that the "structure of society" depended on Christian theology, but disclaimed any interest in "personal piety"—for the most part rejected.[88] If a Christian is—as in Evangelical Protestant theology—one who consciously and explicitly professes faith in the Christian God, Wimsey is *not* a Christian; in the final pages of the series, he is still wondering whether "there *is* a God" (italics Sayers's).[89] But in her theological works, Sayers suggests that conscious religious profession and existential belief are neither identical nor necessarily coterminous. She observes, "What we in fact believe is not necessarily the theory we most desire or admire. It is the thing that, consciously or unconsciously, we take for granted and act on."[90] If a Christian is, rather, one who is hailed by the Christian definition of humanity and actively participates in the Christian community, then Wimsey *is* a Christian. In this context, Sayers's apparently contradictory statements about Wimsey's faith—that he is an agnostic "doubtful whether any claim to possess a soul is not a rather vulgar piece of presumption" and that he is "only the most conventional sort of Christian"—may not be contradictory at all.[91] Or, to put it another way, the Wimsey of Sayers's final novels may not personally be a Christian, but he certainly *is* culturally an Anglican. He is as Anglican as Oxford, where he attends the University Sermon in *Gaudy Night*.[92]

Based on *The Nine Tailors* alone, a reader might conclude that the unified, religious society that Sayers posits as an alternative to the divided, alienated world of industrial capitalism amounts in the end to nothing more than a restoration of the *ancien régime*—albeit in a slightly updated and more gender-equal form. But Sayers's final novels show a broader religious and social vision, a desire for national wholeness, unity, and inclusion that pushes well beyond the boundaries of Fenchurch St. Paul.

In this regard, Sayers's work is of a piece with some of the central intellectual directions in interwar Anglicanism as a whole. After World War I, the Church of England had faced charges that it was an anachronistic institution that embodied a social vision that had properly perished in—and perhaps had partly caused—the war.[93] Many Anglicans attempted to rebut these accusations by envisioning a renewed and revised national church that would be truly contemporary and would embrace the diversity and complexity of English society. This project took on liturgical form, as the Church of England made its first attempt in over two hundred-fifty years to revise the Book of Common Prayer. As the preface to the Revised Prayer Book asserted, if the Church was to speak meaningfully to "a new world" of urbanization, white collar labor, democracy, and an international commonwealth, it needed to use new "forms of speech." In 1920, the Committee to Revise the Prayer Book was appointed and in 1927 it presented the new Prayer Book for the approval of Convocation, which it received.[94] The Revisers retained the elevated and highly formal style of language associated with the Prayer Book. Nonetheless, the Church of England was about to speak in a more modern voice and to allow for slightly more diversity in the interpretation of its rites.

These efforts at revision emphatically adhered to the ideal of a Book of *Common* Prayer: the nation would speak a shared religious language and live according to a collective religious vision. The parliament intended that adherence to the new Prayer Book would be legally enforced with an Act of Uniformity, just as adherence to the old Prayer Book had been; it was to become the sole licit form of worship in the Church of England.[95] Groups ranging from moderate Anglo-Catholics to the Liberal Broad Church produced model Prayer Books intended to influence the committee's final proposal, while the Evangelicals and the higher Anglo-Catholics opposed any form of revision.[96] Since each group assumed that nothing less than the nation's future spiritual direction was at stake, polemical arguments over the issue were frequent and sometimes vicious. In the end, the House of Lords approved the new Prayer Book, but the Evangelicals persuaded the members of the House of Commons that the revised Prayer Book represented a betrayal of traditional

Protestantism. The House of Commons voted against the Revised Prayer Book in both December 1927 and June 1928; it was never legally approved for general usage.[97] But the dream of the Revised Prayer Book that would speak to and for the modern world remained for decades to become and would help to inspire the liturgical reform movement after World War II.

Sayers's feelings about the Revised Prayer Book were conflicted. Most Anglo-Catholics opposed the Revised Prayer Book as insufficiently Catholic in content and too tolerant of liturgical diversity.[98] Sayers herself objected particularly to the unpoetical, inexact, and jargon-filled character of its language. She complained in a letter to her father—himself an Anglican priest—that "I do not know why the efforts of modern liturgists should sound so much like a journalese report of a scientific lecture."[99] But the most important influence on Sayers's Anglo-Catholic thought was Bishop Charles Gore, and Gore endorsed the project of Prayer Book revision. He recognized that throughout England individual parishes—Anglo-Catholic, Broad Church, and Evangelical—were increasingly deviating from the Prayer Book in an effort to construct a form of worship that spoke to the concerns and needs of the congregation. Gore thought a Revised Prayer Book offered the only chance of preserving a truly national form of worship.[100] Even if the proposed Prayer Book were imperfect, the social and metaphysical consequences of a possible loss of common worship itself were far worse. Despite her reservations, Sayers also supported the Revised Prayer Book on the grounds of national spiritual unity. In her principal lecture on the liturgy, "Worship in the Anglican Church," she praises "the revision of the Prayer-Book" as it brings the work "more nearly in line with the wishes of the majority of Anglicans" and faults the secularists and non-conformists in parliament for blocking its implementation.[101]

In her fiction, Sayers expresses her longing for a renewed Anglicanism that could reconcile the factions of interwar English society through her use of the marriage plot. She admired the works of Jane Austen, and in her literary criticism encouraged other writers to explore a synthesis of detective fiction with "the novel of manners."[102] The Wimsey series itself owes as much to the novel of manners as to the mystery novel; Wimsey's great gift as a detective is his preternatural ability to read social cues and social signs. The classic marriage plot, in the hands of such authors as Austen and Elizabeth Gaskell, projects a future of national unity, where the divisions of the present are healed. Typically, two characters representing valid and important sectors and/or geographical regions of English society that are presently at odds fall in love and unite in marriage; implicitly, their children will embody a new, undivided England.

In this context, it is significant that Wimsey's love interest is Harriet Vane: an Oxford graduate, a popular writer, an economically self-made woman, and a bohemian. She is also scandalously famous in the popular press as the principal suspect in the murder of her live-in lover, a modernist poet. Harriet, who is fiercely independent and resents Wimsey's easy assumption of privilege, represents the elements of twentieth-century England that could never be contained in the *ancien régime*. It takes Harriet three novels (and considerable change in Wimsey) to be convinced that she can marry an aristocrat and still be herself, that a unity of synthesis and not subjection (a music of counterpoint, in *Gaudy Night*'s analogy[103]) is possible. The unlikely union of this self-made, bohemian, feminist author and a belated eighteenth-century Whig gentleman conveys a hope for a future English society that will be as united and communal as (although very different in shape from) Fenchurch St. Paul.

And, when Peter and Harriet marry, they do so quite consciously and deliberately in an Anglican service conducted according to the forms of the 1662 Book of Common Prayer. Peter has "insisted on being married in church."[104] Peter's sister-in-law tries to convince him not to use the "old, coarse Prayer-Book form," but he is equally uncompromising on this point, since he finds more honest truth about human nature in the traditional rite—which remains, after all, the common worship of England—than in modern attempts to improve on it.[105] If Harriet has, as she thinks, "married England,"[106] she has done so in an Anglican ceremony; the English past and present are united and reconciled through the language of the Book of Common Prayer.

In *Busman's Honeymoon*, the vision of the Revised Prayer Book is fulfilled using the language of the old rite. The guests at the wedding and wedding breakfast span the full range of possible levels of social class, education, and respectability. As Wimsey's officious sister-in-law complains, "There were all kinds of queer people in the church," from policemen to retired burglars, from impoverished spinsters to female college professors, from dirty old men to members of the diplomatic core.[107] The cast of characters is sufficiently wide and unconventional as to represent in microcosm a unified English society—or perhaps the Kingdom of God. The legendary literary critic Queenie Leavis grasped the social significance of Wimsey's marriage quite acutely (if unsympathetically), complaining that while Sayers writes "with an air of unconventionality and play of analysis," and seems to enjoy the cynicism and immorality of her characters, the final message of the series is that whatever you might happen to believe or however you may happen to act, "you MUST go to Church and be married in it" (Leavis's emphasis).[108]

In fact, by the end of *Busman's Honeymoon*, Wimsey is himself dragging Harriet to church (to avoid offending the Anglican sensibilities of the rural English). As Wimsey awkwardly explains to Harriet, "I'm terribly sorry and all that, but could you possibly bear being hauled off to church? . . . I mean it'll be kind of well thought-of if we turn up in the family pew."[109] He immediately backpedals and offers to let her out of it, but for once, he has misread his audience. As part of her immersion in a women's college, Harriet has attended chapel throughout *Gaudy Night* and has even spent the University Sermon admiring despite its limits "the great Anglican Compromise" that allows such disparate sectors of society as the church and university to "kis[s] one another in righteousness and peace."[110] She replies, "Of course I'll come to church."[111] At the morning service, Wimsey even serves as the lector for the first lesson. In a stunning transformation from the man who at the beginning of *The Nine Tailors* barely followed the Anglican service, he now enacts the liturgy himself, playing a ceremonial part or role.

In her lecture on Anglican worship, Sayers insists that liturgy is not primarily emotional, moral, or petitionary in nature. Rather, the liturgy is a "drama," "it is something done, something acted, and performed."[112] In this drama, "the people" are "representing that redeemed humanity" that they are also becoming by performing the part.[113] In this way, Wimsey is redeemed, and represents a redeemed England. To participate in the liturgy is to create community, to act in a common space where conflict between divinely made but inevitably flawed people can be reconciled. As the atomistic 1930s end and World War II is about to begin, the Book of Common Prayer can still give a meaning to time and serve as the basis for authentic community. For the liturgy enacts and creates the incarnational community that is—as much for Sayers as for Catherine Pickstock—the only alternative to the community of economic exploitation. As Wimsey himself, about to leave on a secret mission during World War II, evaluates the options: "Fall into the hand of God, not into the hand of economic humanity."[114] *Murder Must Advertise* collapses in the end into a cacophony of advertising slogans. But the final words of *The Nine Tailors* are uttered by "[t]he voice of the bells of Fenchurch St. Paul": "Nine Tailors Make a Man."

NOTES

1. Wilde, "To Read," 21–22.

2. The poem "Symbol" is identified as reflecting the "Pre-Raphaelite School," and quite obviously imitates the Pre-Raphaelite manner as it describes a corpse lying "in the church yard . . . ./ With white lilies above him, / And a hemlock by his side" (lines 1, 3, 4).

3. Sayers, "Epiphany Hymn." In *Catholic Tales and Christian Songs* (Oxford: B.H. Blackwell, 1918; *Christian Classics Ethereal Library*, 1996), 9–10; https://www.ccel.org/ccel/sayers/cathtales/files/cathtales.html. Text citations are to line numbers from this edition.

4. Twenty-four years later, Sayers would make this argument explicitly in her principal essay on the liturgy, "Worship in the Anglican Church." Here Sayers

suggests that since the sacrificial instinct—the instinct to be united with the deity by materially offering something of ourselves or our possessions—is shared by virtually all human cultures, it must form "a true expression of the divine part of man's nature" (Sayers, "Worship," 37–38). In the Sacrifice of the Eucharist, which embodies the sacrificial instinct "in a pure and perfect form," Anglicans are joined with those who believe in other religions, whose own longings are fulfilled in the Eucharist (though they know it not) (Sayers, "Worship," 38).

5. Canon John Thurmer, who has published more on Sayers's theology than any other author, identifies Sayers as "one of the inheritors of *Lux Mundi* theology" (Simpson, "Some Views," 30). The Lux Mundi group was very influential at Oxford in Sayers's time there; Charles Gore—the leader of the *Lux Mundi* group—was then Bishop of Oxford. Canon Thurmer deduced Sayers's connections to the *Lux Mundi* group based solely on the similarity of their theological thought. Sayers's recently published collected letters provide material evidence to confirm his deductions, as Sayers recommends Bishop Gore's writings to L. T. Duff in a letter of May 10, 1943 (in *Letters*, 2: 405).

6. For the story of the ritualist slum priests, see John Shelton Reed's chapter "Ritualism and the Urban Poor" in his study *Glorious Battle: The Cultural Politics of Victorian Anglo-Catholicism* (Nashville: Vanderbilt University Press, 1996).

7. See especially the poem "Sacrament: Against Ecclesiasts."

8. As Catherine Simpson notes, an appreciative reviewer in *The Challenge* praised the volume's religious poetry, but found it very daring, even bordering on sacrilege ("Some Views," 99). The most negative review, accusing the volume of heresy, was found in G. K. Chesterton's *New Witness*.

9. As Simpson records in "Some Views," the *Times Literary Supplement* enjoyed Sayers's neo-medievalism, observing, "These pieces reproduce in graceful religious fantasies the childlike spirit and familiar intimacy with Christ characteristic of the Middle Ages" (101).

10. Hone's perspective on Sayers's second volume of poetry is one of many quoted and summarized in Simpson, "Some Views," 101–2.

11. Sean Latham records that the volume "sold 100,000 copies in Britain in just over seven weeks" (Latham, *Am I a Snob?*, 173). For the story of the award, see Bury, "Agatha Christie," paragraph 5.

12. Sayers, *The Nine Tailors*, 84. For Hilary Thorpe's poetic ambitions, see page 237.

13. Sayers, "Gaudy Night," 77.

14. Haberman, *Myth, Memory*, 29, 34.

15. Sayers, *Mind of the Maker*, 131.

16. See Sayers, "The Incredible Elopement," 325.

17. See Wolffe, *God and Greater Britain*, 193–94.

18. See Wolffe, *God and Greater Britain*, 214, 227–28. See also C. Brown, *The Death*, 6–7.

19. On Anglicanism's numerical issues and crisis of morale, see Wolffe, *God and Greater Britain*, 70, 261–62. On the rise of metaphysical skepticism in England as a response to the war, see for instance, Samuel Hynes, *A War Imagined,* 115, 188.

20. On the time frame of the composition of these novels, see Sayers's letter of September 14, 1932, to Victor Gollancz (in *The Letters of Dorothy L. Sayers*, ed. Barbara Reynolds, Vol. 1, *1899–1936* (New York: St. Martin's Press, 1996), 322–23. More specifically, *Murder Must Advertise* was written quickly during a hiatus from *The Nine Tailors*, which thus both predates and postdates it.

21. Sayers, "Gaudy Night," 77.

22. The quotation is from page 188 of Dorothy L. Sayers's novel *Murder Must Advertise* (New York: Harper Paperbacks, 1995). Text references are to chapter and page numbers from this edition.

23. Debord, *The Society*, 26.

24. Sayers, "Creed or Chaos," 100–101.

25. Sayers, *Begin Here*, xi. As I will discuss in more length in my concluding chapter, this concern explicitly drives her early public arguments for Anglicanism.

26. Many historians have written about the collapse of "Liberal England," following World War I. The vision of a unified, mutually beneficent society that the Liberal Party represented was replaced by a vision of a society of competing interest groups (the Conservatives for the upper classes, Labour for the workers) (Perkin, *The Rise*, 16). For a detailed account of the role that mass strikes, and consequent reprisals, played in this process even in the years just prior to the war, see George Dangerfield's classic work *The Strange Death of Liberal England*, pp. 260–73, 290–94.

27. Downing, *Writing Performances*, 5.

28. Baudrillard, *Simulacra and Simulation*, 87.

29. See page 4 in Dorothy L. Sayers, *The Nine Tailors* (San Diego: Harvest/Harcourt, 1966). Text references are to chapter and page numbers from this edition.

30. Crystal Downing has noted that, in addition to the bells, "[t]he church of Fenchurch St. Paul operates as a synecdoche . . . projecting the artistry of its spatial form on the temporality of the narrative that contains it" (Downing, *Writing Performances*, 80)—an observation that she does not, however, relate to the Book of Common Prayer.

31. See Sayers, *The Nine Tailors*, 71, for a discussion of the Harvest Festivals, and of the rector's wife's mixed feeling about them.

32. Charles Taylor also suggests that in parts of rural England an *ancien régime* form of religion and society survived "right up to the twentieth century" (Taylor, *A Secular Age*, 439–40), which fits Sayers's depiction of Fenchurch St. Paul.

33. Hezekiah Lavender blames "eddication" for the lack of a coherent world order, for the entrance of England into a world of "puzzlement" that has replaced the "straight-forward an' proper" world of his youth (Sayers, *Nine Tailors*, 125).

34. See, for instance, when Hezekiah Lavender responds to the announcement of a death by immediately saying, "In the midst of life we are in death" (Sayers, *Nine Tailors*, 46). After this quotation from the Anglican burial service, he quickly goes to toll the passing bell. For children fighting over their prayer-books, see Sayers, *Nine Tailors*, 235.

35. The quotation is found in Sayers, "The Undignified Melodrama," 80; the details cited are found in Sayers, *Strong Poison*, 66–67; and Sayers, *Unnatural Death*, 188 ff. Wimsey's knowledge of Anglicanism deserves a more detailed account than

space in the argument permits. In the first Wimsey novel, *Whose Body?*, Wimsey does some investigating in the cathedral town of Salisbury, a city where even the food "seems faintly flavoured with prayer-books" and as a matter of course "step[s] round to hear Evensong" once he has concluded his work (82, 89). In the third novel, *Unnatural Death*, Wimsey consults a High Church Anglican priest when faced with a moral quandary and displays an ability to identify the precise date in the liturgical year (The Feast of St. John, June 24) simply by observing ecclesiastical décor (188 ff.). In the first Harriet Vane novel, *Strong Poison*, Wimsey is depicted as able to quote the most obscure passages of the Book of Common Prayer from memory. Wimsey meets a highbrow literary publisher who claims to publish works only for their artistic integrity (not for profit), while he is actually commercially exploiting the recent murder of one of his authors. Wimsey ironically comments, "Quite religious, isn't it—you know, the bit about 'plenteously bringing out good works, may of Thee be plenteously rewarded.' [The Collect from the] Twenty-fifth [Sunday] after Trinity"; the narrator informs us this jab is received "with a certain lack of enthusiasm" perhaps because the publisher, unlike Wimsey, "was imperfectly acquainted with the Book of Common Prayer" (Sayers, *Strong Poison*, 66–67). In *The Five Red Herrings*, we find that Wimsey is concerned with maintaining his public Anglicanism even while on vacation in Scotland, as he attends charitable fundraisers for the local "Episcopalian Church" (187). The Wimsey we see in *Busman's Honeymoon*, the expert on all things Anglican who pronounces "I collect vicars," and who can deduce any clergyman's theology from a casual glance at his wardrobe, is carefully established throughout the series (91).

36. Sayers, to her parents, December 6, 1911, and November 1914, in *Letters* 1: 63, 105.

37. For the internal and external evidence on which Geoffrey Alan Lee has identified Tyack's *A Book about Bells* as Sayers's primary source, see *Lord Peter Rings*, 5–6. I find his argument entirely persuasive.

38. Tyack, *A Book about Bells*, 184.

39. See Tyack, *A Book about Bells*, 238, 211, 239–40, 185, 187, 189, 170 ff.

40. For the passing bell for the dead, see pages 46, 77. For reference to the villagers' ecclesiastical celebration of the Harvest Festival, see page 71. For the bells ringing in warning during World War I, see page 76. For the epitaph on a village tombstone that uses the bells as a metaphor for human life, death, and resurrection, see pages 307–8.

41. Bergson, *The Creative Mind*, 220. Sayers references Bergson's ideas about time, and Bergson by name, in the novel *The Documents in the Case*, page 65.

42. Church of England, The Book of Common Prayer, x. Naturally, the bells also perform this basic function of summoning the villagers to church throughout the novel; see, for example, Sayers, *The Nine Tailors*, 123.

43. Sayers, "Worship," 37, 44, 47.

44. Basney, "*The Nine Tailors*," 27, 28.

45. Sayers, "Worship," 47.

46. The Book of Common Prayer evening prayer readings for December 31 are pointedly directed toward establishing a new order, including the description of

the New Jerusalem from Isaiah 66 and the description of the abolition of time from Revelation 22:1–6. Catherine Kenney notes in passing that the "time sequence" of *The Nine Tailors* "follows the church calendar"; in the rest of the chapter, I have attempted to pursue this insight more thoroughly than her focus allowed (Kenney, *The Remarkable Case*, 207).

47. The centrality of the Book of Common Prayer to *The Nine Tailors* has been noted only by Ralph E. Hone, who mentions it in passing in an article on Sayers's intertextual poetics (50).

48. The Church of England, The Book of Common Prayer, 18.

49. For the quotation, see Sayers, "What Do We Believe," 10. She purses this idea further in *Mind of the Maker*, 16–17 and *Making Sense*, 10.

50. As Gillis notes, the novel is based around two crimes, the theft of an emerald necklace in April 1914 and a murder "some twenty years later. World War I temporally separates the crimes yet proves to be *the* glue in bringing them together and solving them both" (Gillis, "Consoling Fictions," 191).

51. Brassley, "British Farming," 188–89, 192–93.

52. Howkins, "Death and Rebirth?" 11. Although Brassley and Howkins write in order to complicate the typically bleak picture of rural England between the wars, their statistics confirm that it was a general period of agricultural decline that was mitigated by the rise of factory farming and suburban migration; the period marks, as they admit, the end of the traditional rural social order.

53. Howkins, "Death and Rebirth?" 15, 24.

54. Church of England, The Book of Common Prayer, 332.

55. In this regard, Wimsey exemplifies Catherine Bell's claim that "[t]he ultimate purpose of ritualization" is "the production of ritualized agents, persons who have an instinctive sense of these schemes embedded in their bodies, in their sense of reality, and in their understanding of how to act in ways that both maintain and qualify the complex microrelations of power" (Bell, *Ritual Theory, Ritual Practice*, 221).

56. See, for example, Kestner, *The Edwardian Detective*, 21, and Dove, "The Detection Formula," 35–36.

57. See Thomas, *Detective Fiction*, 3, 5, 17–25 and Kestner, *The Edwardian Detective*, 16.

58. As Basney has noted¸ throughout the novel, change ringing has functioned as "an explicit image, figuring order in apparent disorder, harmony in chaos, skill and intention manifested superficially as monstrous confusion—the promise of justice within the flux of phenomena" ("*The Nine Tailors*," 28).

59. Church of England, The Book of Common Prayer, 144, 146.

60. Gillis, "Consoling Fictions,"187.

61. Gillis, "Consoling Fictions," 185–86.

62. Sayers argues explicitly in her theological works that Christianity gives "the pattern of the universe" that allows "things that seemed meaningless and irrational" to "click into place" and make sense (*Making Sense*, 13). At times, she even puts this point in explicitly liturgical terms. The sacramental worship, "embodied" in the "liturgy" of "the Church of England, "leaves nothing in the universe to be discarded as useless or meaningless: it gives meaning to the whole"; "it tries to give an explanation

and a full expression—not merely to one bit of man, but to the whole of the universe" (Sayers, "Worship," 48).

63. Sayers, "Worship," 48.

64. Sayers, "Creed or Chaos," 54.

65. Sayers, "Strong Meat," 79.

66. Sayers, "Strong Meat," 79.

67. See Sayers "Worship," 45–46, and "Creed or Chaos," 66.

68. Moberly, "The Incarnation," 215. See also Sayers's own explanation of liturgical worship: Christ "instituted the Eucharist, as a means by which we may . . . solemnly offer the whole of humanity to God" ("Worship," 39).

69. For an analysis of Sayers in these terms, see Watson, "Dorothy Sayers," 29. Sayers's incarnational thought is notably similar to, and also possibly influenced by, the work of Bishop Charles Gore (see Gore, "The Holy Spirit," 270, 282).

70. Sayers, "Worship," 48.

71. Sayers, "Creed or Chaos," 68.

72. For the quotation, see Church of England, The Book of Common Prayer, 61. This quotation is from the collect for the day, which Sayers does not explicitly reference. The same point is made, although less succinctly, by the epistle for the day, Galatians 4:1–7, which she does explicitly reference (see Church of England, The Book of Common Prayer, 62, and Sayers, *The Nine Tailors*, 235. For Wimsey's Christmas services, see Sayers, *The Nine Tailors*, 229, 235, 377.

73. Church of England, The Book of Common Prayer, 264.

74. Gore, "The Holy Spirit," 269.

75. Pagett, "Sacraments," 351.

76. Church of England, The Book of Common Prayer, 264. Geoffrey Alan Lee notes Sayers's dependence on medieval typology in her identification of "the Ark, and Noah" with "the Church and . . . Christ," and the flood with baptism (Lee, *Lord Peter Rings*, 25, 45). The suggestion that the Book of Common Prayer serves to mediate these connections is my own.

77. Kenney, *The Remarkable Case*, 77–78. Kenney astutely notes the symbolic significance of the church as "the ark, the place that cannot be taken" where "those who make the journey to it—good, bad, or indifferent—will not die." She also, I think rightly, sees the ending of *The Nine Tailors* as prefiguring Sayers's World War II–era attempts to reconstruct English society on a theological basis. See also Basney, "*The Nine Tailors*," 33.

78. Sayers, *Murder Must Advertise,* 188.

79. Sayers, *Busman's Honeymoon*, 7, 21.

80. Basney, "*The Nine Tailors*," 33.

81. On this pattern, see Haberman, *Myth, Memory*, 136.

82. Esty, *A Shrinking Island*, 43.

83. Mary Donahoe observes a similar pattern in Sayers's religious plays, though she is apparently unfamiliar with the concept of typology. She writes that in Sayers's plays "history is 'sacramentalized' or reordered into a significant pattern of events foreshadowing a fulfillment in the future"; in this manner, Sayers connects "time-sequence to eternity" (Donahoe, *The Sacramental Aesthetic*, 66, 76).

84. For examples of this debate, see Basney, "*The Nine Tailors*," 27; Kenney, *The Remarkable Case*, 65; and Patterson, "A Ring," 51–52.

85. See, for example, Basney, "*The Nine Tailors*," 25, 31, and Gaillard, *Dorothy L. Sayers*, 65.

86. Nancy-Lou Patterson has noted the Christological overtones of the imagery in this scene, though not the philosophical shift that it suggests in Peter Wimsey ("A Ring," 52).

87. See Gillis, "Consoling Fictions," 191–92.

88. Sayers, "Creed or Chaos," 50–51.

89. Sayers, *Busman's Honeymoon*, 401.

90. Sayers, "What Do We Believe," 10.

91. For the denial of Wimsey's Christianity, see Sayers, *Mind of the Maker*, 105. For the affirmation of Wimsey's faith, see Sayers's letter to Stephen Hobhouse in April 1943 (in *Letters* 2: 399).

92. Sayers, *Gaudy Night*, 302.

93. See Wolffe, *God and Greater Britain*, 261–62.

94. Spinks, "The Prayer Book 'Crisis,'" in Hefling and Shattuck, *The Oxford Guide*, 241–42.

95. Spinks, "The Prayer Book 'Crisis,'" in Hefling and Shattuck, *The Oxford Guide*, 240.

96. Spinks, "The Prayer Book 'Crisis,'" in Hefling and Shattuck, *The Oxford Guide*, 241.

97. Spinks, "The Prayer Book 'Crisis,'" in Hefling and Shattuck, *The Oxford Guide*, 239, 241–42.

98. Hylson-Smith, *High Churchmanship*, 181.

99. Sayers to her father, November 24, 1927, in *Letters* 1: 264.

100. See Hylson-Smith, *High Churchmanship*, 273–74.

101. Sayers, "Worship," 47.

102. Sayers, introduction, 43.

103. See Sayers. *Gaudy Night*, 499.

104. Sayers, *Busman's Honeymoon*, 6.

105. Her attempts prompt a satirical tirade from Wimsey on the euphemisms of modern liturgists. As his mother, the Dowager Duchess of Denver, narrates in a letter, Peter "said he knew all about the 'procreation of children'"—one of the purposes of marriage according to the traditional rite—"in theory though not in practice, but that the 'increase of mankind' by any other method sounded too advanced for him" (Sayers, *Busman's Honeymoon*, 21–22).

106. Sayers, *Busman's Honeymoon*, 98.

107. Sayers, *Busman's Honeymoon*, 20–21. The "dirty old man" is Wimsey's maternal uncle Paul Delgardie, whose unconventional sexual relations and uninhibited talk about sex offend younger female relations throughout the series.

108. Leavis, "The Case," 95–96.

109. Sayers, *Busman's Honeymoon*, 387.

110. Sayers, *Gaudy Night*, 300–1.

111. Sayers, *Busman's Honeymoon*, 387.

112. Sayers, "Worship," 43.
113. Sayers, "Worship," 43.
114. Sayers, *Wimsey Papers—IV*, 810.

Chapter 4

"Forced to Bear Witness"

T. S. Eliot's Liturgical Assault on 1930s England

In the preceding chapter, I have shown how the works of Dorothy L. Sayers refashion the Anglo-Catholic liturgical long poem for an England that had absorbed the cultural shock of World War I. *The Nine Tailors* illustrates that although the events of the war had undermined traditional ideas about both literary structure and social order, the Anglican liturgical calendar could still be used to reimagine both literature and society. But Sayers's literary attempt to reunite England by means of the Prayer Book may be belied by cultural divisions endemic in the interwar publishing industry that so effectively promoted her work. Sayers's literary detective fiction, adored by the Book-of-the-Month-Club and despised by Queenie Leavis, is a decidedly middlebrow accomplishment, and speaks only for a particular sector of the factionalized interwar literary landscape.[1]

Like many middlebrow authors of the period, Sayers artistically set herself against a high literary culture that was dominated by modernism. She critiques in *The Mind of the Maker* the early poems of T. S. Eliot and the later novels of James Joyce for employing literary allusion to such "excess" that they devolve into an "instructional kind of cross-word" puzzle, rather than a moving and persuasive work of art.[2] More memorably, in the novel *Strong Poison* (1930), her detective Lord Peter Wimsey infiltrates an avant-garde artists' party in order to investigate the murder of a modernist poet. He joins a discussion about classical music, and eggs the experimentalists on:

> A diatonic scale, bah! Thirteen miserable, bourgeois semi-tones, pooh! . . . I would dispense with all definite notes. After all, the cat does not need them for his midnight melodies, powerful and expressive as they are. The love-hunger of the stallion takes no account of octave or interval in giving forth the cry of

passion. It is only man, trammelled by a stultifying convention—(Sayers, *Strong Poison*, 84)

At this point, Wimsey is interrupted, and he never resumes his mock-theorizing. But Sayers's satirical point is clear: to dispense with shared structure and convention is also to dispense with music (and thereby poetry), is perhaps even to dispense with one's humanity. A common culture and set of conventions enriches rather than constricts life; culture and convention are to be revised, refined, and perfected, not jettisoned or violently remade. Sayers's critique of modernism is of a piece with her defense of the Book of Common Prayer. She seeks a broad shared culture and is a popular author by design. In their conflation of the *Common Prayer* and common culture, Sayers's works may also imply that the "old, coarse" Anglican liturgy is itself too lowbrow or middlebrow to suit the highbrow literary culture of modernism.

The early stages of modernism, from its developmental era in the 1910s to its "high" period in the 1920s, seem to confirm this conclusion. It is difficult to delineate precisely the contours of a literary movement as complicated as modernism; some measure of simplification is always involved. But as a serviceable generalization, it is fair to describe high modernism as a movement skeptical of mass culture, collective identity, and received forms.[3] World War I resulted in a general crisis of confidence in European national institutions, exemplified by the decline in Anglican affiliation and Anglican cultural authority traced in the last chapter, a crisis of confidence that modernism reflected rather than resisted. Many modernists blamed a "herd mentality" for the general enthusiasm for World War I; for them, collective identity meant a mindless "massification" and collective thinking led to slaughter.[4] They held that an uncritical absorption of received cultural forms—such as emotionally charged, highly rhetorical popular literature and a ritualized popular religion—helps to create the collective consciousness so easily manipulated by war-hungry politicians.[5] Modernism is literature written for and redolent of a fragmented culture and world apparently devoid of inherent meaning, which are realities to be faced and depicted rather than evaded or denied. For reasons as much political and ethical as aesthetic, the modernists created a literature that critiques received cultural forms, demands a critically engaged individual reader, and resists a mass audience.[6] If Sayers affirms the Book of Common Prayer as a collective text that constitutes a received cultural form capable of ordering and reshaping the self and the world, high modernism might object to it on exactly the same grounds.

Virginia Woolf's early novel *The Voyage Out* subjects the Anglican liturgy to just such a critique. The Anglican liturgy drives Woolf's protagonist Rachel Vinrace to lose her faith, an event that she experiences as a liberation, a replacement of collective consciousness with original thought. The narrator observes that on one particular Sunday, during church "[f]or the first time in her life, instead of slipping at once into some curious pleasant cloud of emotion, too familiar to be considered, Rachel listened critically to what was being said."[7] Critical analysis immediately destroys Rachel's affection for the liturgy. The liturgy's structure, its "irregular" movement between disparate genres, "from prayer to psalm, psalm to history, from history to poetry" suddenly strikes her as arbitrary, and the ancient Hebrew Psalms as merely the productions of an "old savage."[8] From her new perspective, she looks around at the other congregants and concludes that their collective responses to the liturgy are being performed in bad faith or false consciousness.[9] The liturgy is making them worse people rather than better. In horror at this instance of Anglican worship, which she deems a "loathsome exhibition," Rachel "reject[s] all she had implicitly believed" about religion as a whole.[10] Having dismissed the liturgy as a received collective form that is oppressive of the individual subject, Rachel is now well on her way to modernism. Pericles Lewis has carefully charted the general tendency of modernist authors to depict churches as both hopelessly antiquated and literally and metaphorically empty.[11] For most modernists, he suggests, a legitimate spiritual experience—if such exists—must be individual in nature, and consequently can be embodied more effectively in experimental literature than in received forms of worship.[12] Rachel Vinrace's rejection of the Prayer Book of the Established Church can perhaps stand in for early and high modernism as a whole.

As far as I have been able to determine, modernism begins to employ the Anglican liturgy for constructive—rather than satirical—ends only after the transition from high modernism to late modernism in the 1930s. Although he did not produce explicitly liturgical poetry until several years later, T. S. Eliot in 1927 became the most prominent literary modernist to convert to Anglo-Catholicism. But since Eliot insisted on the originality and catholicity of his tastes and was averse to literary and cultural provincialism, he had some ambivalence to identifying himself too simply with any particular group or party. In the preface to *For Launcelot Andrewes*, he declared himself to be an "anglo-catholic," but he generally preferred the term "Catholic," and typically pledged his allegiance to "the Universal Church," rather than the national/imperial Anglican Church.[13] However, as his recently released letters and previously uncollected prose attest, Eliot was deeply committed to the Anglo-Catholic subculture of the 1920s and 1930s. He was ardently involved in the Anglo-Catholic gatherings and conferences of his day, and even (despite his hatred of committee work) served on the Publications Committee of the activist group the English Church Union.[14] He was converted as much by his older contemporary Viscount Halifax, the President of the English Church Union,[15] as by the writings of the seventeenth-century Anglican divines that he was more prone to reference publicly.[16] He knew the Victorian literary contributions to the High Church movement all the way from Edward Pusey's *Prayers* and John Henry Newman's *Apologia* down to Joseph Henry Shorthouse's cult classic *John Inglesant*.[17] And, as I have shown in the introductory chapter, he was familiar with John Keble's liturgical poetry and literary theory[18] and well versed in Christina Rossetti's late, explicitly Anglo-Catholic poetry.

About the time Dorothy L. Sayers was publishing *The Nine Tailors*, Eliot began his own campaign to reassert the centrality of the liturgy in English literary culture. In April 1934, the magazine *Time and Tide* asked him to write a column for its New Year's issue, giving him an absolutely free hand as to what topic he would address. He took the occasion to ask his readers to reflect on the liturgical calendar, a subject in which he assumes they have no interest. He opens by observing, "Today (December 29th) is the Feast of St. Thomas of Canterbury, better known to most people as Thomas Becket; and I seize the opportunity to mention that fact, because it is hardly likely that anybody else will."[19] In the rest of the essay, Eliot uses the story of St. Thomas, martyred by the agents of King Henry II, to reflect on the complicated relationship between the church and state in the 1930s and makes a case for the church as "the last asylum" for the legitimate "sceptic," who distrusts his or her own beliefs as thoroughly as everyone else's.[20]

He credits an obscure Anglo-Catholic liturgical manual with inspiring the article and launching him on this analysis of contemporary culture: "I have discovered his [St. Thomas Becket's] Mass in a curious volume called The English Missal. . . . The Introit is Gaudeamus, 'Rejoice we all in the Lord'; but I suspect that St. Thomas himself might have preferred to be remembered with the Introit for Boxing Day: Sederunt principes, 'Princes, moreover, did sit and did witness falsely against me.'" In this article, the liturgy and liturgical time have resurfaced as keys to understanding the world, but with a radical shift in their relation to the audience, which is now imagined to be so secularized as to be both ignorant of and uninterested in them. The possession of liturgical knowledge now belongs to the literary artist and is part of the cultural gap between artist and audience. In Eliot's work we find an Anglo-Catholic liturgical poetics reconstructed for the modernist era, what remains of the tradition once the assumption of a common culture has collapsed.

I will focus my discussion of Eliot on his 1935 verse drama *Murder in the Cathedral*, which continues the Anglo-Catholic tradition of structuring poetic works around the Christian Year (and which, unlike his agnostic high-modernist poetry, Sayers admired). This poetic play comprises Eliot's most ambitious attempt to use the liturgy to reconstruct community, reorder time, and re-enchant the world. *Murder in the Cathedral*, which narrates the martyrdom of the medieval English archbishop Thomas Becket, has been among the best received and is certainly the most frequently revived of Eliot's verse dramas. In this play, Eliot first summons a typically modernist world of chaos and unmeaning, and then reorders it—not, as one might expect, according to the received patterns of the Book of Common Prayer, but according to the patterns of the *Anglican* (or *English*) *Missal*, an interwar Anglo-Catholic liturgical experiment that combined Thomas Cranmer's literary language with Tridentine Roman Catholic liturgical forms.[21] Faced with such horror and beauty, traditionally passive theatrical spectators become real, if involuntary, witnesses to religious martyrdom and religious meaning, and must ultimately determine whether to testify for or against the liturgical world they have witnessed. Eliot considers his audience to be so far removed from the liturgy that it can be reached only through such shock tactics, through what amounts to an immersion experiment. Eliot often asserted that his "Catholicism . . . is revolutionary" in nature,"[22] and in his work—unlike that of his Anglo-Catholic poetic forebears—shared meaning and a shared culture are not so much rediscovered as newly, violently, and abruptly created. *Murder in the Cathedral* is Eliot's Anglo-Catholic revolt against secular time and the secular world order.

I

An explication of *Murder in the Cathedral*'s assault on the audience should begin by analyzing the play's late modernist construction of this audience. Critics have distinguished "late modernism" from "high modernism" especially with regard to audience dynamics, and have often classified Eliot's drama—as opposed to the bulk of his poetry—as late modernist.[23] Though the precise dates of late modernism are contested, many critics locate its emergence in the 1930s—when the global economic and political threats posed by the Great Depression and the totalitarian state began to make the artistic detachment of earlier modernism seem naïve—and its zenith during the equally troubled years of World War II and the beginning of the Cold War.[24] Whereas high modernism refrains from explicit political engagement and insists on the independence of the work of art from the reader, late modernism directly addresses contemporary political and social issues and seeks to persuade, challenge, and "reorient" its audience.[25] Eliot's turn toward both religion and the theater can be retrospectively classified as a movement from high modernism to late modernism. As early as a May 1927 letter, Eliot asserts that events have rendered Ezra Pound's posture of artistic detachment obsolete: "I think that the time for a definite aestheticism, as of Ezra . . . has passed by; and I think that the whole Ezra point of view about art is as out of date as the Yellow Book. And I agree that in whatever direction you go nowadays you buck up in the end against economics and religion."[26] Beginning in the mid-1930s, Eliot largely abandoned conventional poetry in favor of verse drama, as his new efforts at cultural engagement led him to desire the more direct relationship with the audience that theater provided.[27]

Murder in the Cathedral is most akin to other interwar works of experimental theater in its flamboyantly direct confrontation with the audience, its desire to break the fourth wall. As Randy Malamud has noted, *Murder in the Cathedral* is a play dominated as much by its chorus as by its protagonist.[28] The play employs a Greek-style chorus that serves the functions of, in Eliot's terms, "mediat[ing] between the action and the audience" and serving as a surrogate for the audience.[29] The chorus, putatively a group of medieval peasants, is actually and explicitly "the type of the common man" watching the play, a point reinforced by its deliberately anachronistic references to twentieth-century cultural phenomena (such as "sightseers . . . with guide-books").[30]

Eliot's chorus or common man feels nostalgia for a traditional understanding of the world, one based on the rhythms of religious faith and the cycle of the seasons. But, like England itself after World War I, the chorus also feels a deep sense "of separation from the past";[31] for it, the traditional methods of interpreting existence have lost explanatory value. The cycle of the seasons can no longer serve as a source of human meaning as humanity lives disconnected from nature and the natural order itself is breaking down.[32] In imagery that recalls *The Waste Land*, the chorus laments that "[t]he land" has become "brown sharp points of death in a waste of water and mud" (175). The chorus fears that "[s]ome malady is coming" that will replace the cyclic renewal of the seasons with mere dissolution (176). It sees signs of the "death of the old" year but not of birth of the new (201). As Rasma Virsis notes, the chorus' "agony" derives in part from its "perception of the instability of time" and in part from its perception of "the instability of the world."[33]

As the chorus experiences it, modernity is in its essence a break or a void, the loss of a center for both world and self. In an image which my students have complained causes nightmares, the chorus cries out that "our brains [are] unskinned like the layers of an onion, our selves are lost lost / In a final fear which none understands" (181). Thomas Becket often favors the honest reactions of the chorus over those of the priests who assist him, and in the temptations that precede his martyrdom, he too must face the dilemma that haunts modernism: the possibility that human life lacks any identifiable central meaning.[34] The Tempters in chorus mock the idea that meaning could *ever* be truly present in human life:

Man's life is a cheat and a disappointment;
All things are unreal,
Unreal or disappointing:
The Catherine wheel, the pantomime cat,

The prizes given at the children's party,
The prize awarded for the English Essay,
The scholar's degree, the statesman's decoration.
All things become less real, man passes,
From unreality to unreality (194)

The use of deliberate anachronism connects the Tempters' speech to the experience of the chorus and the audience. *All* markers that people use to invest their lives with shape and significance—whether political ("the statesman's decoration"), academic (the "scholar's degree"), familial ("the children's party"), or merely diversionary ("the pantomime cat")—are ultimately empty signifiers, designating nothing, deferring meaning, sending them on a perpetual quest "[f]rom unreality to unreality." Since it does not even attempt verisimilitude, the pantomime cat is more real than anything else in human life.

Modernity as the chorus lives it is above all this state of radical indeterminacy, in which meaning is always deferred and nothing is certain. The play is set in November and December, and each of the characters nervously awaits the coming of the as yet "unshapen" New Year and the new order it may (or may not) bring (176). As the chorus exclaims, "The New Year waits, destiny waits for the coming" (175). The chorus fears this indeterminacy, preferring the known evils of "oppression and torture" (under which it is still possible to "buil[d] a partial shelter") to the unknown future, where even this might be impossible (195–96). As the chorus says in its rumination on death, what it fears most, even more than "active shapes of hell," is "emptiness, absence, the Void" (210).

The chorus possesses little hope that traditional means of social ordering, such as government or religion, are capable of creating meaning or resolving the crises of modernity. It considers governmental action to most often result in "oppression"; its great hope is to be "mostly" ignored or "left alone" by the state (176). Becket, who will be martyred by the state, confirms the chorus in its political skepticism, reading authoritarian government as a misguided attempt to impose order on the modern void through sheer political will:

Those who put their faith in worldly order/ . . .
In confident ignorance, but arrest disorder,
Make it fast, breed fatal disease,
Degrade what they exalt. (187)

As even in a totalitarian state, power can never be completely all-encompassing, the endeavor to exert absolute power is unable to eliminate disorder—it will merely "degrade" culture and society.

But if the chorus shares Becket's doubts about the state, it seems equally skeptical about the transformative power of religion. The chorus shares in the general crisis of confidence in the value of the Established Church that marked England between the wars. The chorus still performs its religious duties; it has "kept the feasts, heard the masses" (180). But it finds no more meaning in religious observance than in having "brewed beer and cyder" (180). Each of these duties is part of a giant list of seasonal activities that the chorus performs mechanically in a universe of reduced meaning and significance; they are part of a pattern best described as "[l]iving and partly living" (180). The chorus's experience corresponds with Eliot's description of modernity as "a condition" in which "life seems to have lost all meaning and value."[35] And amidst the troubles of modernity, the chorus feels sure that "[t]here is no danger / For us, and there is no safety in the cathedral" (175). In a world devoid of meaning, religion is simply irrelevant, a source neither of hope nor of fear, seemingly incapable of either inflicting oppression or bringing liberation.

Yet only Eliot's Archbishop Thomas Becket—the episcopal ordinary of the cathedral—senses a possible solution to the problems of modernity that the chorus endures and suffers. He alone realizes that the indeterminate character of modernity is neither self-interpreting nor definitive. In the philosopher Richard Kearney's phenomenological definition, "divine kenosis" describes a "moment of nothingness" and emptiness, the meaning of which depends upon the broader context in which it is understood, and which is just as capable of producing "a mystical epiphany of renewal" as existential despair.[36] Eliot's Becket similarly understands that emptiness can designate a mere absence—or it can indicate divine kenosis.

As the play opens, Thomas Becket has been living in exile in France as a result of his refusal to accept King Henry II's authority over the church. England has been without spiritual governance and has been, in essence, a secular state. Becket's return to England marks the rebirth of meaning and the resumption of sacramental time, the invasion of the temporal by the spiritual. By kenotically entering into the emptiness and suffering of the chorus and deliberately refusing the temptations of political force, Eliot's Becket transforms the meaning of modernity. Each of Becket's four Tempters offers him some version of exaltation and power, a different method of refusing the spirituality of kenotic self-emptying that—as Richard Kearney notes—must of its nature be opposed to exploitative power.[37] The first tempter suggests hedonism, the second political power, the third political pragmatism, and the fourth spiritual vanity. In each case Becket refuses; his will be the path of emptiness. As he explains shortly before his martyrdom, he is "not here to triumph by fighting, by stratagem, or by resistance" (212). Rather, if he and others "conquer / Now, by suffering" the world will witness "the triumph of the Cross" over the forces of brute power (212).

Becket is aware from the moment of his entrance to the play of the costs of this approach. Jesus said that anyone who claims to follow him must "deny himself, and take up his cross . . . . For whosoever will save his life shall lose it: and whosoever will lose his life for my sake shall find it" (Mt. 16:24–25). According to this logic, suffering and self-denial paradoxically comprise the only viable means by which one can find or construct a meaningful life. The life of self-seeking is doomed to fail, since the self is not utterly independent and cannot exist on its own terms alone; *self*-preservation is fundamentally impossible. Self-renunciation, however, is potentially limitless. Charles Taylor discusses the tension between a conception of religion that casts faith as a means of human flourishing and a conception of religion—often found in Christianity and Buddhism—that casts faith as the means toward "final goals" that lie somewhere beyond human flourishing.[38] In Eliot's vision, human flourishing is in any case impossible in the state of modernity; "partly living" is as good as it gets. Only by asceticism, by accepting rather than resisting one's failure to flourish, can meaning be restored.[39]

Jesus's paradox may lie behind one of Becket's own paradoxes: "acting is suffering / And suffering is action" (182). Suffering would seem to be a passive act devoid of agency, something merely endured. Action, by contrast, is the very definition of agency. But as Talal Asad theorizes with regard to the Christian and Shia ideal of the martyr, "Although the living body is the object of sensations (and in that sense passive), its ability to suffer, to respond perceptually and emotionally to external and internal causes, to use its own pain in unique ways in particular social relationships, makes it active."[40] Eliot's Becket suggests that any meaningful action is suffused with suffering, and vice versa. For it is by willed suffering, willed self-emptying, that people connect the chaos of their individual lives to the universal patterns that can give them meaning. As Becket explains, the divine plan is

an eternal action, an eternal patience
To which all must consent that it may be willed,
And which all must suffer that they may will it,
That the pattern may subsist, for the pattern is the action
And the suffering[.] (182)

Here, meaning is both internal and external, both willed and suffered, and comes about only through askesis. The individual quest for personal flourishing (in all its varied forms) can be traded for universal meaning. Thomas Becket kenotically surrenders a life of honor and protection in France for a life of martyrdom in England. By deliberately embracing the suffering and emptiness that the chorus has experienced only involuntarily, Eliot's Becket creates the conditions under which the chorus's fragmented life can be drawn into a meaningful order. Even for the Christian Eliot, the emptiness and meaninglessness characteristic of modernity cannot be denied or evaded. But to choose the void is to reinterpret the void. To accept death is to refuse to go on "partly living." The experience of meaningless can itself be meaningful; emptiness has been reframed as kenosis.

II

St. Paul first introduces the idea of kenosis in an effort to defend and exposit Jesus's incarnation, a theological concept that in Roman eyes was undermined by Jesus's humble life and seemingly ignominious death. Paul explains that the incarnation and crucifixion together comprise an act of divine self-emptying, a deliberate and humiliating descent from eternal power and glory into the transitory and the mundane which—in a dramatic reversal already begun at the resurrection—will ultimately conclude with the restoration of all things under Christ (cf. Philippians 2:5–11). Eliot's Becket similarly in his Christmas sermon asserts that Christ's birth is synonymous with his self-emptying death (198). He also frames his own impending martyrdom as a participation in Christ's example of renouncing all "ambition" and self-will and instead finding "freedom in submission" (199). Completing Paul's trope of ascent by way of descent, he is ultimately confident that "in Heaven the Saints are most high, having made themselves most low" (200).

The incarnational origins of the concept of kenosis also resonate with the play's liturgical and temporal setting. *Murder in the Cathedral* is chronologically and thematically structured around Advent and Christmastide, the liturgical seasons of preparation for and celebration of the incarnation. Becket returns to England just as November passes into December and Advent begins, and he is martyred on December 29, before the octave—eight days of festive liturgical celebration—of Christmas has concluded.[41] From the moment of his entrance, Becket uses the logic of the Advent and Christmastide liturgies to guide his actions. He does not learn kenosis over the course of the play; he enters the play as the embodiment of kenosis, for he enters the play already functioning as a liturgical subject.

Like other Anglo-Catholic thinkers, Eliot praised the liturgy for its role in personal formation, its shaping of individual subjectivity. As Keble taught, the Anglican formed by the public liturgy would develop into a psychologically integrated and spiritually balanced person, an individual free from the excesses and distortions of subjectivistic Romanticism or Dissent. Similarly, Eliot proclaims in a 1932 lecture, "The fall of these words [the liturgy and liturgical readings] upon the ear, as they follow their due and appointed order in the service and the cyclic recurrence of the services according to the seasons, enters into the whole rhythm of the Christian's life with an unconscious compulsion."[42] Eliot's ideal Anglo-Catholic, then, is a liturgical subject, a person whose individual subjectivity has been shaped and refined by the collective liturgy on a level even deeper than consciousness itself.

Unlike Sayers, Eliot does not identify this liturgical subjectivity with the faith of the rural English in the 1930s. He believes that liturgical subjectivity has not been common in England for at least a century and criticizes the normative 1662 text of the Book of Common Prayer generally employed in Anglican worship. He asserts that at present "only a small number of persons" have a life and language shaped by the liturgy, only for a few does the liturgy comprise "the rhythm of life," the "metric in which a man lives."[43] As befits Eliot's modernist sensibilities—and his keen awareness of secularization—liturgical subjectivity is now the conscious, analytical achievement of an individual or small group, not the inherited collective identity of the nation. Thomas Becket enters *Murder in the Cathedral* as this ideal liturgical subject and essentially invades a secularized England. He has internalized the liturgy, and with his every word and action, he is bringing a nihilistic world subject to chronos, the empty march of uniform time, back into kairos, the opportune seasons and graced moments of divine time.

As the perfect liturgical subject, Becket continually (and seemingly unconsciously) speaks words and performs actions that correlate with the *English Missal*'s prayers and scriptural readings for the Advent season. The *English Missal* readings for the First Sunday of Advent prefigure the play's entire plot. Becket arrives in England just as Advent begins, and he is enthusiastically greeted by the populace. Crowds are "[l]ining the road and throwing down their capes, / Strewing the way with leaves and the late flowers of the season (178).

Many critics have noted that Becket's reception echoes Jesus's triumphal entry to Jerusalem, and some have even suggested that Eliot is referencing "the Palm Sunday liturgy."[44] No critic has noted that the Gospel in the First Sunday in Advent in the *English Missal* is Matthew 21:1 ff., which narrates Jesus's entrance into Jerusalem on a donkey as the populace spreads its garments and palm branches on the ground and cries out "Hosanna." The liturgical placement of this text in the first Sunday of Advent is deliberate and symbolic, for in Advent, the faithful are, like the crowds on Palm Sunday, to welcome Jesus's entry into their world and lives and proclaim him as king. When Becket—Christ's representative as head of the English church—returns to his homeland, the Gospel for the preceding Sunday is physically enacted; the liturgy has come to life.

Of course, Becket's triumphal entry in the play, like that of Jesus in the Gospels, is only the prelude to his execution. The readings for the First Sunday in Advent in the *English Missal* also prefigure the difficulties that Eliot's Becket will face and provide inspiration for the martial spirit with which he will confront them. The same gospel reading that narrates the triumphal entry also tells the story of Jesus's assault on the moneychangers in the temple. The "house of prayer" has been corrupted by the forces of power and turned into a mercantile "den of thieves"; it can be purified only through dramatic action and, ultimately, sacrificial death. A conflict is coming, and the Introit for First Sunday in Advent (Psalm 25) gives it voice: "[M]y God, I have put my trust in Thee, O let me not be confounded: neither let mine enemies triumph over me." In similar language, Becket laments that he is surrounded by "eager enemies" who hold him "in bitterest hate" and are "restless" for his undoing (182).

The epistle for the First Sunday in Advent (Rom. 13:8 ff.) offers martial advice for the participant in such spiritual combat. The saint is to use the "armour of light" to oppose the "works of darkness." Paul explains that these "works of darkness" include the lust of the flesh and the violence and strife of power; as Clifford Davidson notes, Paul's "works of darkness" correspond with the offers of Becket's first three Tempters.[45] Over the course of the play, Becket will defeat these enemies with the instruments of light (rather than force or power) and will in consequence reestablish the legitimacy of the church and the viability of the supernatural order. Becket will fight "the battle of the Lord" using only the weapons of the spirit; as he explains, "The church shall protect her own, in her own way" (207, 211). As Richard Kearney suggests, since physical violence is directed to self-preservation rather than self-emptying, a "kenotic faith" must entail a willingness to be killed rather than to kill.[46] Becket will prevent the politicizing of the temple—he "will not have the house of prayer, the church of Christ, / The sanctuary, turned into a fortress"—by cleansing it through martyrdom (211). The First Sunday of Advent has prefigured, and perhaps inspired, the play's entire plot.

In his Christmas sermon, Eliot's Becket explicitly exposits the theory of liturgy that has informed his actions throughout the play. For Becket, the liturgy can reinstate meaning in a seemingly meaningless world in part because it violates and transcends the order of homogenous, empty time. He insists that to celebrate the mass is to break time. "Whenever Mass is said, we re-enact the Passion and Death of Our Lord"; the Eucharist is a sacrifice because it is a re-presentation of the death of Christ (198). Like the Jewish Passover, the mass is a remembrance that renders the past event as present to the assembled community and that renders the assembled community present in the past event. In this Augustinian model of the mass, Christ is physically present in the contemporary church, and the contemporary church community likewise mingles with the apostles. The mass connects otherwise disparate orders of time, incorporating daily quotidian time into the higher times of Christ and the apostles.

Eliot's Becket proceeds to use his theory of the liturgy as the basis for a broader analysis of liturgical time. He both critiques the merely chronological order to which he assumes that the chorus and audience are subject and offers the liturgical calendar as an alternative. He asserts that although the congregation has "probably never thought" about it, it is no mere chance or "accident" that in the liturgical calendar "the day of the first martyr [Stephen] follows immediately the day of the Birth of Christ [Christmas]" (199). As Becket explains, the progression of liturgical days is both deliberate and instructive: rejoicing and mourning, birth and martyrdom, are for Christians to be linked, rather than opposing, concepts. The order of time is not arbitrary but meaningful and liturgical, and meaningful because liturgical. Typology trumps chronology; or, better, liturgically, typology is chronology. As Kurt Tetzeli von Rosador puts it, by this point in the play, "For Becket, time has been transformed: chronological time is metamorphosed into the Church Year."[47]

By the play's end, Becket will pass from being an embodiment of the liturgy to being embodied in the liturgy. He will become a saint celebrated in the Roman and Anglican missals. Like Keble's King Charles I, Beckett dies while unwittingly enacting the readings for his own feast day. In the *Anglican Missal*, the Gospel for the Feast of St. Thomas of Canterbury is John 10:11 ff., which tells the parable of the Good Shepherd who "giveth his life for the sheep." Thomas directly references this text when he sends the priests who are with him away before Henry's knights arrive, so that his followers might escape the assassination reserved for him. He remarks, referring to the knights who have come to kill him, "They shall find the shepherd here; the flock shall be spared" (209).

In his last words, Eliot's Becket synthesizes the liturgical readings for the Feast of St. Stephen on December 26 with those of his own liturgical feast, which will be celebrated only three days later. The First Priest has informed us that "the day of St. Stephen, First Martyr" is "[a] day that was always most dear to the Archbishop Thomas,"[48] and Becket himself has already referenced the feast of St. Stephen in his Christmas sermon. Now he is living the Introit for the Feast of St. Stephen (which the First Priest chants in the original version of the play[49]): "Princes, moreover, did sit, and did witness falsely against me: and the ungodly pressed sore upon me: O Lord, my God, stand up to help me, for thy servant is occupied continually in thy commandments." As Becket explains, though he has been falsely witnessed against—the knights' account of him is "not true" (203)—he will maintain God's commandments. He will "give [his] life / To the Law of God above the Law of Man" (212).

As a celebration of a great evangelist who was also the first Christian martyr, the Feast of St. Stephen thematically reflects the patristic dictum, "the blood of the martyrs is the seed of the Church." Becket sounds this note explicitly in the play, telling the knights,

I am . . .
Ready to suffer with my blood.
This is the sign of the Church always.
The sign of blood. (213)

Finally, weaving together the stories of the Good Shepherd (who dies for the sheep, the church) and St. Stephen (who dies for his love of Jesus), he declares, "For my Lord I am now ready to die, / That His Church may have peace and liberty" (213).

To an even greater degree than Eliot's Magus in "The Journey of the Magi," Eliot's Becket has traded material comfort and prosperity in exchange for spiritual meaning. At the cost of his life, Becket has expressed an understanding of liturgical time sufficiently profound that it successfully extrapolates the present logic of the liturgy out onto the future. Becket's words, like the Canon of the Mass, have the power to break time, rendering both the biblical past and apocalyptic future ritually present.[50] He knows both the victory he has gained and the cost he has paid. Shortly before his death, he declares to his adversaries, "It is not in time that my death shall be known; / It is out of time that my decision is taken" (212).

Becket has, by his own declaration, broken chronological time and the liturgy is the means by which he has triumphed. Inspired by the Advent readings, Eliot's Becket has undergone the ultimate self-emptying of sacrificial death and has in the process reframed modernity's indeterminate emptiness as kenosis and modernity as a movement within kairotic time.

III

In his use of the liturgy to ascribe meaning to time, Eliot stands in continuity with the Anglo-Catholic Victorian poetic tradition. The movement from empty chronology to illuminating typology via the liturgical year remains fundamentally the same in such disparate authors as Keble, Rossetti, Sayers and Eliot. But liturgy—and Eliot's play—is concerned as much with nature of the community as with the nature of time. Becket's martyrdom is an emphatically public event, a murder *in the cathedral*. Although they write over one hundred years apart, Keble and Sayers both provide a bridge between the secular world and the liturgical world. Over the course of their work, the gap between the secular and the liturgical is gradually elided and the former is transformed into the latter. The Christian Year is a pedagogue and the audience learns its lessons alongside a character or speaker who initially mirrors the audience's entrapment in secular time but is gradually converted. Rossetti, by contrast, writes her final volume of poetry for an implied reader who is already a part of or willing to undergo the intellectual work required to enter her Anglo-Catholic rhetorical economy; she is not concerned with or has abandoned the attempt to reach the general or common reader.

Many high modernists, including perhaps the Eliot of the 1920s, approached the question of audience in a manner analogous to Rossetti's. But like late modernists as a group, Eliot the dramatist did wish to engage a broad audience, to write work that "challenged the choice of cultural lens through which [the] audience made sense of the world."[51] Nonetheless, Eliot still retained a modernist suspicion of conventional means of persuasion, and disdained religious literature that possessed an explicit teaching function, considering it to be mere "propaganda."[52] *Murder in the Cathedral* carefully navigates this tension in aims, as it simply assumes—rather than gradually transitioning into or making a case for—a liturgical world.[53] Becket does not become the liturgy; from his initial entrance into the play, he *is* the liturgy. In his person the modern, secularized theatrical audience is directly confronted with an alternate world and an alternate understanding of time and must determine what to make of it. Becket's example challenges the chorus to transform; as he explains, "A martyr . . . is always made by the design of God, for His love of men . . . to bring them back to His ways" (199). But Eliot envisions the audience as skeptical and resistant. His chorus is reluctant to change and in any case is given no time for a gradual transformation.

The chorus would prefer to remain the group of passive spectators that they, like the audience, have been throughout the play. The members of the chorus have begged Thomas not to draw them "into the pattern of fate" (181). It is too painful and dislocating to be drawn into a larger pattern of liturgical meaning. They would have preferred "to perish in quiet" and "do not wish anything to happen" (180). But Becket's very public martyrdom suddenly places the chorus and passive theatrical spectator in an untenable position. The chorus involuntarily views Becket's corpse and hears the speeches his killers have made in their defense. In both a legal and religious sense, they become "witnesses" and must "testify"—for one cause or the other. The play demands an active reader or viewer.

Like the plays of Bertolt Brecht or Samuel Beckett, *Murder in the Cathedral* attempts to eliminate the possibility of objectivity; the audience participates in the action.[54] One hallmark of interwar avant-garde art is a refusal to accept any line that cordons life off from art, the spectator from the literary work.[55] In his criticism, Eliot distinguishes "A devout person, in assisting at Mass" from "a person attending a drama" primarily on the grounds that the former is "*participating*" and not merely observing (Eliot's emphasis).[56] Just as Eliot's play—which is set in a cathedral and actually contains a mass—blurs the line between liturgy and drama, it also breaks the binary separating active liturgical participant and passive theatrical spectator. Becket points directly at the audience members and informs them that for every evil and indifference "you, and you, / And you, must all be punished" (197). Like the chorus, the audience is "forced to bear witness" (175) as Becket is stabbed and stabbed and stabbed—an excruciatingly long sequence that my students find disturbing even in the film version—and cannot remain comfortably detached.

Eliot's positioning of the audience and chorus as "witnesses" rather than passive theatrical spectators owes as much to liturgy's emphasis on active participation as it does to a modernist ideal of the active reader. As the play moves further into liturgical time, its concept of audience also comes to be defined by the lectionary readings for the season. I have discussed above the role the Feast of St. Stephen (December 26) plays in Becket's self-understanding. The second reading for the Feast of St. Stephen in the *Anglican Missal* is Acts 7:55 ff., which includes the story of the stoning of Stephen. Saul, later to become the Apostle Paul, consents to the death of Stephen, and watches over the cloaks of "the witnesses." The "witnesses" here do not merely observe the stoning as passive spectators; they are the legal witnesses of Stephen's putative act of blasphemy in proclaiming Jesus's deity, and as such actively participate in the stoning itself. To be a "witness" in this passage is to be involved, is to be implicated, is to be anything but neutral.

The chorus, and the audience, cannot help but be witnesses in this sense; their neutrality removed, they are "compelled."[57] But the chorus does get to choose whether it will be a witness like Saul, the willing accomplice of the powerful, or like Paul, whose later testimony to Christ redeems and purifies his guilty memory. Eliot gives the knights who murder Becket a chance to defend themselves to the audience and makes identifying with them—choosing the path of Saul—a disturbingly real possibility; the knights' speeches are far closer to the common reasoning and rhetoric of interwar England than is Becket's sermon.[58] Quite literally, in this verse drama they speak in prose. William de Traci appeals to English nationalism; he explains "We are four plain Englishmen who put our country first," "disinterested" patriots who reluctantly removed a cause of division in the nation (Becket) by the only means possible (assassination) (215–16). Hugh de Morville appeals to English Erastianism, the sense that the church is merely a department of the fundamental social unit, the political state, and charges Becket with violating this value. He informs the audience that "if you have now arrived at a just subordination of the pretensions of the Church to the welfare of the State, remember that it is we who took the first step" (217). Richard Brito appeals to Freud's atheistic model of human psychology, in which excessive religiosity constitutes not holiness but disorder. He explains that Becket was not a saint, but a "monster of egotism" with a "mania" for martyrdom (218); as such, he is responsible for his own fate.

As the knights speak, the chorus and audience encounter their moment of temptation and must decide what sort of witnesses they are.[59] They must decide whether to continue to live and move in the limited but reassuringly comprehensible world of nationalism, materialism, and secularism, or to take a leap into a largely foreign and bafflingly transcendent liturgical world. The knights are confident enough in their case that they frankly inform the audience that to sympathize with them—to be a witness in their cause—is to participate in their guilt and to live in the world they have created. They conclude, "we merit your applause; and if there is any guilt whatever in the matter, you must share it with us" (218).

Eliot retains a modernist preference for indeterminate endings and a modernist aversion to both rhetorically forceful authors and their passive audiences. Conventional rhetoric is left to the knights; the function of the play is simply to clarify the existential decision the audience must make. As *Murder in the Cathedral* ends, the audience's decision remains open, and only in its final speech does the chorus seem to reach a decision. The chorus utters its last lines not in the knights' contemporary, jargon-ridden prose, but in the archaic language of the liturgy. For such foreign (and un-Freudian) concepts as legitimate guilt and longing for forgiveness can be expressed only in an alternate language; modernity has no words for them. The chorus grants that the blood of the martyrs "[i]s upon our heads," and then immediately breaks into the Kyrie said at every mass: "Lord, have mercy upon us" (221). The liturgy provides the terms—repentance, redemption, sanctification—that make the transformation of the self conceptually possible.

The play's ending implies a hope that if the audience, like the chorus, makes the leap into a liturgical world, a new epoch and a new England may be possible. A new year conventionally represents both a new movement in time and the beginning of a new order in the world. Throughout the play, the chorus has wondered what world the new year will bring. The central role the *Anglican Missal*'s readings for January 1 play in the transformation of the chorus suggests that this new world will be liturgical in nature. January 1 (being eight days after Christmas) is the Feast of Jesus's Circumcision. The Gospel for this day is Luke 2:15 ff., which focuses in part on Mary's attempt to remember, interpret, and understand the ineffable. The shepherds have told Mary and Joseph stories of events—such as an angelic host making proclamations about the child—which they cannot comprehend, but at which they may only "wonder." But Mary will, famously, "ponde[r] them in her heart"; she will mull them over and come to understand them later.

Like Mary, Eliot's chorus knows that it is unable to understand the events unfolding around it; Becket is as alien a figure to the chorus as to the audience and his actions are initially incomprehensible. The chorus is also aware of its own passivity. It simply cannot face martyrdom with Thomas, and begs his forgiveness for its inactivity, its mere spectatorship. Thomas forgives the chorus and then wishes it peace, explaining,

This is one moment,
But know that another
Shall pierce you with a sudden painful joy
When the figure of God's purpose is made complete. (207)

The chorus will later "remember" these moments "droning by the fire / When age and forgetfulness sweeten memory" (208–9). The memory will be transformed, "changed" in the telling into something beautiful, which is at once real (reflecting "God's purpose") and not real (for "Human kind cannot bear very much reality"); it will bear a mythic truth, exactly like "a dream" retold (209).

Previous critics have seen no connection between the Virgin Mary and Eliot's chorus. Susan Colón perceptively analyzes the basic trajectory of Becket's remarks; Becket is promising that the chorus will experience a "participatory echo" of his "martyr's ecstasy."[60] But, by using the verb "pierced," Becket suggests that he is actually making a very specific parallel between the present moment and an earlier martyrdom. Simeon, at Jesus's dedication, predicted that when the pain of Jesus's life and death was made manifest a sword would "pierce" Mary's heart (Lk. 2:35). In Catholic art, the Immaculate Heart of Mary is always depicted as pierced with a sword, and church tradition has always seen in Mary a type of the church. By the end of *Murder in the Cathedral*, the chorus has ceased to be a group of isolated spectators and has become the church congregation actively uttering the words of the mass.[61] As the church, the chorus now shares Mary's task of preserving, pondering, and reshaping memory to give meaning to time. This is the work of the liturgy, as reflected in the readings that begin the calendar year on January 1. Eliot seems to suggest that in England, community does not presently exist—just an aggregation of individuals "living and partly living"—but the liturgy could create one.

Eliot famously remarked that the Church Year contains "the full drama of creation."[62] Despite its narrow time frame and compact setting, *Murder in the Cathedral* consistently points outward, suggesting a larger redemption of time and nature, the construction of a community and world that participate in "the full drama of creation." The play gestures beyond its chronological setting in Advent and Christmastime by referencing holy days that as the play ends have yet to transpire, and which if included would complete the cycle of the liturgical year—such as, for instance, Easter and the Feast of All Saints.[63] The play begins as November ends, and the Feast of All Saints would bring the year once more back to November. Similarly, the chorus's final speech looks beyond the play's plot and physical setting, and addresses the whole natural order.

A liturgical, sacramental world is also a re-enchanted world. Through the language of the liturgy, both time and place possess a meaning. The chorus explains that the world possesses coherent significance because the martyrs have inscribed meaning on the earth with their blood: "For the blood of Thy martyrs and saints / Shall enrich the earth, shall create holy places" (221). Although modernity in both its insidious and banal forms is, in this book, oriented toward the erasure of meaning, the message written in the martyrs' blood is indelible. The martyrs have created meaning through their kenotic lives of deprivation and self-renunciation; modernity cannot empty out their emptiness. Their message remains—"Though armies trample over it, though sightseers come with guide-books looking over it" (221)—and the meaning the saints have inscribed on the earth can be understood by those who use the liturgy as an interpretive key. As the cult of saints began with the cult of the martyrs, the *sanctorale* might be seen as kenosis projected out over the temporal year. The members of the chorus end the play by exclaiming, "Blessed Thomas, pray for us"; they are impossibly or prophetically paraphrasing the Postcommunion prayer for Becket's feast day in the *Anglican Missal*, in which the congregation pleads to be "cleanse[d]" from "all our sins . . . at the intercession of blessed Thomas." They are participating in the act of liturgical remembering.

The liturgy also infuses the natural world with meaning. The chorus, which earlier found no real meaning or hope in nature, now proclaims,

> We praise Thee, O God, for Thy glory displayed in the all the creatures of the earth,
> In the snow, in the rain, in the wind, in the storm; in all of Thy creatures, both the hunters and the hunted . . .
> all things affirm thee in living[.] (220)

In seeking re-enchantment, Eliot has not abandoned the modernist rejection of Romanticism. The order his chorus has found in nature and the world is not wholly comforting and is not wholly comprehensible. It is written in the blood of the martyrs and includes both "the hunters and the hunted." It includes both darkness and unbelief: "Thy [God's] glory is declared even in that which denies Thee; the darkness declares the glory of light" (220). The chorus intuits a larger rhythm and pattern, but there is no theodicy; meaning remains slippery and evasive, yet the world is full of meaning. And in a world previously devoid of meaning altogether, this intuition may be enough. Humanity cannot explain or understand everything, but as the species alone capable of conceptual abstraction, it can affirm existence as such, the quality without which it could neither blame nor praise anything. Hence, humanity can serve as, in Eliot's words, the "conscious" voice of Creation's praise of God, its explicit worship a synecdoche for the implicit worship of the whole: "Even in us the voices of the seasons, the snuffle of winter, the song of spring, the drone of summer, the voices of beasts and of birds, praise Thee" (220–21). The song of the chorus translates and renders audible the song of time itself.

If the chorus is now capable of ascribing meaning to the world and its times and seasons, if it can unite all creation in a hymn of praise, it is only because the language and logic of the liturgy have enabled it to do so. The chorus's celebration of the natural order deliberately echoes the liturgical language and logic of "Benedicte, omnia opera," the Song of the Three Holy Children from the Apocrypha, which sings, "Let the heavens, the earth, the sea, and all that is in them, bless thee. And praise thee and magnify thee above all forever." The Benedicte fits the temporal structure of the play, as it is recited by Anglo-Catholics each Advent.[64] In encountering the Anglican prayers for the season, the audience is also encountering a foreign vision of the world. As Charles Taylor suggests, to live in liturgical time, to live in contact with higher times, is generally also to live in an enchanted world.[65] The chorus's final speech presents the audience with a vision of the possible benefits and paradoxes of the liturgical world it has briefly—and possibly involuntarily—witnessed. And the members of the audience will leave the theater to determine what sort of witnesses they will be. Eliot's mass has ended, and they may go in peace.

IV

Eliot's poetic project in *Murder in the Cathedral* is, then, much more ambitious than the work's narrow time frame and confined setting might suggest. Like the liturgical work of Keble and Sayers, Eliot's liturgical verse drama is a daring attempt to reorder time, re-enchant the world, and re-sacralize community. *Murder in the Cathedral*, which is often seen as a conservative exercise in medieval nostalgia,[66] is also much more radical than critics have generally realized—as radical as it is liturgical, and radical because liturgical.

Although critics typically treat the post-conversion Eliot as a political and religious conservative, Eliot hated this label. He insisted that that "the Catholic" like himself was a fundamentally different creature than "the conservative—who is usually confused as to what he wants to conserve."[67] Conservatives by definition preserve what exists, and Eliot did not think that England had a functioning national faith to preserve; "religious faith," he observes sardonically in a 1932 radio talk, is now "a mere extra, like French and Music, which a minority of people treat themselves to."[68] The writings of John Keble and Dorothy L. Sayers contain scathing and perceptive social criticism. But Keble and Sayers are both broadly conservative in political philosophy, though Sayers's moderately progressive and reformist conservativism and Keble's rather reactionary conservatism are by no means identical. They both write to connect deracinated modern English individuals with a spiritual and communal order that they assume—if only in rural England—has remained perpetually in place.

Both more pessimistic and more radical than Keble and Sayers, Eliot lacks faith in the collective order. Despite the Book of Common Prayer, England possessed no shared religious vision or language; in Eliot's words, England was devoid of "common agreement on ethical and theological matters."[69] For Eliot, as for most modernists, social and spiritual renewal begins with an individual or a subculture, not with the culture as a whole.[70] As I have shown, Thomas Becket enters an England where liturgical time and organic community have collapsed and restores both by personally defying the political establishment.

Just as Becket restores liturgical time to England by decisive individual action, Eliot forcibly superimposes a liturgical order on modern England by means of a dissident liturgy. For Keble, Rossetti, and Sayers, the 1662 Book of Common Prayer was a sacred text, the central point of contact with a divine order that could reinstate organic community and re-enchant the world. Eliot, however, had no particular attachment to the Book of Common Prayer and attended only parishes that, contrary to English civil and ecclesiastical law, declined to use it. For the most part, critics have analyzed Eliot's use of the liturgy by assuming either that he is referencing the Latin Roman Catholic liturgy, or that he is referencing the 1662 Anglican Book of Common Prayer, or that he is employing liturgy as a generic sociological construct.[71] But to use either the 1662 Book of Common Prayer or the Roman Rite would be to endorse the kind of collective consciousness that Eliot so often critiques.

Murder in the Cathedral actually draws most of its liturgical references from the *Anglican* or *English Missal*, an avant-garde Anglo-Catholic liturgical experiment combining the form of the Latin Roman Rite with the language of the Book of Common Prayer. The *English Missal*'s advocates imagined it as the liturgical future and thought it would help to bring about a world where Rome and Canterbury were again at one.[72] Like modernist poetry, the *English Missal* combined disparate literary traditions to create a new work, at once ancient and contemporary, culturally specific and international. Like modernist poetry, it appealed only to a relatively small but ardent coterie (who sometimes went so far as to denigrate and ridicule the established Book of Common Prayer).[73] To the average churchgoer, the *English Missal* was entirely unknown, and its use was even technically illegal. Though prosecutions were rare, the use of the *English Missal*—and any other alternative to the Book of Common Prayer—in public worship was legally proscribed in England until after Eliot's death.[74] The two Anglo-Catholic parishes Eliot regularly attended were frequently in trouble with their bishops and the principal Anglo-Catholic organization he supported, the English Church Union, spent much of its resources defending High Church priests from ecclesiastical prosecution.[75] Further, the cult of St. Thomas of Canterbury was banned during the Reformation Era and his feast has no place in any version of the Book of Common Prayer.[76] The veneration of Becket was a fringe Anglo-Catholic practice.[77]

In *Murder in the Cathedral*, then, the secularized audience is without transition thrown into an alternate world, a world that functions according to the logic of an Anglo-Catholic liturgy of which it has never heard. By using the *English Missal*, *Murder in the Cathedral* presents the audience with a defamiliarized Anglican liturgy. Eliot seems to assume that the audience will truly hear the ancient words of the liturgy only after these words have been freed from the banality of repetition that so oppressed Woolf's Rachel Vinrace and have been made to sound as strange and foreign as they are. The chorus and audience are forced to choose between the language and values of the all-too-twentieth-century knights and the language and values of the liturgical Becket. All other options are regarded as fundamentally untenable and neutrality is regarded as an illusion. As Eliot himself wrote with regard to Blaise Pascal's *Pensées*, since neither the religious point of view nor the "unbelieving point of view" can be conclusively substantiated, "in the end *we must all choose* for ourselves between one point of view and another" (italics mine).[78] Each individual is "forced to bear witness," compelled to choose. And thereby Eliot hopes to begin, on a small scale, the remaking of the world.

In the second half of his career, Eliot preferred verse drama to conventional poetry in part because a play creates a community of shared experience.[79] In *Murder in the Cathedral*, Eliot hopes to create a community that reflects divine meaning by causing an audience for a few hours to participate in divine time. In his essay "Poetry and Drama," Eliot explains the role art plays in establishing a community's shared perception of a meaningful world. He writes, "For it is ultimately the function of art, in imposing a credible order upon ordinary reality, and thereby eliciting some perception of an order *in* reality, to bring us to a condition of serenity, stillness, and reconciliation."[80]

Murder in the Cathedral is Eliot's boldest and most explicit attempt to enact this theory. He attempts through poetic drama to create the liturgical and Anglo-Catholic future he in the 1930s imagined for England. Like avant-garde "little magazines" of the period, *Murder in the Cathedral* attempts to create a "counterpublic spher[e] whose ultimate aim was to influence the dominant public sphere," a subculture that might one day reshape the dominant culture.[81] Anglo-Catholicism could become Anglicanism itself; as Eliot openly hoped in 1931, the Church of England could cease to be "the English Church" and find itself instead "more and more coming to be . . . 'the Catholic Church in England.'"[82] And the process could begin with a skeptical crowd of people gathered in a theater.

In what is probably the most overtly religious of major works of twentieth-century English theater, Eliot abandons the Book of Common Prayer, which has historically stood as the center of Anglican worship and identity. Eliot thereby recognizes that even in England Anglicanism is now only one of many voices and interpretations of reality; for every Becket, there will be four knights, and no appeal to consensus or precedent can be successful. But at least in this play, Eliot embraces this situation. If much of existence is linguistically constructed and nature of the universe for the most part indeterminate, then no intractable obstacles prevent the choice of faith, and tradition itself can be rediscovered and (as in the *English Missal*) reimagined. Eliot allows the liturgical Becket to be merely one voice among many, trusting that the audience will find the unfamiliar rhythms and motions of liturgy to comprise a compelling new experience, a different mode of being than those offered by contemporary drama, politics, or advertising; as Eliot often observes, practically speaking, experience is the test of faith[83]. Thus, maybe, just maybe, the community of the theater might become the community of faith, and the community of faith might become the community of England, and modernity itself a transitional state toward a new liturgical order.

NOTES

1. On this divided literary landscape, see Ina Haberman's study *Myth, Memory, and the Middlebrow*, which also addresses the conflict between the modernists and the middlebrow authors.
2. Sayers, *The Mind of the Maker*, 121, 152–54.
3. On the repudiation of received traditions and forms as a response to World War I, see Hynes, *A War Imagined,* 191.
4. For an example of the connection between a fear of "the herd" and a repudiation of World War I, see, for example, Pound, "Pastiche," 358.
5. See Sherry, *Ezra Pound, Wyndham Lewis*, 4, 53–54.
6. See Sherry, *Ezra Pound, Wyndham Lewis*, 46; see also, Carey, *The Intellectuals*, 16–17, 71–72.
7. Woolf, *The Voyage Out*, 227–28.
8. Woolf, *The Voyage Out*, 226–27.
9. Woolf, *The Voyage Out*, 228–29.
10. Woolf, *The Voyage Out*, 233, 228.
11. Lewis, *Religious Experience*, 19.
12. Lewis, *Religious Experience*, 4–5, 29–30.

13. For an example of this terminological preference, see Eliot, *The Idea*, *43*.

14. On his affiliation with the English Church Union, Eliot to Mary James Power, December 6, 1932, in *Letters*, 6: 518. On his work on the Literature Committee, see Eliot, to Charles Harris, September 15, 1932, in *Letters*, 6: 533.

15. In a letter to Jean de Menasce on May 22, 1928, Eliot admits, "I owe a great deal in my present position to conversation with Lord Halifax" (in *The Letters of T. S. Eliot*, ed. John Haffenden and Valerie Eliot, Vol. 3: 1926–1927 (New Haven: Yale University Press, 2012), 169.

16. Eliot cites Laud as a principal reason for his conversion in a letter to Richard Aldington on May 16, 1927 (in *Letters*, 3: 519–21).

17. Eliot references Newman repeatedly; for a specific reference to the *Apologia*, see his letter to S. Dudley of May 24, 1929, in *The Letters of T. S. Eliot*, ed. John Haffenden and Valerie Eliot, Vol. 4: 1928–1929 (New Haven: Yale University Press, 2013), 509–10. On Pusey, see Eliot to Ottoline Morrell, December 27, 1928, *Letters*, 4: 361. On Shorthouse, see Eliot to Charles A. Siepman, February 24, 1929, in *Letters*, 4: 449.

18. On Eliot's knowledge of Keble's literary theory, Eliot to Charles Harris, September 15, 1932, in *Letters*, 6: 443–44. As the letter indicates, Eliot knew Keble's literary criticism—unlike his poetry—only at second hand, having read a submission to Faber and Faber that addressed the subject.

19. Eliot, "Notes on the Way," 154.

20. Eliot, "Notes on the Way," 154.

21. Barry Spurr has conclusively established based on interview data that the Anglican Eliot invariably attended parishes *English* (or *Anglican*) *Missal*, as the order of service (Spurr, *Anglo-Catholic in Religion*, xi, xiii). Eliot's recently published letters lend further support to Spurr's claim. In a January 7. 1931 letter to Bishop George Bell, Eliot describes his devotion to the Anglo-Catholic services devised by the Society of Sts. Peter and Paul, which were collected and compiled as the *Anglican Missal*. He writes, "[T]he form of Lenten Offices to which I am accustomed (and to which I am strongly attached) is in *The English Holy Week Bk* published by the Society of SS. Peter and Paul (2/6)"; he observes also that this order of service was used "at St. Mary the Virgin's," his personal parish (in *The Letters of T. S. Eliot*, ed. John Haffenden and Valerie Eliot, Vol. 5: 1930–1931 (New Haven: Yale University Press, 2015), 457).

Spurr is also the first critic to notice Eliot's dependence on the *English* or *Anglican Missal* in *Murder in the Cathedral*. He notes, for instance, that the titles the priests use to describe the three days after Christmas in Eliot's play are nearly identical to that which is employed in the *English Missal* (rather than the Book of Common Prayer or the Roman Rite) (Spurr, "Liturgical Anachronism," 5).

22. See Eliot to John Middleton Murry, November 23, 1931, in *Letters*, 5: 753.

23. For the classification of Eliot's plays as works of late modernism, see, for example, Esty, *A Shrinking Island*, 158.

24. For a good summary of both late modernism's historical context and literary scholarship on late modernism, see Cheryl Hindrich's article "Late Modernism, 1928–1945: Criticism and Theory," *Literature Compass* 8 (2011), 840–855.

25. On the connection between late modernist style and the culture of the 1930s and 1940s, see Davis, "Late Modernism," 328–33 and Hindrichs, "Late Modernism,"

851–52. On late modernism in the 1950s and the rhetorical dimension of late modernism, see Genter, *Late Modernism,* 5, 12.

26. Eliot to F. S. Flint, May 24, 1927, in *Letters* 3: 533.

27. See Chinitz, *T. S. Eliot*, 169.

28. Malamud, *Where Words Are Valid*, 74.

29. Eliot, "The Need For Poetic Drama," 405.

30. The lines quoted are from page 221 of T. S. Eliot, *Murder in the Cathedral.* In *Complete Poems and Plays: 1909–1950* (New York: Harcout, Brace, and Company, 1967). Unless otherwise noted, text references are to page numbers from this edition. On the contemporary nature of Eliot's chorus, see also Colón, "'This Twittering World,'" 81.

31. Hynes, *A War Imagined*, 261.

32. Malamud, *Where Words Are Valid*, 82; Robinson, "*Murder in the Cathedral*," 35.

33. Virsis, "The Christian Concept," 405–6.

34. I believe that this dynamic makes Becket's own modernity and fragmented psyche part of the play's redemptive logic. In his I differ with critics such as Krystyna Michael ("Neomedievalism," 35), who have seen these traits of Becket as subversive of any direct religious purpose in the play.

35. Eliot, "Building Up," 464.

36. Kearney, *Anatheism*, 5, 55, 137.

37. Kearney, *Anatheism*, 53.

38. Taylor, *A Secular Age*, 17.

39. On the need for askesis in the modern world, see Eliot's essay "Religion without Humanism," 39.

40. Asad, *Formations of the Secular*, 89.

41. On the exact temporal setting of the play and its liturgical implications, see Davidson, "T. S. Eliot's *Murder*," 166; Fjordbotten, *Liturgical Influences of Anglo-Catholicism*, 256; Spurr "Liturgical Anachronism," 4.

42. Eliot, "The Bible as Scripture," 698. Eliot is speaking particularly about the 1549 Prayer Book, but he is making a larger point about the role of liturgy in the formation of individual subjectivity as well.

43. Eliot, "The Bible as Scripture," 698–99.

44. Davidson, "T. S. Eliot's *Murder*," 164.

45. Davidson, "T. S. Eliot's *Murder*," 166.

46. Kearney, *Anatheism*, 136.

47. Tetzeli von Rosador, "Christian Historical Drama," 521.

48. See T. S. Eliot, *Murder in the Cathedral* (New York: Harcourt, 1963), 54. I have generally employed the later version of the play used in Eliot's *Complete Poems and Plays*, as it reflects Eliot's final judgment. Occasionally, however, the play's liturgical vision is clearer in the earlier version.

49. See T. S. Eliot, *Murder in the Cathedral* (New York: Harcourt, 1963), 54.

50. See Davidson, "T. S. Eliot's *Murder*," 157.

51. Genter, *Late Modernism*, 12–13.

52. Eliot, "Religion and Literature," 99–100.

53. In its preference for religious experience over religious argument, *Murder in the Cathedral* corresponds nicely with Eliot's theoretical approach in his essay "Religion and Literature," which was published in the same year. In its acute consciousness of and attempt to remedy the audience's secularity, the dramatic work violates Eliot's critical dictates, however (cf. "Religion and Literature," 100).

54. Davidson, "T. S. Eliot's *Murder*," 157–58.

55. Rainey, *Institutions of Modernism*, 2.

56. Eliot, "A Dialogue," 36.

57. Colón, "'This Twittering World,'" 85.

58. On this point, see Pike, "Liturgy and Time," 282–83.

59. See Jones, *The Plays of T. S. Eliot*, 61–62.

60. Colón, "'This Twittering World,'" 84.

61. Primarily, the chorus quotes the Agnus Dei and, as I shall shortly discuss, paraphrases the Postcommunion prayer for Becket's feast day.

62. Eliot, "A Dialogue," 35.

63. For the references to All Hallows and Easter, see pages 175 and 201, respectively.

64. See the lessons for Ember Saturday in Advent. To my knowledge, only one critic has noted that the chorus' epiphany about the nature of the material world is itself liturgically derived. Grover Smith rightly sees echoes of the "Benedicte, omnia opera," the Song of the Three Holy Children season (Smith, *T. S. Eliot's Poetry*, 193). The connection between the *English Missal* Advent readings and the "Benedicte, omnia opera" is my own.

65. See the introductory chapter of this book, particularly pages 28–29.

66. On the tendency of critics to see the play as a conservative exercise in nostalgia, see Michael, "Neomedievalism," 35.

67. Eliot, "Christianity and Communism," 425; "The Modern Dilemma," 812.

68. Eliot, "Religion and Science," 439.

69. Eliot, "Religion and Literature," 97.

70. On the stance of opposition to "prevailing social values" as typical of modernism as a whole, see Baldick, *The Social Mission*, 76.

71. For instance, Robert Ayers assumes that Eliot employs the Tridentine Catholic liturgy (Ayers, "*Murder in the Cathedral*," 581 ff.); Clifford Davidson uses the Book of Common Prayer approach (Davidson, "T. S. Eliot's *Murder*," 162, 167), and Paul Stanwood treats liturgy simply as a metaphor (Stanwood, "Time and Liturgy," 91).

72. On the *English Missal*, see Spurr, *Anglo-Catholic in Religion*, 84–85. For evidence of Eliot's desire to reunite the Anglican and Roman churches, see, for instance, his remarks to the Anglo-Catholic Summer School of Sociology: "I assume that we are all of one mind about the deplorable consequences of the schisms of Christianity, and are convinced of the vital importance of the reunion of Christendom" (Eliot, "Catholicism and International Order," 534).

73. Spurr, *Anglo-Catholic in Religion*, 84–85.

74. Corbett and Davage, *Defend and Maintain*, 76.

75. On the difficulties of Eliot's parishes, see Frith, *A History of St. Cyprian's*, 10; Spurr, *Anglo-Catholic in Religion*, 81–82. On the English Church Union, see Corbett and Davage, *Defend and Maintain*, 22.

76. On the proscribed nature of the feast, see Davidson, "T. S. Eliot's *Murder*," 153.

77. See Fjordbotten, *Liturgical Influences of Anglo-Catholicism*, 277–78.

78. Eliot, "The *Pensées* of Pascal," 343.

79. See Chinitz, *T. S. Eliot*, 80; Malamud, *Where Words Are Valid*, 4.

80. Eliot, "Poetry and Drama," 87.

81. On this goal of the "little magazines," see Morrison, *The Public Face of Modernism: Little Magazines, Audiences, and Reception, 1905–1920*, 11–12.

82. Eliot, "Thoughts after Lambeth," 337.

83. See Eliot's comment that he became a Christian in part because "the Christian scheme seemed the only possible scheme which found a place for values which I must maintain or perish"; he insists that while a belief is not justified solely by its practical effects, these effects may attest to its veracity (Eliot, "Christianity and Communism," 428).

Chapter 5

Anglo-Catholic Liturgical Poetry from the Christian Social Order to Post-Christian England

This book has traced the poetic project of reordering time and re-enchanting the world by means of the Anglican liturgy from the era of Romanticism and the prospect of Catholic Emancipation through to the age of modernism and the threat of international fascism. As England hovered on the brink of World War II, Anglo-Catholicism stood at what might be considered the height of its popularity and influence. The adherence of figures like T. S. Eliot had given the movement a renewed cultural prominence. The Anglo-Catholic Congresses of the 1920s and 1930s—multiday conferences at which up to thirty thousand people assisted at outdoor high mass, marched in Eucharistic processions, and attended lectures—constituted the largest mass gatherings the movement had ever known.[1] And the new Viscount Halifax, the son of the longtime president of the English Church Union of the same title, was foreign secretary and was rumored to be the next prime minister.

Both Dorothy L. Sayers and T. S. Eliot imagined that World War II would serve as the catalyst for the creation of a more organic, more Anglican, more liturgical England. The war, as they saw it, was the moment when their literary dreams would come to be embodied in concrete reality, when the world would be renewed and remade in fact, and not just imagination. Sayers and Eliot's plans for a renewed Anglican England constitute a real-world climax for the project of the Anglo-Catholic liturgical long poem. Consequently, this conclusion first outlines these plans and the logic behind them, then charts Sayers's and Eliot's literary responses to the postwar failure of their hopes, and finally concludes with a retrospective analysis of Anglican liturgical poetics in light of the massive changes in English religiosity and the Anglican liturgy in the last sixty years.

I

As many historians have noted, a general English consensus during World War II held that the nation should emerge from the conflict fundamentally changed. The "People's War" had been defined by the government and the press as a fight for freedom (as opposed to Nazi totalitarianism), and that freedom was typically defined so as to include both personal economic security and opportunities for self-fulfillment and self-assertion.[2] As the bestselling writer J. B. Priestley told his enormous worldwide audience over BBC radio, the war was worth fighting because it would result in "a truly civilised world of fully co-operating free men and women."[3]

For the members of the once popular but now forgotten Christian Social Order movement, a freer England meant a more Christian England. The movement included many prominent politicians, intellectuals, and religious leaders, but was most visibly represented by the Archbishop of Canterbury serving from 1942 to 1944, William Temple.[4] Temple had written the influential manifesto *Christianity and Social Order* (1942), which argued for the creation of a new model of society that was neither capitalist individualism nor totalitarian collectivism, one devoted to "freedom, social fellowship, and service."[5] As archbishop of York, Temple had also organized the 1941 Malvern Conference to gather Christian intellectuals from all fields to participate in the endeavor of imagining a new society. In an analogous effort, from the late 1930s to the mid-1940s the noted ecumenist J. H. Oldham assembled "the Moot," a reoccurring discussion group of theologically diverse Christian intellectuals, which he hoped would evolve into an interdenominational religious order capable of shaping and reforming the postwar world.[6]

The Christian Social Order movement brought Dorothy L. Sayers and T. S. Eliot together for the first time in person. Both spoke at the Malvern Conference, and both contributed to the discussion groups and periodicals (such as *The Christian News-Letter*) affiliated with the Moot.[7] Sayers and Eliot also wrote books and articles, such as Sayers's *Begin Here* and Eliot's *Idea of a Christian Society*, that helped to spread the movement. Eliot contributed an essay to the provocatively titled collection *Prospect for Christendom*, and Sayers worked to ensure that women's rights were included in what she called "the various plans for a Christian Social Order."[8] All in all, Eliot was one of Christian Social Order's most influential theorists, and Sayers was one of its most forceful popular voices.

As is typical of their work of the war and postwar era, Eliot carefully articulates the philosophy behind their common endeavor, and Sayers—who was greatly influenced by Eliot's religious ideas but doubted his ability to communicate them to the masses[9]—applies it much more flamboyantly and directly. In his influential and controversial *Idea of a Christian Society*—written almost entirely prewar, but first published in book form in wartime with a postscript applying its ideas to the war[10]—Eliot argues for a Christian Social Order as the only viable alternative to the culturally bankrupt Western democracies of the 1930s. The Munich agreement of September 1938, ceding portions of Czechoslovakia to Hitler's Germany, has made him wonder whether England possesses any real principles of any sort: "Was our society, which had always been so assured of its superiority and rectitude, so confident of its unexamined premises, assembled around anything more permanent than a congeries of banks, insurance companies and industries, and had it any beliefs more essential than a belief in compound interest and the maintenance of dividends?"[11] Eliot analyzes each of the ideals that might have some claim to govern England—capitalism, Liberalism, and Democracy—and concludes that none constitutes a meaningful concept around which a healthy society could be constructed.

For both Eliot and Sayers, capitalism is a dehumanizing force, socially harmful and ethically wrong. Eliot argues that "[t]he organisation of society on the principle of private profit," far from benefiting the individual, leads both to environmental destruction and the industrial malformation of the human.[12] Sayers similarly holds that since each individual is created in the image of God the Creator, "work is in itself a sacrament"; hence, the mechanical labor of industrial capitalism is fundamentally anti-sacramental and dehumanizing in nature.[13] Virtually all participants in the Christian Social Order movement shared this critique of the dehumanizing character of unregulated capitalism. Archbishop William Temple, especially, called for both wide-scale social reform and extensive charitable aid; he also wished to respect the human dignity of the underprivileged by distributing this aid through organic local institutions—neighbors helping neighbors—rather than through the faceless central government.[14]

Eliot finds liberal representative government in its common secular and technocratic form to be socially disintegrative. Democracy, Eliot suggests, is not so much a theory or ideal as an administrative technique, and can be used to support virtually any model of society, including totalitarianism.[15] Liberalism is primarily a mode of critique, not a positive ideology around which a society could be arranged, a "habi[t]" rather than a "philosoph[y]"; its effects on society are essentially centrifugal.[16] In Eliot's account, the liberal secular state's attempt to be value-neutral has brought about a society that is managed by bureaucratic experts on a purely pragmatic and utilitarian basis. Such a society must ultimately be fissured and fractured, as no common social ideal or picture of reality exists to which all parties can appeal. As Eliot asserts—and Sayers emphatically concurs—"unless we can find a pattern into which all problems of life can have their place, we are only likely to go on complicating chaos."[17] A secular democracy is inherently a society without a unifying ideal. And, as the Christian Social Order movement generally asserted, England's lack of a such an ideal has rendered the nation weak and indecisive when faced with foes—like Nazi Germany or Stalinist Russia—who do possess a unifying social vision.[18]

The Western democracies, then, can be reformed and placed on a secure foundation only by the rediscovery of a common philosophy and world view in Christianity. Eliot frames his conclusion as the result of a careful logic chain: "As political philosophy derives its sanction from ethics, and ethics from the truth of religion, it is only by returning to the eternal source of truth that we can hope for any social organisation which will not, to its ultimate destruction, ignore some essential aspect of reality."[19] Sayers makes the same point with all the drama of wartime rhetoric:

> the principles to which we are now clinging amid the wreck of the philosophies are the Christian principles of the Western-Mediterranean civilization. . . . [T]hey are rocking beneath us because we have knocked away the foundation of eternal values on which they were built, and that unless we can find some eternal basis on which to rest them, they will founder and our civilization with them. (Sayers, *Begin Here*, 127)

For all these reasons, she believed that "Christianity is necessary for the building of a free and prosperous post-war world."[20]

Although the Christian Social Order movement was a designedly ecumenical endeavor, for Sayers and Eliot, England must be renewed as a Christian nation primarily through the Anglican Church.[21] Both Sayers and Eliot were capable of ecumenical engagement, and Sayers did compose most of her explicitly religious work so as to appeal to a multidenominational audience. But the metaphysical and political centrality they assigned to the liturgy inherently places a certain limit to their ecumenism. Each held that to become an organic and personalist society, England must return to the vision of the person embodied in the liturgy. Sayers theorizes that "[t]he chief peril that confronts a democratic civilization is that of becoming disrupted by an excess of liberal individualism. If it is to survive, it must learn to achieve coherence—not like a dictatorship, by extinguishing the liberality and fettering the individual, but by finding some principle of unity by which individual liberties can be embraced and controlled."[22] The symbiotic interplay between the individual and collective for which Sayers calls resembles liturgical subjectivity as Catherine Pickstock or Catherine Bell defines it. Sayers and Eliot had imagined an alternate, liturgical world in their major mid-1930s works, and their version of Christian Social Order resembles that world come to life. In *The Nine Tailors* and *Busman's Honeymoon*, Sayers had depicted an expansive Anglicanism as capable of sacramentally uniting the disparate sectors of English society and re-enchanting the world. A Christian England that celebrates the individual, embraces diversity, and yet unites all together in a true community would be an exercise in counterpoint, would be the Prayer-Book marriage of Peter Wimsey and Harriet Vane on a national scale.

Eliot is more explicit about the Anglican nature of his vision. Although he freely grants that not everyone in the society will belong to the same church, possess religious faith to the same degree, or believe at all, he feels certain that "[i]f the desirability of unity be admitted, if the idea of a Christian society be grasped and accepted, then it can only be realized, in England, through the Church of England."[23] Without a church that at least aspires to speak for the entire populace, spirituality becomes a private, interior matter and the hope of social renewal becomes impossible. An organic, renewed society must be an Anglican society, viewing the world through the lens of a common liturgy, and moving according to the rhythms of liturgical time. Or, as Eliot puts it more abstractly, for "the great mass of humanity," "religious and social life" must "form . . . a natural whole," one structured around "customary and periodic religious observances."[24] Just as in *Murder in the Cathedral*, in *Idea of a Christian Society,* Eliot confronts a secularized audience with a liturgical vision of the world. Again, he presents "the alternatives" to a liturgical order as appalling—"If you will not have God (and He is a jealous God) you should pay your respects to Hitler or Stalin"—and hopes that faced with such a dilemma the audience might be willing to consider embracing religious, political, and aesthetic ideas that might otherwise seem "alien," impractical, or at least off-putting.[25]

And for both Eliot and Sayers, the war was to be the moment at which secular modernity died of its own self-inflicted wounds, the simulacrum faltered, and the liturgical world was reborn. They imagined that the war would break the old capitalist system—to use Sayers's image, "the whirligig" would finally "slow down"—providing the opportunity for a more organic economic, political, and religious order to take its place. Hence Eliot could calmly but confidently assert, "For a long enough time we have believed in nothing but the values arising from a mechanized, commercialized, urbanized way of life: it would be as well for us to face the permanent conditions on which God allows us to live upon this planet."[26] Sayers positively celebrated the wartime conditions of scarcity, as they restored a world of inherent worth and fixed value by forcing people to abandon excess spending, select their purchases on the basis of utility, and to make things for themselves.[27] The world she satirized in *Murder Must Advertise* seemed to have vanished overnight, and a new world seemed to be on the horizon. She saw Germany as a thoroughly secularized nation, and exuberantly proclaimed in the early days of the war:

> I don't think it's going to be enough merely to keep the Christian flag flying; I fancy that now or never is the time to bring it out and carry it ostentatiously down the street. . . . Materialism is dead, and the people who have been busy for the last fifty years secularising everything are now thoroughly frightened by the results when they see the idea carried to its full conclusion. (Sayers to J. H. Oldman, September 10, 1939, in *Letters* 2:133–34)

Jed Esty's observation about Eliot could apply to Sayers as well: both hoped that "an epochal change in European history might discredit the progressive time of secular modernity in a way that the eloquent protests of high modernism never could," that "the privations of war, depression, and imperial decline could inspire the English to rediscover their Burkean roots as an organic community."[28]

Sayers's hopes perhaps reached a high-water mark when during the war the BBC broadcast her radio play cycle on the life of Jesus, *The Man Born to Be King* (1941–1942), to high ratings and rave reviews. Following the massive success of the initial broadcast, the BBC even planned with Sayers's cooperation a rebroadcast that would have timed the episodes to coincide with appropriate dates on the Anglican liturgical calendar.[29] Valerie Pitt has suggested that the invention of radio also comprised the birth of the first "regular and nationally uniform experience of the English language" alternative to that of the King James Bible and the Book of Common Prayer, weakening the hold of these sacred texts on English speech and identity.[30] But here, we have the possibility of Prayer Book Radio, if you will: the nation gathered around the radio to listen to the events of the life of Jesus as presented in the Gospels and organized structurally by the liturgical calendar. A postwar England both ancient and modern, liturgical and technological, must have seemed at that moment entirely possible.

II

Of course, the postwar future that actually transpired was quite different. The political story is well known. Britain's 1945 Labour government adopted many of Archbishop William Temple's specific policy proposals—such as affordable housing for individuals, some measure of guaranteed economic security for families, a longer period of mandatory education for children, and more rights and recreational holidays for workers—in its attempt to create a more humane society that was neither simply capitalist nor simply socialist.[31] In fact, many historians credit Archbishop Temple with having prepared the British public to accept on religious grounds the postwar welfare state.[32] But Temple himself did not live to see the end of the war, and the

Labour government rejected perhaps the key element of his social vision: the idea that the local organic community—especially in the form of the parish church—was to be a key agent of socialization and social change, so that individuals in want would be empowered through dialogic encounters with their neighbors, and not simply made subject to the mercy of the state.[33] The Labour government gave rise to an increasingly bureaucratic and monolithic state, which also began to marginalize the role of religion in public life.

The accelerated pace of secularization in postwar Europe has many causes and should not be oversimplified. But many cultural historians have concluded that the postwar rise of the welfare state and consequent decline of mediating social institutions is one important factor in this development; from education to aid for the underprivileged, the government began to assume the role previously occupied by the churches.[34] We witness, then, a strange irony. If capitalism had remained in its relatively unmodified prewar state, the churches would have retained a vital social role—and English capitalism might never have been modified if not for the Christian Social Order movement. By critiquing a capitalist democracy that failed to exercise charity and by emphasizing the need for a set of political values that transcended mere individualism, the Christian Social Order movement inadvertently advanced the cause of secularism.

The Christian Social Order movement's emphasis on individual self-expression and self-fulfillment possesses an ironic legacy for Anglicanism as well. After the war, England began to enter what critics have often described in literary terms as the Postmodern Era and Charles Taylor has described in religious terms as "the Age of Authenticity" (the concepts overlap and are in some important aspects identical).[35] I am concerned with these terms not as descriptors of a body of literature—neither Sayers nor Eliot wrote "postmodern" work—but rather as descriptors of the state of culture that emerges in Western Europe and America following World War II. As Tyrus Miller and Robert Genter have both noted within their somewhat different frameworks, literary late modernism—such as Eliot's—and literary postmodernism temporally overlap and in many ways constitute differing artistic responses to a shared set of cultural conditions.[36] To avoid the confusion that could arise from thus differentiating between the "Postmodern Era" and "postmodern literature," I will typically prefer Taylor's terminology in the analysis that follows.

Both the common literary critical account of postmodernity and Taylor's narrative of the rise of the Age of Authenticity note that in the postwar period advertising culture began idealizing "choice" and the power of the individual consumer, and collective allegiances—whether religious, national, or simply cultural—gradually came to be seen as oppressive to the individual.[37] The very idea of a shared national story and identity, of a united Englishness, now fell under suspicion.[38] Modern life seemed flat and empty; collective norms appeared to be the problem and personal choice was seen the answer, a trend that accelerated in the 1960s.

Taylor's term "Age of Authenticity" refers especially to way in individual lives come during the 1950s and 1960s to be defined and shaped by neo-Romantic quests to throw off social expectations and discover a genuine, authentic selfhood; the hippie movement serves as an extreme example of a much broader trend.[39] As Taylor notes, this expressive individualist quest often does not take explicitly religious forms, and when it does take a religious form can give rise to movements as diverse as religious syncretism, spirituality without religion, and Pentecostalism. In each case, the quality of a faith comes to be judged by its degree of resonance with and its capacity to produce a sense of personal wholeness for a particular individual, rather than by the degree to which an individual's faith and practice embody the judgments and collective wisdom of a particular religious tradition.[40] In Taylor's "Age of Authenticity," the dominant churches of a nation remain important as a point of reference, but the precise role of "collective connections" in the individual's "relation to the sacred" is being renegotiated; individual religious "choice" is the order of the day.[41]

Taylor suggests that European state churches, which drew much of their force from their official role in collective society, have been particularly weakened by the rise of the Age of Authenticity.[42] The postwar history of Anglicanism fits this paradigm quite exactly. The health of a church is perhaps best registered in its marriage and baptismal records, the extent to which it establishes the domestic society embodied in the family and the future church embodied in its offspring. Church of England baptisms per 1,000 live births steadily fell from 668 in 1927, to 602 in 1956; to 466 in 1970; to 365 in 1981; to 228 in 1997.[43] The percentage of marriages solemnized in the Church of England has also been in steady decline since the early 1950s.[44] All told, as John Wolffe records, "[a]fter the Second World War," the Church of England suffered "an absolute reduction in numbers."[45] After the year 1956, the rate of religious observance begins to fall in England in almost every measurable demographic category.[46] By the end of the century, "less than 8 percent" of the population of England will attend "Sunday worship in any week."[47] T. S. Eliot himself considered England to have entered a state of "apostasy" in the postwar period.[48]

Rossetti's late poetry, which articulates an idiosyncratic vision of an enchanted world only to those already within its rhetorical economy, might be well suited to a fragmented, individualistic age that lacks shared religious forms. *Verses* aspires to reinvest the material world with liturgical meaning but seems to possess no such hope for English culture. Sayers and Eliot, by contrast, shared Keble's basic goal of a restored common culture and they lived to grapple with the complexities and quandaries that the dawning Age of Authenticity posed for liturgical poetry. The death of Sayers's and Eliot's dream for a renewed organic society inspired their final pieces of liturgical writing, and caused these works to take a very different form than their more hopeful works of the 1930s. Characteristically flamboyant, Sayers approaches a secularized postwar world through the tactic of head-on assault, even mockery; her final work of liturgical poetry is published in the popular British humor magazine *Punch*.

In her series of *Punch* essays collectively titled "The Pantheon Papers" (1953–1954), Sayers offers a satirical depiction of the religion of the post-Christian world that she perceives around her.[49] As the first essay begins, she claims to have found a plate of a stained-glass window representing an unknown cult; a "Professor of Comparative Irreligion" has informed her that this window perfectly embodies the beliefs and practices of the "Polar Cult"[50] The "Polar Cult" turns out to be an open secret, a religion not often discussed but which actually "embraces almost the whole population of the Western World (with the exception of a few strict Jews and fanatical Christian sects)."[51] Around the periphery of the stained-glass window we see hagiographical depictions of (in clockwise order) St. [Karl] Marx the Evangelist, St. Julian [Huxley] the Polymath, Fiery Loins of Lawrence, D. H.; St. Sigmund (Freud), Sub-Limine; the Venerable Bernard Shaw; and the Beautification of St. Henna. In the center of the image glows "The Apotheosis of the Common Man" in his bowler hat.[52]

This hagiographical image, on which the initial essay is presented as anthropological commentary, sums up Sayers's critique of the Age of Authenticity; to help explicate the image, she also supplies the Polar Cult's creed and detailed liturgical calendar. The Polar Cult takes its name from "polarity," and its adherents desire to be as divided and isolated from other human beings as possible—living as if up on a pole. Hence, they are a community that "specifically repudiates communion."[53] An alienating individualism is the essence of the religion. In the religion's High Church, liturgical form, the religious calendar culminates in isolation: "Pole-Star Sunday, devoted to the cult of Isolation, ushers in the season of Polarity, a period of peculiar an awful sanctity, in which the cycle of the year completes its revolution."[54] The religion's Low Church devotees object to the liturgical calendar, and insist that so long as one is isolated from all others the essence of the religion is performed, regardless of specific forms of ritual and belief.[55] Isolation is achieved by an exaltation of individual opinion, impulse, and identity. As the hagiographical stained-glass window suggests, polar devotees are taught to embrace their individual sexual nature and sexual identity, to throw off traditional social mores and ideas of sin, and to remake themselves artificially.

St. Sigmund Freud will free them from traditional morals and lead them to sexual self-acceptance, after which, like St. Lawrence, D. H., they will experience the beatitude of releasing their "Fiery Loins." They will also remake, recast, and revise themselves and their physical bodies perpetually, a process celebrated in the Beautification of St. Henna.

But Sayers's hagiographical image also suggests the paradoxical collectivism of expressive individualist society, the rise of the welfare state at the precise moment when individualism is most valued. For now, as St. Karl Marx would explain, individual problems are to be understood as the product of social laws, not of individual choice. The figure of the Venerable Bernard Shaw, the ultimate Fabian, clarifies the point. We are to seek the solution to our problems neither in religious conversion nor in Marxist revolution, but in the gradual development of the bureaucratic state as managed by technocrats. Science, in the figure of St. Julian Huxley, serves not so much as the arbiter of truth as the handmaiden of the technocratic state, debunking rival belief systems such as religion and defending the dominance of the expert over every area of life and society. Ultimately, then, Sayers's satire suggests that there is no conflict between the simultaneous rise of individualism and collectivism. Postwar private life will be ever-more self-expressive, to the point of destroying the idea of a common life, and isolated individuals who admit no common mores or common creed will increasingly require the bureaucratic state to address their needs and arbitrate their conflicts. This synthesis of unbridled individualism and the collective state is summed up in the final articles of the new religion's Euthanasian Creed (which has replaced the Athanasian Creed): "And I believe in the Spirit of Progress, who spake by Shaw and the Fabians; and in a modern, administrative, ethical and social Organization; in the Isolation of Saints, the Treatment of Complexes, Joy through Health, the Destruction of the Body by Cremation (with music while it burns), and then I've had it."[56]

The central image of Sayers's stained-glass window, the Apotheosis of the Common Man, visually depicts the effect of this new social order on individual subjectivity. The Common Man glows with a heavenly light and seems about to ascend to heaven. He glows because, above, an angel on a cloud is bathing him in stage lights, while another angel films the transformation for BBC-TV (as the label on his camera indicates). A third angel plays a saxophone, while a dove descends carrying a newspaper titled *Daily Dogma*, as befits a religion that celebrates the feast of the newspaper baron Alfred Lord Northcliffe, under the title "St. Northcliffe-in-the-Fleet (January 26)."[57] The only unity, the only vision of common life, possible in the Age of Authenticity is that which has been artificially created by television and the press. The Anglican liturgy, with its careful balance of the individual and collective, has been replaced with what T. S. Eliot would in his final play call the "liturgy / Of the Press."[58]

The liturgical calendar for the new religion includes a season of Advertisement—it replaces Advent[59]—and "The Pantheon Papers" suggests that all of Sayers's fears from *Murder Must Advertise* have now come true. The material world and the individual have both been abandoned along with the Christian liturgy. In the new liturgical calendar, the feast of All Hallows (or All Saints) is replaced with "All Hollows."[60] The physical world has been hollowed out and deprived of meaning; the new liturgy reverses the old liturgy's attempt to sacralize materiality and time. Similarly, the world has now neither real music (which requires shared notions of order and beauty) nor meaning; the new religion has replaced the feast of the Epiphany with the "Feast of Cacophony."[61]

In a point that should have particular resonance in an Age of Authenticity, Sayers suggests that a world without meaning or beauty also inevitably becomes a world without interiority. Without an authentic liturgy, individual authenticity also ceases to exist. Sayers's final piece of liturgical poetry—a mock hymn "For an Evening Service" of the new religion, a new evensong—ironically celebrates this process:

The day that Nature gave is ending,
    The hand of Man turns on the light;
We praise thee, Progress, for defending
    Our nerves against the dreadful night . . . .

We thank thee that thy speed incessant
    Provides upon this whirling ball
No time to brood on things unpleasant—
    No time, in fact, to think at all.

Secure amid the soothing riot
    Of crank and sound-track, 'plane, and car,
We shall not be condemned to quiet,
    Nor left alone with what we are.

By lavish and progressive measures
    Our neighbour's wants are all relieved;
We are not called to share his pleasures,
    And in his grief we are not grieved.

Thy winged wheels o'erspan the oceans,
    Machining out the Standard Man . . .

All bars of colour, caste, and nation
Must yield to movies and the mike;
We need not seek communication,
For thou dost make us all alike.

So be it! let nor sleep nor slackness
Impede thy Progress, Light sublime;
Nor ever let us glimpse the blackness
That yawns behind the gates of Time.
(in Sayers, "The Pantheon Papers," 7–8)

The ethos of a religion is best expressed in its hymnody. Evensong has been one of the most beloved of Anglican liturgical services, and John Keble's poem for evensong became a well-known hymn. In Sayers's poem for evensong, the speaker unconsciously explains both the reasons why England has abandoned the Anglican liturgical order and the social and psychic costs of this decision. The postwar welfare state encourages the process of individualistic fragmentation, by teaching people to see themselves as autonomous social units whose desires and needs are not to be reconciled but bureaucratically managed. Individual or group charity or even sympathy are precluded by state action; "lavish and progressive measures" assure that we "share" neither others' "pleasures" nor "grief" (lines 17, 19–20). This isolated individualism does not subvert but rather abets the production of the artificial "Standard Man" who is both created and summoned by the voice of television and radio. Lacking both meaningful dialogic "communication" with others and the opportunity for introspection—never "condemned to quiet, / Nor left alone with what we are" (lines 15–16)—the individual has no real means of resisting interpellation by mass media. The individual lives in a world of surfaces devoid of depth. Constant artificial light precludes the thoughts of death and mortality traditionally associated with night. Continually enclosed, distracted, and managed, the postmodern individual exists in a relentlessly and exclusively finite world, Charles Taylor's closed Immanent Frame. Whereas the Christian liturgical year bridges time and eternity, the function of this liturgical hymn is to permanently sever time from eternity; as the faithful beg Progress, "Nor ever let us glimpse the blackness / That yawns behind the gates of Time" (lines 31–32).

Despite the affirmative and inclusive nature of her earlier liturgical vision, Sayers meets the rising Age of Authenticity with not appeasement but satirical resistance. Sayers's purpose in composing "The Pantheon Papers" was to hold a mirror up to the age. Liturgies depict an ideal social world, to which the culture aspires and in which the individual participates. The purpose of a satire is to persuade and to change minds; it is essentially a hopeful and rationalistic art form. Sayers attempts to reveal to her readers the ideal social world in which they have been unconsciously participating. She describes the Polar Religion as a Gnostic cult in which the masses "practice the rites" and behaviors of the religion, but only the educated inner elite have "access to the Mysteries," the philosophical ideas that justify these practices.[62] In the mass market magazine *Punch*, she makes a populist case against secularity by depicting its social implications in the form of collective religious ritual.

By doing so, she also questions the very possibility of an authentic secularity; if secularity has itself a cultus, then a truly secular, post-liturgical world does not and cannot exist. Individuals will continue to accept on faith ideas that they cannot personally, empirically verify, whether they accept these ideas on the authority of the Apostolic Fathers or the *Daily Dogma* newspaper. The tension between the individual self and the collective social ideal that the liturgy attempts to mediate will continue to exist. The only question is whether a culture devoid of transcendence, a purely immanent liturgy, can offer a model of life that is experientially worth living and intellectually capable of accounting for the complexities of reality. Sayers's withering comedy strongly asserts that it cannot.

The Book of Common Prayer retains a normative status in Sayers's late satire. The Prayer Book can no longer be assumed as the center of English life and identity; indeed, it is explicitly Sayers's thesis that it has been supplanted and replaced. But the Prayer Book remains the register by which change can be measured. Sayers's satire is a running gag imagining what a Prayer Book of postwar secularism would look like. The problems and follies of the culture can be measured by their deviation from the Prayer Book; for instance, the nihilism of the Feast of Cacophony registers precisely in comparison with the prospect of the Feast of the Epiphany upon which it puns. Without the Prayer Book, Sayers's juxtaposition of secular and liturgical language would be postmodern pastiche rather than satire, a combination of literary forms that pointed nowhere beyond itself rather than a comic call for cultural change. The satire also assumes that the audience possesses a lingering memory of the Prayer Book, and a vestigial deference to it; otherwise, the Prayer Book could not reveal to the audience how ridiculous it has become. In "The Pantheon Papers," the Book of Common Prayer becomes a weapon of protest.

III

T. S. Eliot's late liturgically inflected poetry and poetic drama approach the quandary posed by 1940s and 1950s secularism more delicately. Unlike Sayers, Eliot declines to directly confront a secularized postwar England with the Anglican liturgy; instead, he grapples with the issue of whether and by what means a liturgical picture of the universe can be communicated to a post-religious world. How can the liturgy's vision of an enchanted, sacramental world that moves in kairotic time be communicated to a postwar era of nuclear armaments and expanded industrial production, where time is measured by the factory time clock and the Doomsday Clock? Eliot, in fact, begins to change his approach to religious poetry before the war is even over, most notably in his final major work of non-dramatic poetry, *Four Quartets* (1943).

Eliot's *Four Quartets* are his most explicit and perhaps his most famous rumination on the nature of time. As Jed Esty observes, they collectively constitute an "attempt to pose meaningful, shaped, or eschatological time against mere chronology."[63] Although a full analysis of the work is outside my purpose, I will briefly show that *Four Quartets* shapes time and imagines society in a manner that mirrors the Anglo-Catholic liturgical long poem as I have interpreted it. The speaker of the poem wishes to be liberated from the march of empty, homogenous clock time, and to relate to time in an older and more organic way; he speculates about "a time / Older than the time of chronometers."[64] He critiques, as a source of the emptiness characteristic of clock time, a belief in linear chronological progression (a "mere sequence") or simple evolutionary "development."[65] He wishes, instead, to gather times together, to form moments into a pattern, a dance, that would both transcend (clock) time and be within (organic) time; to defeat time through time. "The saint" is one able "To apprehend / The point of the intersection of the timeless / With time," one who understands that "Only through time time is conquered."[66] Eliot imagines this dance as a resumption of an earlier organic society (depicted as a rural village dancing) and as fundamentally sacramental in nature.[67] Only an oral defense shy of a Harvard Ph.D. in philosophy, Eliot offers a philosophical summary of the literary tropes I have traced over the course of this book.

But a major change has occurred here—one so obvious that it could easily be missed. The concerns of liturgical poetry remain, but the liturgical structure is absent. A few critics have argued that the *Four Quartets* is implicitly structured around the Anglican liturgical calendar.[68] But this argument is doubtful—it holds only if a liturgical poem can rearrange the order of the liturgical calendar to fit its own progression, rather than vice-versa[69]—and ultimately beside the point. In the *Four Quartets*, the liturgy and liturgical calendar have unquestionably faded into the background. One cannot argue about whether *The Christian Year* is structured around the liturgical calendar, or about whether the liturgical processions in *Murder in the Cathedral* are liturgical in nature. In *Four Quartets,* Eliot analyzes the marriage rite, mentions major feasts like the Annunciation, and even (without naming the figure) briefly discusses, like Keble, the death of King Charles I.[70] But these are passing references in a work that is just as likely in its quest to reestablish meaning in the modern world to employ Buddhist imagery (the lotus) or Hindu ideas (illumination and analytical meditation), narratives (the story of Krishna), and ethical philosophy (acting without desiring the fruit of action).[71] The poem no longer attempts to pull the audience into an explicitly liturgical world, or assumes that the Anglican liturgy can construct a shared community.

For all its philosophical ambition, the poem's goals are more modest. The *Four Quartets* derive their structure from the natural seasons and Eliot's personal experience and family history. As this structure suggests, meaning is now either private and shared intersubjectively or perhaps natural and inevitable, if only our gaze were not diverted from it (as a flood forces us to notice the river over which we usually drive on a bridge in a car). The poem can perhaps be seen as a kind of philosophical preamble to the liturgy, schooling the audience in the kind of questions to which the liturgy can serve as a meaningful answer. But the liturgy itself—a shared communal meaning, consciously constructed but also organic—has been pushed to the margins of the text, either dissolving into its background or lingering just beyond its horizon. The final quartet, "Little Gidding," is named for an Anglican monastic community, in which both celibates and married couples lived a life strictly focused around the liturgy.[72] But "Little Gidding" is an abandoned structure that is as dead as Charles I, and has been for about as long. Eliot's hope for a Christian society, a liturgical world, has faded.

To look at why, I turn to Eliot's principal publication of 1943 besides the *Four Quartets*, his largely forgotten pamphlet *Reunion by Destruction: Reflections on a Scheme for Church Union in South India.* In *Reunion by Destruction* Eliot expresses his fears that the Church of England is for reasons of polity abandoning its claims to be organic and divine. Christian leaders in South India were seeking to bring Protestant bodies as various in doctrine and ecclesiastical structure as the Methodist, Presbyterian, Congregationalist, and Anglican churches into a single communion. The hope was that a united witness would help efforts at evangelization in India and better reflect the Gospel's vision of Christian unity. But the proposed terms of union for the Church of South India allowed, out of a respect for ecumenical diversity, clergy who had not been ordained by bishops possessing apostolic succession to consecrate the Eucharistic elements in Anglican parishes. The new church would not require its members to believe in the principle of apostolic succession and would postpone a definitive decision as to whether it would adopt an episcopal structure until a period after reunion had been achieved. And, regardless of these concessions, the newly formed Church of South India would remain part of the Anglican Communion.

For Low Church and Broad Church Anglicans, these may have been minor compromises, or even ecumenically desirable developments. But for Anglo-Catholics, as Eliot observes, apostolic succession is tied to "the validity of orders and the validity of the Sacraments," and even the sacred character of the church itself.[73] As the title of his pamphlet suggests, Eliot saw this deliberate abandonment of the principle of apostolic succession in the name of ecumenism as tantamount to the end of the Anglican Communion as a divine, organic entity, as "a living member of one visible Church"; henceforth, the Anglican Church would be merely a political arrangement, not a "church" properly called, but simply a "society."[74] Eliot argues that when a church is willing for purposes of practical expediency and polity to compromise its organic structure it then becomes "an organ of the totalitarian state, charged with the preservation of morality in the interest of that state. It would be a National Church, not in the sense of representing the true religious spirit of the people, but as a department of the Board of Education. As a Church, it would be only a shell."[75] He writes his lengthy pamphlet protesting the proposed Church of South India because he is "concerned . . . that the Church of England should not be *destroyed* (Eliot's italics).[76]

Eliot lost his protest, and while he never left the Church, his hopes that it could renew the community and world began to fade. He had earlier asserted that "the idea of a Christian society . . . can only be realized, in England, through the Church of England."[77] And now the Church of England had deliberately weakened and perhaps lost its vertical tie to the higher times of Christ and the apostles and had compromised its sacramental structure, and thereby its plausibility as a synecdoche of a sacramental world. Eliot was logically consistent enough to recognize the probably mortal blow offered by this development to his hopes for an organic, liturgical England. He continued to worship in the Church of England, but (until his late second marriage) planned ultimately to withdraw from the world into an Anglican monastery[78]; he sought an alternate world of liturgical meaning now that the possibility of England itself becoming that world had collapsed.

The *Four Quartets* sets the tone for Eliot's postwar verse dramas. His works will continue to reflect the vision that a meaningful world and a meaningful approach to time must ultimately be liturgical in nature. But his hope that the audience could share this vision, that a liturgical immersion experiment could create a shared community, that the Anglo-Catholic subculture could become the common culture, has disappeared. The need for liturgical meaning can still be depicted—and the audience is summoned to recognize this need, this lack, in itself—but a liturgical world lies beyond the margins of the text. If Sayers will directly confront the postwar world with the liturgical universe it has lost, Eliot will approach postwar audiences obliquely and indirectly, gesturing toward values and concepts he believes they need but which he assumes they presently can neither imagine nor understand. He enacts this approach most explicitly in his first major postwar work, *The Cocktail Party*, which debuted on Broadway in January 1950.

The Cocktail Party was Eliot's most successful postwar production, both commercially and critically; it was a Broadway hit that, with Sir Alec Guinness as the unconventional existential psychologist Sir Henry Harcourt-Reilly, won the Tony Award for best play. Reilly is initially identified merely as the "Unidentified Guest" at a party to which no one seems to have invited him. He enjoys this status, observing, "It's easier to talk to a person you don't know."[79] Reilly continues to keep the other characters, and the audience, off-balance. For most of the play he peppers his fellow party-goers with perceptive questions about their motives and proffers devastating critiques of their behavior. He makes them question both their actions and what they think they know about human identity (308), but until act 2 his own identity and philosophy cannot be determined. He will keep the other main characters in the dark. And, as he observes,

There is certainly no purpose in remaining in the dark
Except long enough to clear from the mind
The illusion of having ever been in the light. (309)

The Cocktail Party assumes the death of the traditional English social order, which lingers merely as a simulacrum; the play's only aristocratic manor house has decayed and is now being reproduced in California as a film set (377–78). In the character of Reilly, Eliot grapples with the rhetorical challenge of enunciating a religious and liturgical vision to this changed England. Eliot seems to suggest that in postwar England a voice that speaks from a specific religious position will be automatically dismissed before it can be heard; the audience can hear the truth only from a stranger. Reilly's few explicit religious references tend to be eclectic and syncretic in nature.[80] Instead of religious discourse, Reilly uses poetry, a heavily revised version of psychoanalysis (one that emphasizes the present moment and distrusts childhood memory), and the categories of existential philosophy (such as the subject/object distinction) to make the play's other characters realize that they are "nothing but a set of obsolete responses" and shake them out of their habitual ways of living and perceiving (383, 348, 307–8).

Alone among Reilly's patients, the poet Celia Coplestone discovers the possibility of depth or transcendence on her own. Reilly assists Celia, who has just ended a love affair with a married man, primarily by affirming the authenticity of her experience. In her affair, she felt what it meant to break from egocentrism and embrace the Other (363) and to live in a world charged with meaning where chronological time had come to a complete stop. She tells her lover at the conclusion of their affair,

I abandoned the future before we began,
And after that I lived in a present
Where time was meaningless[.] (324)

She finds that the phenomenological significance of her experience remains, even if she now realizes that the relationship itself was an illusion. She laments that her lover was

a projection—
I see that now—of something that I wanted—
No, not *wanted*—something that I aspired to—
Something that I desperately wanted to exist.
It must happen somewhere—but what, and where is it?
(327, Eliot's italics)

What she needs from Reilly are conceptual terms to describe her transcendent experience and to validate its phenomenological legitimacy; otherwise, she will attempt to dismiss it as madness and return to the quotidian as the only reality (363).

Reilly is in the difficult position of trying to help characters who live in this postwar world of surfaces, devoid of depth or substance, to find their own depth and substance. Reilly's patients, like the play's California-movie manor house, exist primarily "in the phantasmal world" (365). For the most part, their attempts to seek self-discovery or to reveal their dark, hidden depths simply mimic a preexisting social script (355, 348). And they are deeply post-Christian. As Celia explains, "Well, my upbringing was pretty conventional— / I had always been taught to disbelieve in sin" (361).

Morality is passé, and violations of social norms are now condemned either as "bad form" or the result of psychological "kinks." But, as Celia realizes, these condemnations have no force, and an age of expressive individualism is coming or is now here; in practice, individuals are already left alone to work out their desire-based identities. She explains that

I don't worry much about form, myself—
But when everything's bad form, or mental kinks,
You either become bad form, and cease to care,
Or else, if you care, you must be kinky. (360)

In sum, Reilly addresses characters prey to the problems of a postwar Age of Authenticity not through a specifically religious discourse but by employing each of the principal secular discourses of the time capable of rehabilitating the notion of depth. Like *Murder in the Cathedral*, *The Cocktail Party* constitutes a late modernist attempt to make the audience reexamine the frame through which it perceives the world. But unlike the earlier work, *The Cocktail Party* lacks an alternative shared frame to offer the audience. Reilly possesses only fragments of liturgy.

Reilly is acutely aware of the limits of his approach. The influence of Søren Kierkegaard on *The Cocktail Party* has often been noted,[81] and like one of Kierkegaard's pseudononymous authors, Reilly offers an interpretation of the world that is coherent on its own terms but that also gestures toward a religious vision that he cannot articulate within its frame. He sends each of his patients on the way with the benediction "Go in peace . . . / Work out your salvation with diligence" (366). This parting blessing is the closest he approaches toward the language of the Authorized Version of the Bible and the Anglican liturgy. St. Paul tells the Philippians—in the King James Version—to "work out your own salvation in fear and trembling" (2:12) and mass in the *Anglican Missal* ends with the priest proclaiming, "Depart in peace." Reilly's words are almost a priestly proclamation. But they are his culminating words—he says nothing to each patient beyond them—and he does not feel that he himself fully comprehends their meaning. Speaking of Celia, he observes,

And when I say to one like her,
"Work out your salvation with diligence," I do not understand
What I myself am saying. (368)

He can lead people to the brink of a liturgical understanding of the world, but like Moses on Pisgah he cannot quite cross over. Poetry, psychanalysis, and existential philosophy can perhaps articulate the need for liturgical meaning, but they are not conceptually capable of articulating that meaning, or of imagining what a liturgical subject would look like.

Celia is the one character in the play who, unlike Reilly, is capable of herself becoming a liturgical subject. The play's attempt to depict her can serve to represent the quandaries involved in attempting to enunciate liturgical subjectivity in the postwar era. The play depicts her transformation from a character of surfaces to a character of depth, and her desire to retain this sense of depth although the affair that first triggered it has ended. Reilly tells her that she can preserve her sense of depth and heightened meaning if she chooses to enter what he calls in psychological terms "the sanatorium" (365–66). This particular "sanatorium," in which people seeking psychological wholeness lead a collective life focused around a transcendent meaning, is actually a convent. But the audience is never informed of this fact until after Celia has exited the play near the end of the second act, and never sees her life as a nun. The third act opens two years later, at another party, with guests whose conversations relate the remainder of Celia's life in summary form: she first became a missionary nun, then was assigned to nursing work (which she had also performed as a volunteer in World War II), and finally was martyred (380–81, cf. 375). She was crucified at the hands of cannibals, perhaps in part cannibalistically consumed, and then eaten by ants (380–81). The original version of the play adds the detail that native population afterward out of guilt began venerating her as a saint, "erect[ing] a sort of shrine for Celia" and placing offerings before it.[82]

Ultimately, Celia is as much an embodiment of the liturgy as Eliot's Thomas Becket; she *is* the mass. After her liturgically centered life as a nun, she reenacts Christ's death, is consumed in Eucharistic fashion, and venerated like a saint with ritual prayers and offerings (albeit of dubious orthodoxy). But the audience stands in a very different relation to Celia than it did to Thomas Becket. In *Murder in the Cathedral*, both the chorus and audience were confronted with the liturgical figure of Becket and made to watch his execution in a gruesome extended scene. In *The Cocktail Party*, no one is "forced"—or even allowed—"to bear witness." Literally and figuratively, Eliot has abandoned the chorus, a central element of both of his prewar plays but absent from all his postwar drama. Celia's entire liturgical and religious life occurs off-stage and is narrated long after the fact in summary form by third parties. Even more: she consummates her status as the embodiment of the liturgy precisely at the moment when she becomes literally disembodied. As her friend Peter Quilpe complains about an earlier absence, "She has simply faded—into some other picture— / Like a film effect" (315). Celia's transformation is incapable of being depicted in the world of the play. She belongs in another story, told in another time. The liturgical subject is difficult to envision and enunciate in the Age of Authenticity. In the figure of Celia, Eliot gestures toward liturgical subjectivity, but he has given up on asking the audience to experience it, leaving the matter to the rare theatergoer who like Celia herself is already capable of imagining transcendence but lacks the terms to enunciate it.

The Confidential Clerk of Eliot's play of the same name, his last popular success (1953), will undergo the same transformation, equally off-stage. Colby Simpkins discovers the possibility of depth and an inner life through his love of music, and—the play's most reliable character predicts—after the play is over will become an Anglican priest.[83] The need for a world of depth rather than mere surfaces is again fulfilled only in the liturgy, and again this liturgical subjectivity exists only beyond the frame of the play. Each play prods the individual viewer already in the proper existential position to consider questions it cannot within its restrictions answer and worlds it cannot within its genre depict. In this manner, Eliot attempts to continue to convey his liturgical vision to a postwar audience, even as his hopes for a revived community and remade world fade.

And, more than Sayers, he has a certain measure of ironic success. Eliot's postwar work spoke to many and, to a certain extent, continues to speak to many in an Age of Authenticity. His existentialism, his religious eclecticism, even his injunction to reject convention and look past the surface of things could mark him as an "authentic" figure. He was the most celebrated literary figure of the postwar epoch, his status not fading until the massive literary critical upheavals of the 1970s.[84] *The Cocktail Party* was the toast of Broadway, and was seen by over one and a half million people in its initial theatrical runs in England and America.[85] Via Andrew Lloyd Webber, Eliot has remained the toast of Broadway. *Cats* (1982), Lloyd Webber's adaptation of Eliot's children's poetry into an adult theatrical musical, is still the fourth-longest-running play in Broadway history, and has been recently revived. And when Lloyd Webber wished to insert a moment of contemplation and profundity into the world of *Cats*, he naturally turned to the *Four Quartets*, transforming a complicated philosophical rumination from "The Dry Salvages" into a short musical number with the incredibly un-Eliotic title "The Moments of Happiness." Any quick journey through the blogosphere will attest that many self-proclaimed religious "seekers" of a more introspective and less music hall turn of mind are still fond of quoting the *Four Quartets*.

But it was Eliot's secular discourses of depth, not the larger liturgical world to which they pointed, that attained a certain vogue. In a word, Reilly, not Celia. Eliot's liturgical vision has been bracketed off and forgotten. No one has been quite sure what to make of Celia, who has confused readers and theater-goers since the play was released and who (as a silenced female poet) has also drawn the ire of feminist critics.[86] Most readers could not conceive—much less seriously entertain—the possibility that she is not so much silenced as silent, and that her kenotic silence points toward presently unspeakable liturgical mysteries. The world she represents lies too far outside our conceptual horizon to be seriously contemplated. When Eliot is being attacked by a literary critic or blogger, he is typically dismissed as "a conservative Christian" or "an Anglican traditionalist." When he remains an authority, he is praised as an inter-religious philosopher or seeker.[87] Dorothy L. Sayers's wartime and postwar creative work has been largely forgotten, ironically preserved only by an American Evangelical Protestant subculture that rejects both her sacramental theology and her social vision.[88] Her publisher presents Sayers in the sole terms in which she is remembered by the general public; she is "the Mistress of the Golden Age Mystery." The later Eliot survives—but only as edited into a reflection of the Age of Authenticity.

IV

As Dorothy L. Sayers and T. S. Eliot struggled to enunciate a liturgical vision to the postwar world, the Anglican Church was itself was wrestling with the question of whether a new age required a new liturgy. What sort of liturgy could speak to a world where collective forms were themselves suspect? The answers at which the Anglican Church arrived mark both the termination and the ironic consummation of the project of Anglican liturgical long poem.

In the second half of the twentieth century, the liturgical reform movement idealistically unraveled the received liturgies of most major Western churches. By the 1950s, Catholic and Anglican liturgical reformers had come to view the medieval liturgies from which both the Book of Common Prayer and the Roman Rite were derived not as an ideal form of worship originating in a lost Age of Faith, but as a corruption of a simpler primitive liturgy. They postulated that this primitive liturgy had possessed no single, original form, but rather a basic common shape that was flexible and adaptable to local variation.[89] The liturgical reformers employed the rhetoric of a return to origins to question and undermine the forms of liturgy with which the laity were familiar, but simultaneously dismantled the idea that the Christian liturgy originated in a higher time, fundamentally different from the present era. Both diversity of rite and intercommunal conflict had marked Christianity from the beginning. The type of liturgical thought that informed Keble and Rossetti's poetry was now held to be mistaken at the root; no divine, apostolic liturgy existed for the faithful to preserve or recover. The received liturgies of both Anglicanism and Roman Catholicism began to lose their prescriptive force, and liturgical revision became the order of the day. If liturgies had originally been designed to speak to specific communities in specific local circumstances, then liturgy should now be correspondingly "updated" or "modernized," adapted to fit the new epoch.

The often-repeated goal of the liturgical movement was to renew the liturgy by producing "full, conscious, and active" lay participation.[90] Previously, the liturgy's authority had been connected to the sacred—set apart—character of its language; its beauty and otherness would transform the auditor. The Latin Roman Catholic liturgy is an obvious case in point, but similar claims were made for Cranmerian English. But now, to encourage full participation, the liturgy would (to use the common expression) meet people where they were; it, too, would try to resonate with the individual and achieve authenticity. On a basic level, this principle requires the use of an informal, colloquial liturgical language—which itself requires a state of continual liturgical revision, since informal language is constantly changing.[91] Although she was not in principle opposed to liturgical reform, Dorothy L. Sayers had earlier warned the colloquializers about the pragmatic difficulties their project would entail:

"I agree to some extent about the archaic words and unreal sentiments, only I think this is rather a matter for explanation in sermons and instructions than for alterations in the liturgy. It's no good running anxiously out with new words, trying to keep pace with changes in language—it takes all the running we can do to make words stay in the same place."[92]

On a more philosophical level, the liturgical reformers have entirely reversed Keble's liturgical theory. Keble thought that the Prayer Book possessed a divine music which itself reflected the music of heaven; the believer could through careful listening bring himself or herself into tune with its music, thereby renewing self and community and gaining a new vision of the world. Now the service is to be altered to come into tune with the rhythms of the worshipper (quite literally in the state of contemporary church music).

T. S. Eliot had supported the *English Missal*, an experimental liturgy that attempted to connect Anglican worship to liturgical forms that were seen as both more ancient and more universal than those contained in the Book of Common Prayer. But he acutely sensed the dilemma that liturgical "updating" posed for the liturgical poet. After in old age he had already abandoned poetry, Eliot to his annoyance was chosen by the Church of England to serve on a committee charged with updating the Anglican Psalter. Eliot was the only respected poet in a body that consisted largely of clergy schooled in Hebrew or lay theologians like C. S. Lewis. Each of the poets in this study has grappled with the difficulty of translating the liturgy into poetry. The liturgy derives its force from the fact that it is a collective sacred text rather than an individual creation. But in an age of expressive individualism, an Age of Authenticity, this power threatens to be transformed instead into alienation, the collective text seeming to erase the individual. Liturgical poetry, for each of the authors in this study, tries to bridge the gap between the individual and the collective by depicting the vision of liturgical subjectivity. But this poetic project could easily—and accidentally—transfer the locus of textual and spiritual authority from the liturgy itself to the poetry that reframes it. In a provocative essay, John Henry Newman suggests that Keble's *The Christian Year* actually sacralizes the Book of Common Prayer rather than the reverse. He writes of Keble, "[H]is poems became a sort of comment upon its [the Anglican Church's] formularies and ordinances, and almost *elevated* them into the dignity of a religious system" (italics mine).[93] The publication history of *The Christian Year*, which was issued in a series of editions increasingly physically indistinguishable from the Prayer Book itself, may bear Newman out.

Whether Newman's claim is accurate or not, he has expressed the nightmare of the liturgical poet, a fundamental deconstruction of his or endeavor. In the era of liturgical revision, T. S. Eliot was destined to live this nightmare. The poet is now explicitly commissioned to rewrite the liturgy, his or her poetry is to become the liturgy, and even lend its credibility to the liturgy. Eliot was conscious of the difficulty this task posed for the authority of the liturgy. While he did contribute his poetic gifts to the *Revised Psalter*, his most frequent role in the proceedings was to argue for the poetic superiority of the wording of Coverdale's Psalms to that of any of their proposed replacements. Much more than any other member of the committee—even the conservative C. S. Lewis—he was aware of the vexed nature of the task at hand, and continually sought a definition of the committee's work that would emphasize preservation over revision.[94] The more progressive committee members both complained about Eliot's supposed lack of contribution to the revision of the Psalter and hoped to use his name to "sell" the *Revised Psalter*.[95] And this is the difficulty of the Anglo-Catholic liturgical poet at the end of the tradition: he must insist that the Anglican liturgy stands apart from and above him, ordering the world in which he lives, but the bishops think the *Revised Psalter* will sell only if people think he wrote it. The liturgy is now to be evaluated primarily in terms of public response, and the Nobel-Prize winning Eliot possesses a level of cultural capital that the Book of Common Prayer now lacks.

This emphasis on public response logically requires not just the constantly shifting liturgical language that so dismayed Sayers and Eliot, but a potentially infinite number of liturgies. The premise that individual resonance is the measure of a faith inherently undermines the idea of a collective national worship, as the colloquial language and felt needs of no two congregations are exactly the same. And the trajectory of the Anglican liturgy over the course of the last fifty years has been correspondingly centrifugal. As befits the Age of Authenticity, "Flexibility, options, and alternatives" are the order of the day.[96] The 1662 Book of Common Prayer is still legally normative in England, but provisionally since 1966 and permanently since 1974, parishes are no longer required to use it in worship; the Acts of Uniformity have been legally repealed.[97] Liturgical experimentation began on an ad-hoc basis in the late 1960s; by 1980 and the *Alternative Service Book*, the Anglican Church had begun to provide parishes dissatisfied with the language of the Book of Common Prayer with a variety of official options. The present instantiation of this project, first issued in 2000, is *Common Worship*. The contents of *Common Worship* belie the name; the volume contains multiple liturgies for varying theological tastes, including no fewer than twelve options for the Eucharistic Prayer alone.[98] In fact, *Common Worship* possesses so many different liturgical options that printing it in its entirety has proved impracticable; it is over 3,600 pages long, and its full contents exist only online.[99] It is designed for the priest to pick and choose online a particular approach to worship, and print out only what is desired.[100] In an effort to speak to the Age of Authenticity, the Church of England has abandoned the vision of a uniform national worship. In the era of *Common Worship*, the literary tradition of structuring individual experience and literary form on the basis of a common liturgy not only ceases to exist; it becomes conceptually impossible.

Liturgical reform has also involved alterations to the liturgical calendar, and the altered liturgical calendar of *Common Worship* can serve to conclude this study. The desire to bring the liturgy closer to the worshipper has resulted in a proliferation of Anglican saints' days from some few postbiblical examples, to hundreds of locally admired post-Reformation figures, some of whom (like Dietrich Bonhoeffer) never belonged to the Anglican Communion and others of whom (like John Henry Newman) intentionally left it; worshipers will be more readily inspired, it is thought, by the examples of saints with whom they can more easily identify. In this expanded Anglican *sanctorale*, both John Keble and Christina Rossetti are now venerated with their own feast days (July 14 and April 27, respectively). Like the King Charles the Martyr of Keble's imagination, Keble and Rossetti were shaped by the liturgical calendar, lived and wrote according to the liturgical calendar, and have now been assumed into the liturgical calendar. Ironically, they become part of the calendar only in the volume *Common Worship*, the adoption of which eliminated the liturgical world to which they belonged; they are canonized the moment their poetic projects become impossible and cease to challenge or trouble us.

NOTES

1. See Hylson-Smith, *High Churchmanship*, 256–57.

2. See Forrester, "A Free Society Today?" in Reeves, *Christian Thinking*, 211; Haberman, *Myth, Memory*, 113.

3. Ina Haberman quotes Priestley's radio broadcasts at some length in *Myth, Memory*, 113.

4. Marsden, "William Temple," 214, 229.

5. Marsden, "William Temple," 227. The slogan is Temple's own.

6. See Reeves and Taylor, "Intellectuals in Debate," in Reeves, *Christian Thinking*, 24–26, 34–35.

7. Reeves and Kaye, "Tracts for War-Time," in Reeves, *Christian Thinking*, 50, 52.

8. Sayers to Maurice Reckitt, November 19, 1941, in *Letters*, 2: 319.

9. Sayers's biographer and friend Barbara Reynolds credits Eliot's *Idea of a Christian Society* with persuading Sayers to join the Christian Social Order movement (*Dorothy L. Sayers*, 295–96). On her skepticism about Eliot's ability to write for children or the masses, see her March 21, 1940, letter to Rev. T. A. O'Neil and Rev. A. M. Stack in *Letters*, 2: 155–57.

For his own part, Eliot—though he corresponded politely with Sayers and worked carefully with her on the Christian Social Order movement—considered

Sayers's openly polemical theological essays to be a degraded form of religious writing. He sent a friend the doggerel poem "Wee Dolly Sayers" to mock her approach (in Ricks and Hue, *The Complete Poems* 2:197).

10. See Eliot, *The Idea*, 51.

11. Eliot, *The Idea*, 51.

12. Eliot, *The Idea*, 48.

13. Sayers, *Mind of the Maker*, 218; "Creed or Chaos," 68.

14. Marsden, "William Temple," 228–29.

15. Eliot, *The Idea*, 14–15, 50.

16. Eliot, *The Idea*, 12–13.

17. Eliot, *The Idea*, 50. See also Sayers, *Making Sense*, 13–14.

18. On this position as one generally held by the Christian Social Order Movement, see Platt, foreword, in Reeves, *Christian Thinking*, ix.

19. Eliot, *The Idea*, 50.

20. Sayers, "Creed or Chaos," 107.

21. Eliot's *Idea of a Christian Society*, for all its nuances, has been judged the least "pluralist" of the major works on Christian Social Order (Forrester, "A Free Society Today?" in Reeves, *Christian Thinking*, 211). For Sayers's insistence that liturgy is indispensable for a meaningful world, see "Worship in the Anglican Church," 48.

22. Sayers, *Begin Here*, x.

23. Eliot, *The Idea*, 37.

24. Eliot, *The Idea*, 23.

25. Eliot, *The Idea*, 50, 18.

26. Eliot, *The Idea*, 49.

27. Eliot, "Why Work," 128, 132.

28. Esty, *A Shrinking Island*, 18, 109.

29. The details of this project are related in Simmons, *Creed without Chaos*, appendix C. I have been unable to determine whether the plan was carried out. But that the project was taken seriously, both by Sayers and others, shows that liturgical radio was not considered a contradiction in terms at the BBC at this point.

30. Pitt's observation is quoted in Rosendale's survey of the cultural impact of the Book of Common Prayer (Rosendale, *Liturgy and Literature*, 7).

31. See Marsden, "William Temple," 214, 228.

32. See Forrester, "A Free Society Today?" in Reeves, *Christian Thinking*, 211.

33. Marsden, "William Temple," 229.

34. On this point, see C. Brown, *The Death,* 5–6.

35. Taylor typically speaks of the Age of Authenticity as a phenomenon of the 1960s and after, but also sometimes references the 1950s as its starting point, particularly as regards postwar individualism and consumerism, and the idealization of "choice" (Taylor, *A Secular Age*, 474, 479).

36. Miller, *Late Modernism*, 9; Genter, *Late Modernism*, 315, 321.

37. Taylor, *A Secular Age*, 474.

38. As Ina Haberman notes, by 1951 "the practice of seeing Englishness as a symbolic form was very much on the wane" and World War II has come to be seen

in English popular culture "as the last time the nation appeared united" (Haberman, *Myth, Memory*, 23, 29).

39. Taylor, *A Secular Age*, 475.
40. See Taylor, *A Secular Age*, 489, 508, 512–14.
41. Taylor, *A Secular Age*, 521–22, 516, 479.
42. Taylor, *A Secular Age*, 515.
43. C. Brown, *The Death*, 6–7.
44. C. Brown, *The Death*, 187.
45. Wolffe, *God and Greater Britain*, 70.
46. C. Brown, *The Death*, 188.
47. C. Brown, *The Death*, 8.
48. Spurr quotes these words of Eliot's in a longer discussion of Eliot's postwar religious beliefs (Spurr, *Anglo-Catholic in Religion*, 193).
49. Where possible, I will cite "The Pantheon Papers" as republished in book form. This version includes a print of the stained-glass window, which is absent from the pages of *Punch* that I have been able to procure. For the portions of "More Pantheon Papers" that have never been published in book form, I will cite the titles of particular articles from the series as it appeared in the pages of *Punch*.
50. Sayers, "The Pantheon Papers," 2.
51. Sayers, "The Pantheon Papers," 4.
52. Sayers, "The Pantheon Papers," 2.
53. Sayers, "The Pantheon Papers," 3.
54. Sayers, "The Pantheon Papers," 5.
55. Sayers, "More Pantheon Papers: The Cosmic Synthesis," 84.
56. Sayers, "More Pantheon Papers: The Cosmic Synthesis," 84.
57. Sayers, "More Pantheon Papers: Kalendar," 60.
58. T. S. Eliot, *The Elder Statesman, 26.*
59. Sayers, "The Pantheon Papers," 5.
60. Sayers, "The Pantheon Papers," 5.
61. Sayers, "The Pantheon Papers," 5.
62. Sayers, "The Pantheon Papers," 4.
63. Esty, *A Shrinking Island*, 18.
64. Eliot, "The Dry Salvages," I, lines 37–38.
65. Eliot, "The Dry Salvages," II, lines 38–40.
66. Eliot, "The Dry Salvages," V, lines 17–18; Burnt Norton, II, lines 43.
67. Eliot, "East Coker," I, lines 23–46.
68. See, for example, Sexton, *Four Quartets*, 279–80.
69. In Sexton's analysis, Eliot's poem moves from the Ascension ("Burnt Norton") to Good Friday ("East Coker") to the Annunciation ("Dry Salvages") to Pentecost ("Little Gidding"). Since the Ascension invariably falls between Good Friday and Pentecost, even if this argument were true, Eliot would not be accepting the liturgical year as a transcendent basis for his literary structure, but rather employing liturgical images in a poem the structure of which is fundamentally independent of the liturgical calendar.

70. Eliot, "East Coker," I, lines 28–30; "Dry Salvages," II, line 36; "Little Gidding," I, line 26.

71. See Eliot, "Burnt Norton" I, line 36; "The Dry Salvages," III; "Little Gidding" III, lines 1–7.

72. Under the leadership of Deacon Nicholas Ferrar, Little Gidding's inhabitants attended daily service and prayed in common each of the Psalms designated for the day in the Anglican calendar (Blackstone, *The Ferrar Papers*, 40). Little Gidding was controversial—and was eventually destroyed by the Puritans—precisely because it took the Prayer Book too seriously as a means of structuring life, becoming what its opponents called an "Arminian Nunnery." For Ferrar, the Church of England is divine, and the Book of Common Prayer is the Church of England. Ferrar's "Commemoration Prayer," recited annually by the community, attributes the authorship of the "heavenly songs" the community recites to the "holy Spiritt it self" [*sic*] and equates the community's liturgical worship with that of heaven (Blackstone, *The Ferrar Papers*, 241).

73. Eliot, *Reunion by Destruction*, 460.

74. Eliot, *Reunion by Destruction*, 458.

75. Eliot, *Reunion by Destruction*, 465.

76. Eliot, *Reunion by Destruction*, 463.

77. Eliot, *The Idea*, 37.

78. On Eliot's intention to enter the Anglican monastery Nashdom Abbey, see Spurr, *Anglo-Catholic in Religion*, 87.

79. The lines quoted are from page 304 of T. S. Eliot, *The Cocktail Party*. In *Complete Poems and Plays: 1909–1950* (New York: Harcout, Brace, and Company, 1967). Unless otherwise noted, text references are to page numbers from this edition.

80. A case in point: if Reilly and his coworkers chant a kind of litany blessing both married life ("the hearth") and religious life (the "travelers"), their words belong to no unknown religious rite, address no specific deity ("the Moon" is invoked as well as "the holy ones"), and evoke a social structure as redolent of the Hindu Upanishads (which affirmed the householder and the wanderer as stages of life) as of medieval Catholicism (368–69).

81. Kierkegaard's influence on Eliot has long been noted, and the recently published collected letters date his knowledge of Kierkegaard's basic ideas back at least to the early 1930s. The echoes of Kierkegaard in *A Cocktail Party* in particularly were observed as early as the 1960 article by Thomas Hazno, "Eliot and Kierkegaard: The Meaning of 'Happening' in *The Cocktail Party* (*Modern Drama 3* [1960]: 52–59). Roger Duncan's more recent article "Drinks and Dinner with Kierkegaard" (Duncan, *Logos: A Journal of Catholic Thought and Culture* 12, no. 2 (May 2009): 125–43) offers a persuasive reading of *The Cocktail Party* in terms of Kierkegaard's aesthetic, ethical and religious categories of development.

82. T. S. Eliot, *The Cocktail Party* (New York: Harcourt, Brace, and Company, 1950), 181–82.

83. Eliot, *The Confidential Clerk*, 50–51, 125.

84. If any support is needed to establish Eliot's cultural pervasiveness prior to deconstruction's rise to critical dominance in the 1980s one might reference Chris

Baldick's history of literary criticism, which notes that Eliot set the terms for literary critical discussion from the early 1920s to the mid-1960s (Baldick, *The Social Mission*, 64). Or one might reference the fact that as late as 1981 even so unlikely a figure as Barack Obama felt the need to engage with and felt some reluctant affinity for his social criticism (for the full text of Obama's comments, see Mendelson, "Obama as Literary Critic," paragraphs 5–8).

85. Smith, *T. S. Eliot's Poetry*, 259.

86. On the audience's confused reaction to Celia, see Smith, *T. S. Eliot's Poetry*, 254. For a feminist critique of Celia, see Laura Severin's article "Cutting Philomena's Tongue: *The Cocktail Party*'s Cure for a Disorderly World" *Modern Drama* 36, no. 3 (Sept. 1993): 396–408.

87. For a summary of recent scholarship on T. S. Eliot that treats him as a poet of "universal religious experience," of spirituality rather than religion, see Glenn Hughes, *A More Beautiful Question: The Spiritual in Poetry and Art* (Columbia: University of Missouri Press, 2011), especially pages 101–4.

88. Evangelical Protestant publishers are responsible for almost all the reprints of Sayers's religious essays that I have cited in this chapter. Sayers's essay "The Lost Tools of Learning" is often cited as the inspiration for the Evangelical Christian "Classical School" movement in the United States (see, for example, Matt Forster's essay, "Dorothy L. Sayers's Surprising Legacy" in *Christian History 113* [2015], https://christianhistoryinstitute.org/magazine/article/dorothy-l-sayers-surprising-legacy).

Evangelical Protestant appreciation for Sayers seems to be popularly based on an appreciation for her flamboyant religious confidence and for her friendship for evangelical icon C. S. Lewis (she is often seen as a kind of honorary female Inkling). Her Anglo-Catholicism is generally ignored.

89. Baldovin, "The Liturgical Movement," in Hefling and Shattuck, *The Oxford Guide*, 254.

90. Baldovin, "The Liturgical Movement," in Hefling and Shattuck, *The Oxford Guide*, 251–52.

91. See Buchanan, "The Winds of Change," in Hefling and Shattuck, *The Oxford Guide*, 236.

92. Sayers, to O'Neil and Stack, March 21, 1940, in *Letters* 2: 157.

93. Newman, "John Keble," 445.

94. Mussachio, "C. S. Lewis, T. S. Eliot," 46.

95. Mussachio, "C. S. Lewis, T. S. Eliot," 50–51.

96. Hefling, introduction in Hefling and Shattuck, *The Oxford Guide*, 5.

97. Lloyd, "The Church of England," in Hefling and Shattuck, *The Oxford Guide*, 413.

98. Baldovin, The Liturgical Movement," in Hefling and Shattuck, *The Oxford Guide*, 257.

99. Lloyd, "The Church of England," in Hefling and Shattuck, *The Oxford Guide*, 416; Jacobs, *The Book of Common Prayer*, 192.

100. Buchanan, "Preserving the Classical," 2 in Hefling and Shattuck, *The Oxford Guide*, 66.

Bibliography

Abrams, M. H. *The Mirror and the Lamp: Romantic Theory and the Critical Tradition.* Oxford: Oxford University Press, 1953.

Alexander, J. Neil. "The Shape of the Classical Book of Common Prayer." In Hefling and Shattuck, *Oxford Guide*, 64–72.

Althusser, Louis. "Ideology and Ideological State Apparatuses: Notes Toward an Investigation." Trans. Ben Brewster. New York, 1970; Marxists Internet Archive, n.d. https://www.marxists.org/reference/archive/althusser/1970/ideology.htm.

Armstrong, Isobel. "Christina Rossetti in the Era of the New Woman and fin de siècle Culture." *Journal of Pre-Raphaelite Studies* 13, no. 3 (2004): 21–48.

Arnold, Matthew. *Literature and Dogma.* London: Smith, Elder, and Co., 1909.

Arseneau, Mary. *Recovering Christina Rossetti: Female Community and Incarnational Poetics.* New York: Palgrave, 2004.

Asad, Talal. *Formations of the Secular: Christianity, Islam, Modernity.* Stanford: Stanford University Press, 2003.

Ayers, Robert W. "*Murder in the Cathedral*: A 'Liturgy Less Divine.'" *Texas Studies in Literature and Language: A Journal of the Humanities* 20 (1978): 579–98.

Baldick, Chris. *The Social Mission of English Criticism: 1848–1932.* Oxford: Clarendon Press, 1983.

Baldovin, John F. "The Liturgical Movement and Its Consequences." In Hefling and Shattuck, *Oxford Guide*, 249–60.

Basney, Lionel. "*The Nine Tailors* and the Complexity of Innocence." In *As Her Whimsey Took Her: Critical Essays on the Work of Dorothy L. Sayers*, edited by Margaret Hannay, 23–28. Kent, Ohio: Kent State University Press, 1979.

Baudrillard, Jean. *Simulacra and Simulation.* Translated by Sheila Faria Glaser. Ann Arbor: University of Michigan Press, 1994.

Bell, Catherine. *Ritual Theory, Ritual Practice.* New York: Oxford University Press, 1992.

Benjamin, Walter. "Theses on the Philosophy of History." In *Illuminations*, edited by Hannah Arendt, translated by Harry Zohn, 255–66. New York: Harcourt, Brace, and World, 1955.

Bergson, Henri. *The Creative Mind.* Translated by Mabelle Andison. New York: The Philosophical Library, 1946.

Blackstone, B., ed. *The Ferrar Papers: Containing* A Life of Nicholas Ferrar, The Winding-Sheet: An Ascetic Dialogue, *A Collection of Short Moral Histories, A Selection of Family Letters.* Cambridge: Cambridge University Press, 1938.

Blair, Kirstie. *Form and Faith in Victorian Poetry and Religion.* Oxford: Oxford University Press, 2012.

———. "John Keble and the Rhythm of Faith." *Essays in Criticism 53* (2003): 129–50.

———, ed. *John Keble in Context.* London: Anthem Press, 2004.

Brassley, Paul. "British Farming between the Wars." In *The English Countryside between the Wars: Regeneration or Decline?*, edited by Paul Brassley, Jeremy Burchardt, and Lynne Thompson, 187–99. Woodbridge, United Kingdom: The Boydell Press, 2006.

Brontë, Charlotte. *Jane Eyre.* 1847. London: Penguin Books, 1996.

Brown, Callum G. *The Death of Christian Britain: Understanding Secularisation, 1800 to 2000.* London: Routledge, 2001.

Brown, Janice. *The Seven Deadly Sins in the Work of Dorothy L. Sayers.* Kent, Ohio: Kent State University Press, 1998.

Buchanan, Colin. "Preserving the Classical Prayer Book." In Hefling and Shattuck, *Oxford Guide*, 261–67.

———. "The Winds of Change." In Hefling and Shattuck, *Oxford Guide*, 229–38.

Bulfin, Ailise. "'The End of Time': M. P. Shiel and the 'Apocalyptic Imaginary.'" In Ferguson, *Victorian Time*, 153–77.

Bump, Jerome. "The Victorian Radicals: Time, Typology, and Ontology in Hopkins, Pusey, and Muller." In *Victorian Religious Discourse: New Directions in Criticism*, edited by Jude Nixon, 27–49. New York: Palgrave MacMillan, 2004.

Bury, Liz. "Agatha Christie Wins Vote to Steal Crown as Crime Writers' Favourite Crime Writer." *The Guardian.* November 6, 2013. https://www.theguardian.com/books/2013/nov/06/agatha-christie-poll-best-ever-crime-writer.

Cantalupo, Catherine Musello. "Christina Rossetti: The Devotional Poet and the Rejection of Romantic Nature." In Kent, *The Achievement*, 274–300.

Carey, John. *The Intellectuals and the Masses: Pride and Prejudice among the Literary Intelligentsia, 1880–1939.* Chicago: Academy Chicago Press, 1992.

Chinitz, David. *T. S. Eliot and the Cultural Divide.* Chicago: University of Chicago Press, 2003.

The Church of England, The Book of Common Prayer. Standard (1662) Edition. Cambridge, England: Cambridge University Press, 2005.

———. *The Book of Common Prayer with the Additions and Deviations Proposed in 1928.* London: Society for Promoting Christian Knowledge, 1928.

Coleridge, Sir John T. *A Memoir of the Rev. John Keble, M. A., Late Vicar of Bursley.* 3rd ed. 1870. Westmead, England: Gregg International Press Limited, 1969.

Colón, Susan E. "'This Twittering World': T. S. Eliot and Acedia." *Religion and Literature* 43.2 (2011 Summer): 69–90.

Comte, Auguste. *The Positive Philosophy of Auguste Comte*. Edited and translated by Harriet Martineau. 3rd ed. Vol. I. London: Kegan Paul, Trench, Trübner and Company, 1893.

Corbett, Philip, and William Davage. *Defend and Maintain: A History of the Church Union 1859–2009*. London: Tufton Books, 2009.

D'Amico, Diane. *Christina Rossetti: Faith, Gender, and Time*. Baton Rouge: Louisiana State University Press, 1999.

———. "Christina Rossetti's *Christian Year*: Comfort for 'the weary heart.'" *The Victorian Newsletter* 72 (Fall 1987): 36–42.

D'Amico, Diane, and David Kent. "Rossetti and the Tractarians." *Victorian Poetry* 44, no. 1 (Spring 2006): 93–103.

Dangerfield, George. *The Strange Death of Liberal England: 1910–1914*. 1935. London: Transaction Publishers, 2011.

Davidson, Clifford. "T. S. Eliot's *Murder in the Cathedral* and the Saint's Play Tradition." *Papers on Language and Literature: A Journal for Scholars and Critics of Language and Literature* 21, no. 2 (Spring 1985): 152–69.

Davis, Thomas. "Late Modernism: British Literature at Midcentury." *Literature Compass* 9 (2012): 326–37.

Debord, Guy. *The Society of the Spectacle*. Translated by Donald Nicholson-Smith. New York: Zone Books, 1994.

Dennis, Barbara. Introduction to *The Heir of Redclyffe* by Charlotte Yonge, vii–xxv. Edited by Barbara Dennis. Oxford: Oxford University Press, 1997.

Dieleman, Karen. "Christina Rossetti, The Communion of Saints, and *Verses*." *The Journal of Pre-Raphaelite Studies* 15 (Spring 2006): 27–49.

———. *Religious Imaginaries: The Liturgical and Poetic Practices of Elizabeth Barrett Browning, Christina Rossetti, and Adelaide Proctor*. Athens: Ohio University Press, 2012.

Donahoe, Mary A. "The Sacramental Aesthetic in the Plays of Dorothy L. Sayers." Ph.D. diss., University of Oregon, 1993. Proquest (DA9238914).

Dove, George. "The Detection Formula and the Act of Reading." In *The Cunning Craft: Original Essays on Detective Fiction and Contemporary Literary Theory*, edited by Ronald Walker and June Frazer, 25–37. Macomb, Illinois: Essays in Literature, 1990.

Dowling, Linda. *Language and Decadence in the Victorian fin de siècle*. Princeton: Princeton University Press, 1989.

Downing, Crystal. *Writing Performances: The Stages of Dorothy L. Sayers*. New York: Palgrave, 2004.

During, Simon. "Completing Secularism: The Mundane in the Neoliberal Era." In Warner, VanAntwerpen, and Calhoun, *Varieties of Secularism*, 105–25.

Edgecombe, Rodney. *Two Poets of the Oxford Movement: John Keble and John Henry Newman*. Madison, Wisconsin: Farleigh Dickinson University Press, 1996.

Eliot, T. S. "The Bible as Scripture and Literature." 1932. In Eliot, *The Complete Prose* Vol. 4, 695–708.

———. "Building Up the Christian World." 1932. In Eliot, *The Complete Prose*, Vol. 4, 464–73.
———. "Catholicism and International Order." 1933. In Eliot, *The Complete Prose*, Vol. 4, 534–46.
———. "Christianity and Communism." 1932. In Eliot, *The Complete Prose*, Vol. 4, 422–31.
———. *The Cocktail Party*. New York: Harcourt, Brace, and Company, 1950.
———. *The Cocktail Party*. In *The Complete Poems and Plays 1909–1950*. New York: Harcourt, Brace, and Company, 1950.
———. *The Complete Prose of T. S. Eliot*. Edited by Jason Harding and Ronald Schuchard. Vol. 4: *English Lion, 1930–1933*. Baltimore: Johns Hopkins University Press, 2015.
———. *The Complete Prose of T. S. Eliot*. Edited by Iman Javadi, Ronald Schuchard, and Jayme Stayer. Vol. 5: *Tradition and Orthodoxy, 1934–1939*. Baltimore: Johns Hopkins University Press, 2017.
———. *The Complete Prose of T. S. Eliot*. Edited by David Chinitz and Ronald Schuchard. Vol. 6: *The War Years, 1940–1946*. Baltimore: Johns Hopkins University Press, 2017.
———. *The Confidential Clerk*. New York: Harcourt, Brace, and Company, 1953.
———. "A Dialogue on Dramatic Poetry." In Eliot, *Selected Essays*, 31–45. New York: Harcout, Brace, and Company, 1950.
———. *The Elder Statesman*. New York: Farrar, Straus, and Cudahy, 1959.
———. *Four Quartets*. In *The Complete Poems and Plays 1909–1950*. New York: Harcourt, Brace, and Company, 1980.
———. "The Idea of a Christian Society." In *Christianity and Culture*, 1–78. New York: Harcourt, Brace, and Company, 1949.
———. *The Letters of T. S. Eliot*. Edited by John Haffenden and Valerie Eliot. Volume 3: *1926–1927*. New Haven: Yale University Press, 2012.
———. *The Letters of T. S. Eliot*. Edited by John Haffenden and Valerie Eliot. Volume 4: *1928–1929*. New Haven: Yale University Press, 2013.
———. *The Letters of T. S. Eliot*. Edited by John Haffenden and Valerie Eliot. Volume 5: *1930–1931*. New Haven: Yale University Press, 2015.
———. *The Letters of T. S. Eliot*. Edited by John Haffenden and Valerie Eliot. Volume 6: *1932–1933*. New Haven: Yale University Press, 2016.
———. "The Modern Dilemma." In Eliot, *The Complete Prose*, Vol. 4, 810–16.
———. *Murder in the Cathedral*. In *Complete Poems and Plays: 1909–1950*. New York: Harcout, Brace, and Company, 1967.
———. "The Need for Poetic Drama." 1936. In Eliot, *The Complete Prose*, Vol. 5, 401–6.
———. "Notes on the Way." Jan. 1935. In Eliot, *The Complete Prose*, Vol. 5, 154–57.
———. "The *Pensées* of Pascal." In *Selected Essays: New Edition*, 355–68. New York: Harcourt, Brace, and Company, 1950.
———. "Poetry and Drama." 1951. In *On Poetry and Poets*, 72–88. London: Faber and Faber, 1957.

———. "Religion and Literature." 1935. In *Selected Prose*, edited by Frank Kermode, 97–106. New York: Harvest Books, 1975.

———. "Religion and Science: A Phantom Dilemma." 1932. In Eliot, *The Complete Prose*, Vol. 4, 436–45.

———. "Religion without Humanism." In Eliot, *The Complete* Prose, Vol. 4, 36–41.

———. *Reunion by Destruction: Reflections on a Scheme for Church Union in South India: Addressed to the Laity.* 1943. In Eliot, *The Complete* Prose, Vol. 6, 447–69.

———. "Thoughts after Lambeth." 1931. In *Selected Essays: New Edition*, 320–42. New York: Harcourt, Brace, and Company, 1950.

———. [Types of English Religious Verse]. 1940. In Eliot, *The Complete Prose*, Vol. 6, 46–62.

———. "Wee Dolly Sayers." In *The Complete Poems of T. S. Eliot*, edited by Christopher Ricks And Jim McCue, Volume II: *Practical Cats and Further Verses*, 197. Baltimore: John Hopkins University Press, 2015.

Esty, Jed. *A Shrinking Island: Modernism and National Culture in England.* Princeton: Princeton University Press, 2004.

Ferguson, Trish, ed. *Victorian Time: Technologies, Standardization, Catastrophes.* New York: Palgrave, 2013.

———. Introduction. In Ferguson, *Victorian Time*, 1–15.

Fjordbotten, A. Lee. "Liturgical Influences of Anglo-Catholicism on 'The Waste Land' and Other Works by T. S. Eliot." Diss., Fordham University, 2000. Proquest. DA9955962.

Forrester, Duncan. "A Free Society Today?" In Reeves, *Christian Thinking*, 210–20.

Francis, Emma. "'Healing relief . . . without detriment to modest reserve . . .': Keble, Women's Poetry, and Victorian Cultural Theory." In Blair, *John Keble*, 115–24.

Fraser, Hilary. *Beauty and Belief: Aesthetics and Religions in Victorian Literature.* Cambridge: Cambridge University Press, 1986.

Frazer, James. *The Golden Bough: A Study in Comparative Religion.* Vol. II. New York: MacMillan and Company, 1894.

———. *The Golden Bough: A Study in Magic and Religion.* 3rd ed. Vol. IX. Part VI: The Scapegoat. London: MacMillan and Company, 1913.

Frith, Ivy. *A History of St. Cyprian's Clarence Gate.* Saffron Walden, Essex: The Talbot Press, 1963.

Gaillard, Dawson. *Dorothy L. Sayers*. New York: Frederick Ungar, 1981.

Genter, Robert. *Late Modernism: Art, Culture, and Politics in Cold War America.* Philadelphia: University of Pennsylvania Press, 2010.

Gibbon, Daniel R. "Rewriting Spiritual Community in Spencer, Donne, and the Book of Common Prayer." *Texas Studies in Literature and Language* 54, no. 1 (Spring 2012): 8–44.

Gibson, William. *The Church of England 1688–1832: Unity and Accord.* New York: Routledge, 2000.

Gillis, Stacy. "Consoling Fictions: Mourning, World War One, and Dorothy L. Sayers," In *Modernism and Mourning*, edited by Patricia Rae, 185–97. Lewisburg: Bucknell University Press, 2007.

Goodwin, Gregory. "Keble and Newman: Tractarian Aesthetics and the Romantic Tradition." *Victorian Studies 30* (1987): 475–94.

Gore, Charles. "The Holy Spirit and Inspiration." In *Lux Mundi: A Series of Studies in the Religion of the Incarnation*, edited by Charles Gore, 263–302. 13th ed. New York: Thomas Whittaker, n.d.

Gregory, Jeremy. "The Parish Church: Restoration to the Oxford Movement." In Hefling and Shattuck, *The Oxford Guide*, 93–105.

Haberman, Ina. *Myth, Memory, and the Middlebrow: Priestly, du Maurier, and the Symbolic Form of Englishness.* New York: Palgrave, 2010.

Hassett, Constance. *Christina Rossetti: The Patience of Style.* Charlottesville: University of Virginia Press, 2005.

Hefling, Charles. "Introduction: Anglicans and Common Prayer." In Hefling and Shattuck, *Oxford Guide*, 1–8.

———. "The State Services." In Hefling and Shattuck, *Oxford Guide*, 73–77.

Hefling, Charles, and Cynthia Shattuck, eds. *Oxford Guide to the Book of Common Prayer*. Oxford: Oxford University Press, 2006.

Hindrichs, Cheryl. "Late Modernism, 1928–1945: Criticism and Theory." *Literature Compass 8* (2011): 840–855.

Holy Bible: King James Version, A Reprint of the Edition of 1611. Peabody, Massachusetts: Hendrickson Publishers, 2005.

Hone, Ralph E. "From Poetaster to Poet, One Aspect of the Development of Lord Peter Wimsey." *VII* 10 (1993): 43–58.

Hönninghausen, Gisela. "Emblematic Tendencies in the Works of Christina Rossetti." *Victorian Poetry* 10, no. 1 (Spring 1972): 1–15.

Hooker, Richard. *Of the Laws of Ecclesiastical Polity.* Vol. 2. London: J.M. Dent, 1954.

Howkins, Alun. "Death and Rebirth? English Rural Society, 1920–1940." In *The English Countryside between the Wars: Regeneration or Decline?*, edited by Paul Brassley, Jeremy Burchardt, and Lynne Thompson, 10–25. Woodbridge, UK: The Boydell Press, 2006.

Hu, Esther. "Christina Rossetti, John Keble, and the Divine Gaze." *Victorian Poetry* 46.2 (Summer 2008): 175–89.

Hylson-Smith, Kenneth. *High Churchmanship in the Church of England: From the Seventeenth Century to the Late Twentieth Century.* Edinburgh: T and T Clark, 1993.

Hynes, Samuel. *A War Imagined: The First World War and English Culture.* London: The Bodley Head, 1990.

Jacobs, Alan. *The Book of Common Prayer: A Biography.* Princeton: Princeton University Press, 2013.

Janes, Dominic. *Victorian Reformation: The Fight Over Idolatry in the Church of England, 1840–1860.* Oxford: Oxford University Press, 2009.

Jeanes, Gordon. "Cranmer and the Common Prayer." In Hefling and Shattuck, *Oxford Guide*, 21–38.

Jones, D. E. *The Plays of T. S. Eliot.* Toronto, University of Toronto, Press, 1960.

Kearney, Richard. *Anatheism: Returning to God after God.* New York: Columbia University Press, 2010.

Keble, John. "Catechism." In Keble, *The Christian Year,* 190–91.

———. *The Christian Year, Lyra Innocentium, and Other Poems, Together with His Sermon on "National Apostasy."* London: Oxford University Press, 1914.
———. "The Danger of Sympathizing with Rebellion." 1831. In Keble, *Sermons, Academical and Occasional*, 105–26.
———. "Easter Day." In Keble, *The Christian Year,* 72–74.
———. "Endurance of Church Imperfections." In Keble, *Sermons, Academical and Occasional*, 292–320.
———. "Eucharistical Offices." In Keble, *Sermons, Academical and Occasional,* 251–72.
———. "Favour Shewn to Implicit Faith." 1822. In Keble, *Sermons, Academical and Occasional,* 2–23.
———. "Fifteenth Sunday after Trinity." In Keble, *The Christian Year,* 126–28.
———. "Forms of Prayer to be Used at Sea." In Keble, *The Christian Year,* 201–2.
———. "Fourth Sunday after Epiphany." In Keble, *The Christian Year,* 35–37.
———. "Fourth Sunday in Advent." In Keble, *The Christian Year*, 13–15.
———. *The Jewish Nation and God's Dealings with Them, Paralleled with Individual Christians, and God's Dealings with Them.* In Keble, *Occasional Papers*, 435–506.
———. "King Charles the Martyr." In Keble, *The Christian Year*, 204–5.
———. Letter XXII. *Letters of Spiritual Counsel and Guidance*, 229–40. Edited by R. F. Wilson. Oxford: James Parker, 1870.
———. "Morning." In Keble, *The Christian Year,* 3–5.
———. *Occasional Papers and Reviews.* Edited by E. B. Pusey. Oxford and London: James Parker and Company, 1877.
———. "Ordination." In Keble, *The Christian Year,* 209–10.
———. "Postscript to the Sermon on Tradition." In Keble, *Sermons, Academical and Occasional*, 341–42.
———. Preface. Introduction to *The Works of That Learned and Judicious Divine, Mr. Richard Hooker with an Account of His Life and Death, by Isaac Walton,* edited by John Keble. 2nd ed. Vol. 1. Oxford: Oxford University Press, 1888.
———. "Primitive Tradition Recognised in Holy Scripture." 1836. In Keble, *Sermons, Academical and Occasional*, 173–231.
———. "Sacred Poetry." 1825. In Keble, *Occasional Papers*, 81–107.
———. "St. Luke the Evangelist." In Keble, *The Christian Year,* 180–82.
———. "St. Matthew the Apostle." In Keble, *The Christian Year,* 175–76.
———. "Septuagesima Sunday." In Keble, *The Christian Year,* 42–43.
———. Sermon XXX. *Sermons Occasional and Parochial*, 355–68. Oxford and London: James Parker, 1868.
———. "Sermon on National Apostasy." In Keble, *The Christian Year,* 539–56.
———. *Sermons, Academical and Occasional.* 2nd ed. Oxford: John Henry Parker, 1848.
———. "Shadows and Substance." In Keble, *Sermons for Christmas and Epiphany*, 202–13. Oxford: James Parker and Co., 1875.
———. "Sunday Next before Advent." In Keble, *The Christian Year,* 147–49.
———. "Third Sunday in Advent." In Keble, *The Christian Year,* 11–13.

———. *Tract 13: Sunday Lessons. The Principle of Selection.* 1833. In *Tracts for the Times by Members of the University of Oxford*, edited by John Henry Newman. Vol. I. London: J. Rivington, 1841. New York: AMS Press, 1969.

———. *Tract 89: On the Mysticism Attributed to the Early Fathers of the Church.* 1841. In *Tracts for the Times by Members of the University of* Oxford, edited by John Henry Newman. Vol. VI. London: J. Rivington, 1840. New York: AMS P, 1969.

———. "Trinity Sunday." In Keble, *The Christian Year*, 98–100.

Kenney, Catherine. *The Remarkable Case of Dorothy L. Sayers.* Kent, Ohio: Kent State University Press, 1990.

Kent, David, ed. *The Achievement of Christina Rossetti.* Ithaca: Cornell University Press, 1987.

Kestner, Joseph. *The Edwardian Detective: 1901–1915.* Aldershot, England: Ashgate, 2000.

Kimaid, Michael. *Modernity, Metatheory, and the Temporal-Spatial Divide: From Mythos to Techne.* New York: Routledge, 2015.

King, Joshua. "John Keble's *The Christian Year*: Private Reading and Imagined National Religious Community." *Victorian Literature and Culture* 40.2 (2012): 397–420.

Landow, George P. *Victorian Types, Victorian Shadows: Biblical Typology in Victorian Literature, Art, and Religion.* Boston: Routledge and Kegan Paul, 1980.

LaPorte, Charles. *Victorian Poets and the Changing Bible.* Charlottesville, University of Virginia Press, 2011.

Latham, Sean. *"Am I a Snob?": Modernism and the Novel.* Ithaca: Cornell University Press, 2003.

Leavis, Q. D. "The Case of Miss Dorothy Sayers." 1937. In *British Women Fiction Writers 1900–1960*, edited by Harold Bloom. Vol. 2. New York: Chelsea House, 1998.

Lee, Geoffrey Alan. *Lord Peter Rings the Changes: A Study of Change Ringing in* The Nine Tailors. Hurstpierpoint, England: Dorothy L. Sayers Historical and Literary Society, 1987.

Lewis, Pericles. *Religious Experience and the Modernist Novel.* New York: Cambridge University Press, 2010.

Lloyd, Trevor. "The Church of England: Common Worship." In Hefling and Shattuck, *Oxford Guide*, 413–19.

Lowe, Peter. "Churches Built and Churches Bombed: T. S. Eliot's Vision of National Loss and Spiritual Renewal." *English Studies: A Journal of English Language and Literature* 94, no. 8 (December 2013): 908–930.

Lysack, Krysta. "The Productions of Time: Keble, Rossetti, and Victorian Devotional Reading". *Victorian Studies: An Interdisciplinary Journal of Social, Political, and Cultural Studies* 55.3 (2013): 451–70.

Malamud, Randy. *Where Words Are Valid: T. S. Eliot's Communities of Drama.* Westport, Connecticut: Praeger, 1994.

Marsden, John. "William Temple: Christianity and the Life of Fellowship." *Political Theology* 8, no. 2 (Apr. 2007): 213–33.

Mason, Emma. "Christina Rossetti and the Doctrine of Reserve." *Journal of Victorian Culture* 7.2 (Fall 2002): 196–219.

Mendelson, Edward. "Obama as Literary Critic." *NYR Daily*. New *York Review of Books*. January 4, 2016. http://www.nybooks.com/daily/2016/01/04/obama-as-literary-critic/.

Michael, Krystyna. "Neomedievalism and the Modern Subject in T. S. Eliot's *Murder in the Cathedral*." *Postmedieval: A Journal of Medieval Cultural Studies* 5, no. 1 (2014): 34–43.

Milbank, John. "A Closer Walk on the Wild Side." In Warner, VanAntwerpen, and Calhoun, *Varieties of Secularism*, 54–82.

Miller, Tyrus. *Late Modernism: Politics, Fiction, and the Arts between the World Wars*. Berkely: University of California Press, 1999.

Mitchell, Leonel. "Sanctifying Time: The Calendar." In Hefling and Shattuck, *Oxford Guide*, 476–83.

Moberly, R. C. "The Incarnation as the Basis of Dogma." In *Lux Mundi: A Series of Studies in the Religion of the Incarnation*, edited by Charles Gore, 181–226. 13th ed. New York: Thomas Whittaker, n.d.

Morrison, Mark. *The Public Face of Modernism: Little Magazines, Audiences, and Reception, 1905–1920*. Madison: University of Wisconsin Press, 2001.

Müller, Max. *Natural Religion*. 2nd ed. London: Longman, Green, and Company, 1892.

———. *Physical Religion*. London: Longman, Green, and Company, 1891.

Mussachio, George. "C. S. Lewis, T. S. Eliot, and the Anglican Psalter." *VII* 22 (2005): 45–59.

Neale, John Mason. *Medieval Preachers and Medieval Preaching: A Series of Extracts Translated from the Sermons of the Middle Ages*. London: J. and C. Mozley, 1856.

Newman, John Henry. "John Keble." In *Essays Critical and Historical*, 421–53. Vol. II. London: Longmans, Green, and Co., 1907.

———. *Tract 90: Remarks on Certain Passages in the Thirty-Nine Articles*. 1841. Oxford: John Henry and James Parker, 1865.

Nietzsche, Friedrich. "On Truth and Lying in an Extra-Moral Sense." In *Friedrich Nietzsche on Rhetoric and Language*, edited and translated by Sander Gilman, Carol Blair, and David Parent, 246–57. New York: Oxford University Press, 1989.

Nockles, Peter Benedict. *The Oxford Movement in Context: Anglican High Churchmanship, 1760–1857*. Cambridge: Cambridge University Press, 2004.

Oakeley, Frederick. *Lyra Liturgica: Reflections in Verse for Holy Days and Seasons*. London: Burns, Lambert, and Oates, 1865.

Oser, Lee. "Coming to Terms with Four Quartets." In *A Companion to T. S. Eliot*, edited by David Chinitz, 216–27. Malden, Massachusetts: Wiley-Blackwell, 2009.

Pagett, Francis. "Sacraments." In *Lux Mundi: A Series of Studies in the Religion of the Incarnation*, edited by Charles Gore, 337–62. 13th ed. New York: Thomas Whittaker, n.d.

Palazzo, Lynda. *Christina Rossetti's Feminist Theology*. New York: Palgrave, 2002.

Patterson, Nancy-Lou. "A Ring of Good Bells: Providence and Judgment in Dorothy L. Sayers's *The Nine Tailors*." *Mythlore* 16 (1989): 50–52.

Pecora, Vincent. *Secularization without End: Beckett, Mann, Coetzee*. Notre Dame, Indiana: University of Notre Dame Press, 2015.

Perkin, Harold. *The Rise of Professional Society: England Since 1880*. London: Routledge, 1989.

Pickstock, Catherine. *After Writing: On the Liturgical Consummation of Philosophy*. Oxford: Blackwell, 1998.

Pike, Lionel J. "Liturgy and Time in Counterpoint: A View of T. S. Eliot's *Murder in the Cathedral*." *Modern Drama* 23 (1980): 277–291.

Lord Platt. Foreword. In Reeves, *Christian Thinking*, ix–xii.

Pound, Ezra. "Pastiche: Regional—XVIII." In *Ezra Pound: Poetry and Prose Contributions to Periodicals,* edited by Leo Baechler, A. Walton Lite, and James Lagenbach, 357–58. Volume III: *1918–19*. New York: Garland Press, 1991.

Prickett, Stephen. *Romanticism and Religion: The Tradition of Coleridge and Wordsworth in the Victorian Church*. New York: Cambridge University Press, 1976.

———. "Tractarian Poetry." In *A Companion to Victorian Poetry*, edited by Richard Cronin, Alison Chapman, and Antony H. Harrison, 279–90. Malden, MA: Blackwell P, 2002.

Pusey, E. B. Preface, *Occasional Papers and Reviews* by John Keble, xxiii. Edited by E. B. Pusey. Oxford and London: James Parker and Co., 1877.

Rainey, Lawrence. *Institutions of Modernism: Literary Elites and Popular Culture*. New Haven: Yale University Press, 1998.

Rappaport, Roy. *Ritual and Religion in the Making of Humanity*. Cambridge: Cambridge University Press, 1999.

Reed, John Shelton. *Glorious Battle: The Cultural Politics of Victorian Anglo-Catholicism*. Nashville: Vanderbilt University Press, 1996.

Reeves, Marjorie, ed. *Christian Thinking and Social Order: Conviction Politics from the 1930s to the Present Day*. London: Cassell, 1999.

Reeves, Marjorie, and Elaine Kaye. "Tracts for War-Time: The Christian News-Letter." In Reeves, *Christian Thinking*, 49–79.

Reeves, Marjorie, and William Taylor. "Intellectuals in Debate: The Moot." In Reeves, *Christian Thinking*, 24–48.

Reynolds, Barbara. *Dorothy L. Sayers: Her Life and Soul*. New York: St. Martin's Press, 1993.

Riede, David. *Matthew Arnold and the Betrayal of Language*. Charlottesville: University of Virginia Press, 1988.

Robinson, James E. "*Murder in the Cathedral* as Theatre of the Spirit." *Religion and Literature* 18, no. 2 (1986 Summer): 31–45.

Roe, Dinah. *Christina Rossetti's Faithful Imagination: The Devotional Poetry and Prose*. New York: Palgrave, 2006.

Rosendale, Timothy. *Liturgy and Literature in the Making of Protestant England*. Cambridge: Cambridge University Press, 2007.

Rossetti, Christina. "Alone Lord God, in Whom Our Trust and Peace." In Rossetti, *Verses,* 181.

———. "And now why tarriest thou?" In Rossetti, *Verses*, 204–5.

———. *Annus Domini, a Prayer for Each Day of the Year, Founded on a Text of Holy Scripture*. Oxford: James Parker, 1874.

———. "'Beloved, let us love one another,' says St. John." In Rossetti, *Verses*, 216.

———. *Called to Be Saints: The Minor Festivals Devotionally Studied*. London: Society for Promoting Christian Knowledge, n.d. [1883].

———. "Christmas Eve." In Rossetti, *Verses*, 213–14.

———. "Earth cannot bar flame from ascending." In Rossetti, *Verses*, 215–16.

———. "Earth has clear call of daily bells." In Rossetti, *Verses*, 265.

———. "Easter Day." In Rossetti, *Verses*, 229–30.

———. *The Face of the Deep: A Devotional Commentary on the Apocalypse*. Second Edition. London: Society for Promoting Christian Knowledge, 1893.

———. "The Flowers appear on the Earth." In Rossetti, *Verses*, 319–20.

———. "The Holy City, New Jerusalem." In Rossetti, *Verses*, 280.

———. "Looking back along life's trodden way." In Rossetti, *Verses*, 335.

———. "Of each sad word which is more sorrowful." In Rossetti, *Verses*, 310.

———. *Seek and Find: A Double Series of Short Studies of the Benedicte*. London: Society for Promoting Christian Knowledge, n.d. [1879].

———. "The Sunday before Advent." In Rossetti, *Verses*, 247.

———. "Thou knewest . . . thou oughtest therefore.'" In Rossetti, *Verses*, 320.

———. *Time Flies: A Reading Diary*. London: Society for Promoting Christian Knowledge, 1902. *Google Book Search*.

———. "Time seems not short." In Rossetti, *Verses*, 273.

———. *The Letters of Christina Rossetti: A Digital Edition*. Ed. Antony Harrison. Charlottesville: The University Press of Virginia, 1997–2004. http://rotunda.upress.virginia.edu/crossetti/.

———. "What are these lovely ones, yea, what are these?" In Rossetti, *Verses*, 289.

———. *Verses: The Complete Poems of Christina Rossetti*. Edited by R. W. Crump. Vol. II. Baton Rouge: Louisiana State University Press, 1986.

———. "'Who hath despised the day of small things?'" In Rossetti, *Verses*, 257.

———. "'Yea, the sparrow hath found her a house.'" In Rossetti, *Verses*, 332–33.

Sayers, Dorothy L. *Begin Here: A Statement of Faith*. New York: Harcout, Brace, and Company, 1941.

———. *Busman's Honeymoon*. 1937. New York: HarperTorch, 2006.

———. *Catholic Tales and Christian Songs*. Oxford: B. H. Blackwell, 1918; *Christian Classics Ethereal Library*, 1996. https://www.ccel.org/ccel/sayers/cathtales/files/cathtales.html.

———. "Creed or Chaos." In Sayers, *Letters to a Diminished Church*, 49–72.

———, with Robert Eustace. *The Documents in the Case*. 1930. New York: Harper Paperbacks, 1995.

———. "Epiphany Hymn." In Sayers, *Catholic Tales*, 9–10.

———. *The Five Red Herrings*. 1931. New York: HarperCollins, 2006.

———. *Gaudy Night*. 1936. New York: Harper Paperbacks, 1995.

———. "Gaudy Night" (essay). In *Titles to Fame*, edited by Denys Kilham Roberts, 73–95. London: Thomas Nelson and Sons, 1937.

———. “The House of the Soul: A Lay.” In Sayers, *Catholic Tales*, 54 ff.
———. “The Incredible Elopement of Lord Peter Wimsey.” In *Lord Peter: A Collection of All the Lord Peter Wimsey Stories*, edited by James Sandoe, 302–28. New York: Harper and Row, 1972.
———. Introduction. *The Omnibus of Crime*, edited by Dorothy L. Sayers, 9–47. New York: Payson and Clarke, 1929.
———. *The Letters of Dorothy L. Sayers*. Edited by Barbara Reynolds. Vol. 1: *1899–1936: The Making of a Detective Novelist*. New York: St. Martins P, 1996.
———. *The Letters of Dorothy L. Sayers*. Edited by Barbara Reynolds. Vol. 2: *1937–1943: From Novelist to Playwright*. New York: St. Martins P, 1998.
———. *Letters to a Diminished Church: Passionate Arguments for the Relevance of Christian Doctrine*. Nashville: Thomas Nelson, 2004.
———. *Making Sense of the Universe. An Address Given at the Kingsway Hall, Ash Wednesday, March 6th, 1946*. London: St. Anne’s Church House, 1946.
———. *The Mind of the Maker*. 1941. New York: HarperCollins, 1987.
———. “More Pantheon Papers: The Kalendar.” *Punch* January 6, 1954: 60.
———. “More Pantheon Papers: The Cosmic Synthesis.” *Punch* January 13, 1954: 84.
———. *Murder Must Advertise*. 1933. New York: Harper Paperbacks, 1995.
———. *The Nine Tailors*. San Diego: Harvest Book/Harcourt, 1934.
———. “The Other Six Deadly Sins.” In Sayers, *Letters to a Diminished Church*, 81–108.
———. “The Pantheon Papers.” Nov. 1953/Jan. 1954. In *Christian Letters to a Post-Christian World: A Selection of Essays*, edited by Roderick Jellema, 2–10. Grand Rapids: W. B. Eerdmans, 1969.
———. “Sacrament: Against Ecclesiasts.” In Sayers, *Catholic Tales*, 8–9.
———. “Strong Meat.” In Sayers, *Letters to a Diminished Church*, 73–80.
———. *Strong Poison*. 1930. New York: HarperTorch, 2006.
———. “The Undignified Melodrama of the Bone of Contention.” In *Lord Peter: A Collection of All the Lord Peter Wimsey Stories*, edited by James Sandoe, 78–136. New York: Harper and Row, 1972.
———. *Unnatural Death*. 1927. New York: Avon, 1964.
———. “What Do We Believe?” In Sayers, *Letters to a Diminished Church*, 9–14.
———. *Whose Body?* 1923. New York: Harper and Row, 1995.
———. “Why Work?” In Sayers, *Letters to a Diminished Church*, 125–46.
———. “Wimsey Papers—IV.” *Spectator* December 8, 1939: 809–10.
———. “Worship in the Anglican Church.” 1942. Ed. Barbara Reynolds. *VII* 12 (1995): 31–48.
Schivelbusch, Wolfgang. *The Railway Journey: The Industrialization of Time and Space in the Nineteenth Century*. Berkeley: University of California Press, 2014.
Society of Sts. Peter and Paul. *Anglican Missal*. London: The Society of St. Peter and St. Paul, 1921.
Sexton, James. “*Four Quartets* and the Christian Calendar.” *American Literature: A Journal of Literary History, Criticism, and Bibliography* 43, no. 2 (May 1971): 279–81.

Sherry, Vincent. *Ezra Pound, Wyndham Lewis, and Radical Modernism*. New York: Oxford University Press, 1993.

Simmons, Laura K. *Creed without Chaos: Exploring Theology in the Writing of Dorothy L. Sayers*. Grand Rapids, Michigan: Baker Academic, 2005.

Simpson, Christine. "Some Views on *Catholic Tales and Christian Songs*." *VII* 20 (2003): 93–104.

Skinner, S. A. "'The Duty of the State': Keble, the Tractarians, and Establishment." In Blair, *John Keble*, 33–46.

Smith, Grover. *T. S. Eliot's Poetry and Plays: A Study in Sources and Meaning*. Chicago: University of Chicago Press, 1956.

Spinks, Bryan. "The Prayer Book 'Crisis' in England." In Hefling and Shattuck, *Oxford Guide*, 239–43.

Spurr, Barry. *'Anglo-Catholic in Religion': T. S. Eliot and Christianity*. Cambridge: The Lutterworth Press, 2010.

———. "Liturgical Anachronism in *Murder in the Cathedral*." *Yeats Eliot Review* 15 (1998): 2–7.

Stanwood, P.G. "Christina Rossetti's Devotional Prose." In Kent, *The Achievement*, 231–39.

———. "Time and Liturgy in Donne, Crashaw, and T. S. Eliot." *Mosaic* 12.2 (1979): 91–105.

Taylor, Charles. *A Secular Age*. Cambridge, MA: Belknap Press, 2007.

Tennyson, G. B. *Victorian Devotional Poetry: The Tractarian Mode*. Cambridge: Harvard University Press, 1981.

Tetzeli von Rosador, Kurt. "Christian Historical Drama: The Exemplariness of Murder in the Cathedral." *Modern Drama* 29, no. 4 (December 1986): 516–531.

Thomas, Ronald. *Detective Fiction and the Rise of Forensic Science*. Cambridge: Cambridge University Press, 1999.

Thompson, E. P. "Time, Work-Discipline, and Industrial Capitalism." In *Customs in Common: Studies in Traditional Popular Culture*, 352–403. New York, The New Press, 1993.

Tyack, George. *A Book about Bells*. 1898. Detroit: Omnigraphics, 1991.

Tylor, Edward. *Primitive Culture*. 3rd ed. Vol. I. London: John Murray, 1891.

Virsis, Rasma. "The Christian Concept in *Murder in the Cathedral*." *Modern Drama* 14 (1971):405–7.

Warner, Michael, Jonathan VanAntwerpen, and Craig Calhoun, eds. *Varieties of Secularism in a Secular Age*. Cambridge, Mass.: Harvard University Press, 2010.

———. Editors' introduction. In Warner, VanAntwerpen, and Calhoun, *Varieties of Secularism*, 1–31.

Watson, Giles. "Dorothy Sayers and the Oecumenical Penguin." *VII* 14 (1997): 17–32.

Westerholm, Joel. "In Defense of *Verses*: The Aesthetics and Reputation of Christina Rossetti's Late Poetry." *Renascence* 51, no. 3 (Spring 1999): 191–203.

Wheatly, Charles. *A Rational Illustration of the Book of Common Prayer of the Church of England: Being the Substance of Every Thing Liturgical in Bishop Sparrow, Mr. L'Estrange, Dr. Comber, Dr. Nichols, and All Former Ritualists,*

Commentators, and Others, Upon the Same Subject. 1710. London: Henry G. Bohn, 1849.

Wheeler-Barclay, Marjorie. *The Science of Religion in Britain, 1860–1915.* Charlottesville: University of Virginia Press, 2010.

Wilde, Oscar. *The Picture of Dorian Gray.* London: Simpkin, Marshall, Hamilton, and Kent and Co., 1891.

———. "To Read or Not to Read." In *A Critic in Pall Mall*, edited by E. V. Lucas, 21–22. London: Methuen and Company, 1919.

Williams, Isaac. *Tract 80: On Reserve in Communicating Religious Knowledge. Tracts for the Times by Members of the University of Oxford.* Edited by John Henry Newman. Vol. IV. London: J. Rivington, 1837. New York: AMS Press, 1969.

———. *Tract 87. On Reserve in Communicating Religious Knowledge. Tracts for the Times by Members of the University of Oxford.* Edited by John Henry Newman. Vol. V. London: J. Rivington, 1840; New York: AMS Press, 1969.

Williams, Rowan. Foreword. In Hefling and Shattuck, *Oxford Guide*, xiii.

Wolffe, John. *God and Greater Britain: Religion and National Life in Britain and Ireland 1843–1945.* London: Routledge, 1994.

Woolf, Virginia. *The Voyage Out.* New York: George H. Doran, 1920.

Wordsworth, William. "Preface to *Lyrical Ballads*." *Prefaces and Prologues.* Vol. XXXIX. The Harvard Classics. New York: P.F. Collier & Son, 1909–14; Bartleby.com, 2001. www.bartleby.com/39/.

Yonge, Charlotte. *The Heir of Redclyffe.* Edited by Barbara Dennis. Oxford: Oxford University Press, 1997.

Zemka, Sue. *Time and the Moment in Victorian Literature and Society.* Cambridge: Cambridge University Press, 2012.

Index

About the Author

Chene Heady is professor of English at Longwood University in Farmville, Virginia, where he teaches courses on both religion and British literature. He has published a dozen academic articles, primarily on religion and literature, and has served as a peer reviewer and book reviewer for the scholarly journal *Religion and the Arts*. He received his PhD from the Ohio State University.